The

INCORRUPTIBLES

The
INCORRUPTIBLES

A Study of the Incorruption of the Bodies
of Various Catholic Saints and Beati

by

Joan Carroll Cruz

*"The bodies of holy martyrs and others now
living with Christ, bodies which were His members and temples of the Holy Spirit, which one
day are to be raised up by Him and made glorious in everlasting life, are to be venerated by the
faithful; God gives men many benefits through
them."*

—The Council of Trent

TAN BOOKS AND PUBLISHERS, INC.
Rockford, Illinois 61105

NIHIL OBSTAT:

> Msgr. Henry C. Bezou
> Censor Librorum
> November 11, 1974

IMPRIMATUR:

> ☩ Most Rev. Philip M. Hannan
> Archbishop of New Orleans
> November 19, 1974

Library of Congress Catalog Card Number: 77-93992

ISBN: 0-89555-066-0

Cover photographs by Dan Paulos. Copyright © by Dan Paulos 1996. Used by permission.

Cover design by Pete Massari

Printed and bound in the United States of America.

TAN BOOKS AND PUBLISHERS, INC.
P.O. Box 424
Rockford, Illinois 61105
1977

ABOUT THE AUTHOR

Writing comes second for Mrs. Joan Carroll Cruz, a New Orleans housewife and mother of five children, not that she is a second-rate writer—far from it. She simply cannot tolerate writing if there is housework left undone. For this reason she usually writes at night, when her regular work is finished. Actually, she writes every other night, during the wee hours of the morning, often rising by 2:00 a.m. to sit down to her typewriter. "That is the only time I have enough uninterrupted quiet to get anything done," she states. She catches up with rest on alternate nights.

The catalyst that initiated her writing career was a challenge from her niece. Already she had done considerable reading in the lives of the saints and was well aware of the phenomenon of incorruption when a family discussion evolved to the subject. She was noting that there are so many contradictions in this area that she would like to see someone write a book to clarify matters. When her niece challenged her to write one, the idea did not seem so far-fetched and she accepted. After working a while on the project, she laid it aside, thinking herself unequal to the task. But later she resumed it with renewed vigor, and *The Incorruptibles* is the result.

During the research on this book, she conceived the outline of a novel inspired by the life of King Edward the Confessor of England, a work she pursued immediately upon completion of *The Incorruptibles*. It is now in print with the title *The Desires of Thy Heart*. Published by Tandem Press in hardbound, it quickly went through two printings and was accepted by New American Library for a pocketbook edition under the Signet label. It was their lead book for November, 1977, with an initial printing of 550,000. Three companies are interested in the movie rights.

Already she has completed a second novel, *Love Endures Forever,* which will appear in the summer of 1978, and two children's stories, *Butterflies Clap Their Wings* and *Fish Fan Their Fins,* which will come out approximately the same time. Books in progress include a novel entitled *The Mustard Seed,* a children's fantasy called *The Crystal Forest,* and a non-fiction Catholic work. "The more I write and research, the more ideas I get for new books," she says.

A native of New Orleans, Mrs. Cruz is the educational product of the School Sisters of Notre Dame, having attended grade school, high school and college under their tutelage. She attended boarding school at St. Mary of the Pines in Chatawa, Mississippi, and went to Notre Dame Junior College in St. Louis, Missouri. She is married to Louis Cruz, who works for a trucking company at the New Orleans Port Authority in various capacities.

Writing for Joan Carroll Cruz is the fulfillment of a long unexpressed drive for creative self-expression. Having already tried her hand at painting and fine needle-work, in an unsuccessful attempt to satisfy her creative urge, she was about to embark upon volunteer work when the possibility of writing a book occurred to her. Once solidly into it, she discovered she had found her medium and now plans to stay with it for some years to come.

Themes for her prose works are all religious, as is the background for her novels, into which she weaves a definite moral lesson. "Fiction without a moral to it is a waste of time," she comments. Her novels are all written without any of the suggestiveness or blatant openness so typical of popular writing today. She maintains "a book does not need this," and she has solidly proved her point.

Table of Contents

List of Illustrations

ACKNOWLEDGEMENTS

I am overwhelmingly indebted to Serena Bodellini Burke who assisted in the translation of the Italian, French, and Spanish books and correspondence, which work was indispensable for the accuracy of the facts mentioned in this volume. No expression in words, no matter how carefully chosen could adequately express my deep appreciation for her gracious and invaluable assistance.

Gratitude must also be extended to my husband, Louis, who assisted with the Spanish translations and to my son, Tommy, for escorting me many times to local libraries during the evening hours.

I am also grateful to Mr. and Mrs. Oswald Bauer for their help with the German translations, to Mr. Said Rafidi for his Arabic translations, and to Mr. Thomas V. Schmidt of the Reference Department of the Catholic University of America.

The following are representatives of the shrines or officials of the religious orders of the saints discussed in this book, who so kindly answered my queries. Their generous and gracious assistance has been an inspiration to me, and to them I extend my profound respect and deepest appreciation.

Austria
Dr. Reginald, Abrkoadjutor, Abtei, Stift Mel; The Kirchenmeisteramt der Domkirche St. Stephan, Vienna.

Belgium
Mons. Coens, Société des Bollandistes; Abbé V. Salmon; l'Abbè R. Doutreligne, Recteur de L'Instituit Notre Dame de la Poterie; Sisters of the Maison du Sacre Coeur, Jette.

England
The Rt. Rev. Msgr. Canon, F. J. Bartlett, Westminster Cathedral; Rev. G. Pritchard, Ely, Cambridgeshire; Rev. Fr. Denis J. Cronin, C.S.Sp.; Rev. F. Murphy of St. Werburgh's; Francis Cutler, Rector, Croyland Abbey Rectory; The Subdeanery of Lincoln Cathedral; Sr. Mary Jude, O.P., Prioress, St. Dominic's Convent; Mr. R. Taylor of the Cathedral Archives, Canterbury; The Chapter Librarian, The College, Durham; W. R. J. Pullen, The Chapter Office, Westminster Abbey; Mr. N. H. MacMichael, Keeper of the Muniments, Westminster Abbey; Mr. James Ogilvie Forbes, London; Mr. H. A. Baker, Custodian, St. Augustine's Abbey, Canterbury.

France

Mon. E. Reillier, Directrice, Institution Notre-Dame, Bordeaux; Fr. Jacques-Marie, le Curé de Pibrac; Fr. M. E. Lauzière, Province Dominicaine de Toulouse; A. Chanel, Curé, Paroisse d'Ars; Fr. Saint-Pierre, S.S.S.; Gabriel Collangettes, Prélat, Saint-Quentin; R. Edet, S.S.E., Les Pères de Saint-Edme; The Sister Archivist of the Visitation of Saint Marie, Annecy; S. Marie-Thérèse, Monastère des Clarisses, Alençon; Sr. Margaret of the Sisters of Charity, Rue de Bac, Paris; J. Depouilly, Conservateur du Musée de Soissons; Paroisse St. Didier, Avignon.

Germany

Abs. P. Mauritius Keller, O.P., Köln; Rev. A. D. Trapp, O.S.A., Tübingen; Dr. Ludwig Vogl, Bischöfl. Ordinariat, Eichstätt; Sr. M. Evangelista, O.S.B., Eichstätt.

India

Fr. Moreno de Souza, S.J., Bom Jesus Basilica, Goa.

Italy

ABRUZZI: P. Gabriele Marini, Superiore, Convento S. Bernardino, L'Aquila.

APULIA: Rev. Vincenzo Campagna, S.J., Taranto; Basilica di S. Nicola, Bari.

BASILICATA: Don Franco Ferrara, Chiaromonte.

EMILIA: Sr. M. A. Paola Marchesi, O.L.C., Superiore, Monastero Del Corpus Domini; Madre M. Benedetta Chiminelli, Abbadessa delle Monache Benedettine; P. Mauro Scopo, Tempio Del Santo, Cotignola; P. Amadis M. Brighetti, Superiore, Santuario S. Pellegrino; Madre M. Benedetta Chiminelli, Abbadessa Monache Benedettine, Ferrara; La superiora delle Suore Minime dell'Addolorata, Le Budrie.

LIGURIA: P. Cassiano da Langasco of the St. Catherine Cultural Centre.

LOMBARDY: Mons. Francesco Delpini, Cathedral of Milan; Dr. Nicola Fiasconaro of the Order of the Dominican Fathers of Mantua; Don Feliciano Righetti, Vice Canc. della Curia Vesc. di Mantova; Fr. Peter Bianchi, Milano; Miss Antonietta Trivi, Villa Biscossi, Pavia; Maria Terese Pezzotti, Casa S. Angela, Brescia.

MARCHE: Abbadessa Mon. Beata Mattia, Matelica; R. P. Paolo Massi, Superiore Santuario S. Pacifico; Don Pierdamiano Buffadini, Fabriano, Ancona; Sr. M. Ildegarde Paesani, Abbadessa Monastero S. Sperandia; P. Domenico Gentili, Tolentino.

PIEDMONT: Suor M. Agnese, Priora, Monastero Domenicane; Don Zucca Giuseppe, Cappellano Chiesa S. Lorenzo.

ROME: P. Paolo Molinari, S.J.; P. Peter Gumpel, S.J.; Fr. David Colella, O.Ss.T.; P. Antonino Silli, O.P., Rettore della Basilica di S. Maria sopra Minerva; Rt. Rev. Msgr. Umberto Dionisi, St. Cecilia's Basilica; Mother General, Pontificio Instituto Maestre Pie Filippini; Sr. Joanna O'Donnell, F.M.M.; Rev. Patrick M. Dalos, C.O.; Fr. E. Cassoni, S.J.; D. Giuseppe Ranocchini, Postulatore Generale, Societas Apostolatus Catholici, Pallottini; Rev. Gualberto Giachi, S.J.; Mons. Pietro Galavotti, Sacra Congregazione per le Cause dei Santi, Vatican; Procura Generale, Benedettini Di Monteoliveto; The Superior General, Congregazione Delle Suore Di Santa Dorotea Della Frassinetti; P. Dossi Sisinio, M.I.; Sr. M. Lodovica Pietropaoli, O.S.C., Viterbo. Suor Assunta Ubertini, Monastero Clausura S. Rosa.

Acknowledgements 17

TUSCANY: P. Cristoforo Testa, O.P., Montepulciano; P. Lodovico Serafini, O.F.M., Cortona; Padre Francesco Banci, Sansepolcro; Suor Maria Letizia Fini, O.P., Prato; Sr. Paola Maria dello Spirito Santo, Firenze; The Prioress of the Discalced Carmelites, Florence; Basilica di S. Frediano in Lucca; Mother Superior of the Passionist Nuns, Lucca; P. Giuseppe Giacomelli, Pistoia.

UMBRIA: Sac. Giovanni Marchetti, Perugia; The Abbess, Monastero Santa Rita; P. Pacifico Brunori, Il Rettore della Basilica, Gubbio; Suor Maria Cecilia Ventotto, Abbess, Ven. Monastero Delle Agostiniane di S. Chiara; Vincenzo Pieggi, Rettore della Chiesa di S. Domenico; The Abbadessa, Monastero Cappuccine, S. Veronica Giuliani; Sr. Chiara Agnese, Abbadessa, Protomonastero di Santa Chiara; D. Aldo Brunacci, Canonico Teologo Cattedrale, Assisi; P. Stanislas Casali, Gubbio; Miss Luigina Cardinali, Gubbio; Fr. Domenico Marconi, Assisi.

VENEZIA: D. Simplicio Toffanin, Padova.

Lebanon
Monastery of St. Maron, Annaya-Djebeil.

Peru
Fr. John J. Lawler, M. M., Lima.

Poland
P. Ladislaus Janczak, S.J., Warszawa.

Scotland
Mr. A. Jackson, Head Custodian, Melrose Abbey, Melrose.

Sicily
Msgr. Salvatore Famoso, Chancellor of the Ven. Curia of the Archdiocese of Catania; P. Luigi Pecoraro, Superiore, Convento S. Maria Di Gesu; Padre Girolamo Ciaramitaro, O.P., Catania; Suor Chiara Costante Centorrino, Messina.

Spain
P. Restituto Fuertes, Madrid; Fr. Matías de Jesús, O.C.D., Prior, Salamanca; Rev. Manuel Garcia Miralles, O.P., Valencia; Sor Maria del Pilar Cubillo, Avila; Carmelitas Descalzas, Alba de Tormes, Salamanca; Fr. Lázaro Simón Cánovas, Superior, Granada; Carmelitas Descalzas, Barcelona; Carmelitas Descalzas de San José, Toledo; Doroteo Fernandez Ruiz, Abad, Alcalá De Henares; Andrés de Lucas, Canciller Secretario del Arzobispado, Madrid.

United States
Father Roger Huser, O.F.M.; Rev. James Prohens, C.R., Provincial; Rev. Rudolph Arbesmann, O.S.A.; Very Rev. Patrick Paschak, O.S.B.M.; Very Rev. Richard Korzinek, O.S.Cam., Provincial; Sr. Agnes Immaculata, Archivist, Sisters of Notre Dame of Namur; Sr. M. Fitz-William, R.S.C.J.; The Sisters of Mother Cabrini High School, West Park, N.Y.; The Sisters of the Convent of St. Walburga, Boulder, Colorado.

*"Blessed are the pure of heart:
for they shall see God."*
Matt. 5:8

This book is dedicated to
the memory of my sister,
ELBA CARROLL MOORE,
who sees God.

PREFACE

How can one begin to explain what motivated her to compile and record such unusual subjects as the death, burial, exhumation, and the condition of the preserved bodies of saints—topics which, to say the least, would at first appear of morbid and macabre interest, but which eventually proved to be stimulating and fraught with mystery? First impulse would claim an inability to explain my attraction for this unusual matter, so far removed from my immediate preoccupations, but I must credit a long-standing interest in the saints, plus the reading of countless biographies, as my introduction, however subliminally, to this subject.

I can recall being greatly impressed on first learning of that great phenomenon of our day, the perfectly preserved and bleeding body of Saint Charbel Makhlouf, but I lay the origins of this book to a sketch that appeared in a Catholic publication which outlined a reclining figure in a glass reliquary. The caption identified the enclosed form as the incorrupt body of St. Francis of Geronimo, a declaration that subsequent research revealed was completely incorrect. Although inaccurate, the sketch of this saint, who was previously unknown to me, stimulated my curiosity regarding the number of saintly preservations in existence, and my interest in this entire subject was immediately kindled.

My preliminary research was abandoned for a year when I was overcome by a feeling of complete inadequacy in the face of so extensive and phenomenal a topic. However, when research was resumed, so many errors and false impressions concerning these preservations were uncovered that a housewifely compulsion for order was aroused, which compelled me once again to undertake, and this time to finish, the compilation of this book.

Initial research involved correspondence with the Library of the Catholic University of America and the Bollandist Jesuits of Brussels. For over three hundred years this order of Jesuit scholars has been reviewing and rewriting the lives of the saints based on documents contemporary to their times. Their work has thus far been published in sixty-eight volumes and is entitled the *Acta Sanctorum*—a work officially accepted as the most accurate record of the saints. Both contacts revealed that not only were there no estimates or compilations of these relics, but also that there was no research material available, except for Father Herbert Thurston, S.J.'s *The Physical Phenomena of Mysticism,* which contains one lengthy and extremely interesting chapter on the incorruption of the saints. This book, unfortunately out of print, also explores other topics, such as levitations, stigmitizations, blood prodigies, mystical fasts, and other subjects which provide very interesting reading.

Having secured with some difficulty a copy of this excellent work, my next steps were made in the direction of four of New Orleans' Catholic university libraries, as well as a number of public libraries. During my visits to these treasuries of information, literally several hundred biographies of saints were scanned to obtain as many names of the incorruptibles as possible. In order to avail myself of other sources, my next field of exploration was the fourteen volumes of the *New Catholic Encyclopedia,* in which every entry of saints, blesseds, and venerables was read for possible mention of their incorruption. I likewise checked, with rewarding results, a number of anthologies, particularly Butler's *Complete Lives of the Saints* (1956 edition).

It must be carefully noted that *the saints included in this present book are by no means the only saints whose bodies have been preserved incorrupt.* Since the incorruption of their bodies was not always mentioned in their biographies, there are perhaps a goodly number of cases unintentionally overlooked; however, I feel certain that the great majority, and certainly the most famous, of these favored souls are included in this volume. To obtain an accurate number of the saints so highly blessed with this unusual dispensation would necessarily constitute a monumental and virtually impossible task.

The next phase of research involved correspondence with the shrines of all those saints reputed to be incorrupt. This was necessary for several reasons:

In a number of European churches there can be found crystal reliquaries which contain reclining statues representing particular saints, the bones of the saints being enclosed in their simulated figures. Because of the techniques employed in reproducing pictures of some of these models, the figures have been frequently mistaken for the actual bodies, producing errors such as that involving St. Francis of Geronimo, mentioned previously, and creating false rumors, as occurred with regard to St. Frances Cabrini, whose body was never found preserved. It was necessary, therefore, to check with the shrines of all those saints reported as being incorrupt to determine if the enshrined figures were the actual bodies of the saints or statues representing them.

Research revealed that the bodies of many saints were reported as being incorrupt when in reality their bodies, which had been conserved for many years, were no longer preserved, due to the effects of floods or accidental fires. Many were also deliberately destroyed by the enemies of the Church during various political upheavals. It was again necessary to obtain verification from the shrines that the bodies were actually intact, as reported.

A third reason for contacting the shrines was to establish the exact location of these relics since many were moved—translated to various places throughout the years. It was frequently found that a relic was reported as being in two or three different churches, only to be found in a fourth. And in two instances, relics were recorded as being in either of two countries and were eventually located in yet another.

A further reason for contacting the shrines was to learn the exact condition of these relics since some, as can be expected, are in a better state than others. It also seemed necessary to obtain verification from the shrines that certain phenomena, including the transpiration of clear oils and perfumes, had proceeded from these relics as recorded. It was also important to obtain certain data concerning the phenomena which are still observed relative to many of these treasured relics.

The final and perhaps most important reason for this correspondence was to learn if the preservations were due to extensive embalming. Of all those saints mentioned in this volume, the preservations of only about one percent are credited to deliberate intervention, and this fact is mentioned in their individual chapters.

In order to report all of this essential information with the greatest accuracy, a reply from the shrines or religious orders involved was established as a requisite for a saint's inclusion in this book. A departure from this norm was allowed in only two instances. Because of the volumes of authoritative information concerning the incorruption of the body of St. Bernadette of Lourdes, correspondence with her shrine seemed entirely superfluous. Contact with the shrine of St. Pascal Baylon was unsuccessful, but due to the availability of a great quantity of documented material and those biographies written by his contemporaries, verifications from his shrine also seemed unnecessary.

The response to my queries was overwhelmingly gratifying. My correspondents were not only pleased to be of assistance but rendered it with detail, supplying me with pictures when these were available and with many definitive works regarding their saints. The responses were so gracious and generous as to fill me with profound and sincerest sentiments of appreciation.

Because some of the material supplied to me from archives and European publications had not previously been utilized by American biographers, and because many interesting facts regarding the lives of these saints, which were given emphasis in these foreign books, had been casually reported or neglected altogether in our editions, I thought it best, in order to bring many of these facts before the reader, that each saint be given his or her own entry. Arranging this work in any other fashion would necessarily limit the amount of data assigned to each one. Organized as it is, this work provides easy access to those saints of particular interest to the reader.

It will be noted that the titles of some of these people are variously stated as *Venerable* and *Blessed* (Beatus) although the author collectively refers to them as saints. It should be explained that *Venerable* is a title given to servants of God after the Congregation of Rites in Rome concludes that they have practiced virtue to an heroic degree. This is the first step toward sainthood. *Blessed* is an official ecclesiastical title, preliminary to sainthood, bestowed on souls after God has testified to their sanctity by miracles performed for others through their holy intercession. Further, it must be mentioned that prior to the bestowal of these titles, the recognition and examination of the remains are made. Incorrupt bodies are medically and scientifically examined, and all phenomena are carefully studied. Since only those souls who have been so recognized by the Church are included in this work, the phenomena reported herein have thus been scrutinized and verified by ecclesiastical authorities.

It is recommended that the entry of Saint Charbel Makhlouf be given particular consideration because many of the unusual circumstances that surrounded the discovery of the incorrupt bodies of saints in past ages were also witnessed not long ago at the tomb of this holy monk. It must be remembered that the pathways which are now seldom trod to the altars guarding the relics of many ancient and medieval saints, were once crowded with scurrying souls in search of a favor or a cure, as countless pilgrims are *now* doing when they climb the cedared hills of Lebanon to the shrine of this perfectly preserved saint. It should be considered that the now-darkened relics of some of these earlier saints were lifelike for many years longer than has been the body of Saint Charbel, now dead but seventy-nine years, and that in many instances the undeniable presence of a heavenly fragrance, which is not noted in the case of this holy monk, further signaled the supernatural quality of other preservations.

May the veneration now deservedly lavished on the memory of Saint Charbel be renewed in equal measure in favor of all those incorruptibles from past ages who await in the shadows of their reliquaries the day of their glorious resurrection.

JOAN CARROLL CRUZ

INTRODUCTION

Preserved bodies found in countries around the world can be divided into three classifications: the *deliberately preserved,* the *accidentally preserved,* and the *incorruptibles.* Specimens of the accidentally or naturally preserved were found even before Egyptian Pharaoh times, when the art of embalming originated, producing for the first time the *deliberately* treated mummies which have survived for as many as three thousand years. The incorruptibles, however, have existed only since early Christian days. Their preservations since that time have challenged the opinions of skeptics and contradicted and defied the laws of nature, all to the dismay of many examining physicians and the admiration of succeeding generations.

The more carefully we consider the preservation of the incorruptibles, the more baffling does the subject become, for their conservation seems to be neither dependent on the manner of burial nor on the temperature or place of interment. Nor were they adversely affected by extended delays between the time of death and their burials, by moisture in the tombs, by rough handling, by frequent transferences, by covering with quicklime, or by their proximity to decaying corpses. The greater majority were never embalmed or treated in any manner, yet most were found lifelike, flexible, and sweetly scented many years after death, in sharp contrast to the specimens of the other two classifications above, who without exception were found stiff, discolored, and skeletal. The mystery of their preservations is further compounded by the observance of blood and clear oils—which have proceeded from a number of these holy relics—a phenomenon which again, needless to say, was never recorded with regard to the deliberately or accidentally preserved.

In order for the reader to appreciate fully the truly phenomenal, highly mysterious, and in most cases, absolutely miraculous aspects of the incorruptibles, it is of the utmost importance that we examine, however briefly, the methods employed in the deliberate preservation of human bodies from ancient times to our modern day, and the conditions favoring the accidental or natural preservation of human remains. Final consideration will be given to the incorruptibles, with an analysis of their attending prodigies.

I

The artificial preservation of human bodies has been of interest to civilization since about the year 3000 B.C. Believed to have evolved from the procedures used to preserve food by drying and salting, the elaborate methods employed to preserve bodies were first applied to satisfy ancient religious beliefs. The Egyptian creators of the art believed that the preservation of the body was essential for maintaining the identity of the deceased on his prolonged journey to his ultimate existence in the other world. In order to maintain this necessary housing of the spirit, they developed a number of embalming methods, some of which were not as successful as the natural preservations which were achieved by placing the remains in hot, dry sand.

There were basically three embalming techniques. The most elaborate and likewise the most expensive method, performed for the wealthier classes, involved the removal of the brain through the nasal passages and the extraction of the internal organs, except for the heart and kidneys, through standardized incisions. The cranial cavity was filled with hot resin and the abdominal cavity, after being cleansed with palm wine and aromatics, was filled with any one of a number of materials including spices, resin, or resin-soaked sawdust. The body was then placed in natron, a sodium carbonate found in the Libyan Desert. After complete desiccation [dehydration or drying], which took as many as seventy days to achieve, the body was cleansed with various spices and oils. Then followed the elaborate wrapping of each digit, each limb, and the entire body with as many as four hundred fifty yards of cotton or linen, into which were tucked bracelets, necklaces, rings, charms, and jeweled amulets, which were intended for the use of the spirit during its hazardous journey. After the linen was sealed with resin or gum, the body was returned to the relatives for storage in mummy cases, familiar to us in the case of the Egyptians.

One of the cheaper processes involved injection of cedar oil into the abdomen by the use of syringes and the desiccation of the body in natron. The oil and intestines were then withdrawn. In the simplest and cheapest method, the intestines were cleared out, and after seventy days in natron the procedure was considered completed. In these simpler methods no wrapping with linen was undertaken.

Many Egyptian mummies have survived to modern times in remarkable states of preservation, as we know, but many were reduced to dust during scientific examinations or putrefied rapidly when the bandaging was removed.

The Incas of South America were also very successful at mummifying human remains, but the procedures used are not known for certain. It is thought, however, that the bodies were desiccated before burial, probably because of the hot, dry climate of the region.

In Tibet, mummification was used upon bodies of the highest lamas. After evisceration [disembowelment], the abdominal cavity was packed with lacquer-saturated padding and the body wrapped in lacquered silk. It was thoroughly dried by placing it in a lotus position in a salt-filled room into which for several days heated air was forced. After cooling and unwrapping, it was covered with gold leaf by experienced craftsmen and then conveyed to the Hall of Incarnations where it was seated on a throne in the solemn company of other gilded lamas of past ages.[1]

Very unusual substances have been used in man's efforts to conserve mortal flesh. In Babylon, preservations are said to have been effected by the immersion of bodies in honey; the remains of Alexander the Great are reputed to have been preserved in this manner. The body of Sir Gerard de Braybroke, who died in 1422, was discovered in the Church of Danbury in 1779, where examining doctors noted with amazement that it was lying in an aromatic fluid which tasted like mushroom catchup spiced with Spanish olives, according to the adventurous soul who partook of it. In 1723 the well-preserved body of a naval commander was found steeped in rum, "as befitted one of his calling."

More modern methods were devised when it became necessary to preserve bodies and various organs for anatomical dissection and storage in medical museums. Several original methods were used which necessitated the use of saltpeter, pitch, resin, tar, salt, camphor, or cinnamon, but alcohol proved to be the most popular, except that it caused undue shrinkage and loss of color. In the nineteenth century the use of formaldehyde came into vogue, and anatomical specimens were treated with this, the color being restored by brief immersion in spirits and storage in a fifty percent solution of glycerine.[2]

[1]*The Third Eye, The Autobiography of a Tibetan Lama.* T. Lobsang Rampa. Doubleday & Co., Inc., Garden City, New York. 1957. pp. 241-245.

[2]*The Disposal of the Dead.* C. J. Polson, R. P. Brittain & T. K. Marshal. Charles C. Thomas, Publisher. Springfield, Illinois. 1962. p. 13.

Modern embalming methods, which are more detailed and scientifically formulated than one would ordinarily suppose, entail basically the drainage of the blood vessels and the injection, under pressure, of a solution of formaldehyde, glycerine and borax, the principle constituents of embalming fluids. These ingredients and many others may be used in various proportions and quantities as the embalmer deems proper and necessary. Depending upon the strength of the arterially injected fluid and the weight of the subject, as many as ten to fourteen pints of a strong solution may be used in an average adult body. If a weaker solution is employed, embalmers generally compensate for this by injecting a larger volume of fluid, which might measure from twenty-four to thirty-two pints, reckoned entirely upon the subject's weight.[3]

The complete dissolution of some bodies may require several years depending upon the strength of the embalming fluid used, but even with these specialized chemicals the majority of tombs are ready for re-use after only one year's occupancy.

Cemetery workers around the world could undoubtedly relate instances in which mummified remains have been discovered. Those sextons with whom the author spoke concerning this subject reported that the finding of such specimens is quite rare. One sexton of a large cemetery who had supervised the opening of vaults both above and below the ground for over twenty-eight years, related that only one such preservation was found during that time and that it was as dry and hard as stone. Other sextons, with as many as fifteen years experience each, had never seen such a preservation but had heard that at least one of these rigid conservations had been found previously in their cemeteries. The mummified condition of these remains is believed by them to have been effected by strong embalming fluids, which halted dissolution until the desiccation of the tissues was completed under prolonged drying conditions.

Undoubtedly the most modern method devised to preserve human bodies might well be said to belong to the realm of science fiction. This is the technique fostered by the Life Extension Society (Cryogenics) in which the bodies of persons dying of incurable ailments are frozen in a state of suspended animation in thermostatically controlled cylinders, to be thawed and reanimated in future ages when science has developed a cure for their particular maladies. Tests in-

---

[3]*Ibid.* pp. 303-305.

volving the freezing and reanimation of animals have failed miserably, and the revival of those persons already frozen is hoped for with an unfounded optimism. The followers of this cult are, nevertheless, looking to the future and investing considerable sums of money in it.

Now that we have examined the methods and materials used during various ages in the deliberate preservation of human bodies, we will consider the conditions and elements favoring the *accidental* or *natural preservation* of human remains. This analysis is very important since the bodies of the incorruptibles have been erroneously classified by many as natural mummies. The origins and differences between the two groups are vastly distinct as further exploration of this subject will disclose.

II

Moisture is the principle deterrent in the formation of natural or accidental mummies. Contrarily, interment in a warm, dry atmosphere, particularly in warm dry sand, permits the rapid evaporation of the body fluids, completely arresting the dissolution of the internal organs, where the process of corruption usually begins. During the drying process, the skin loses its elasticity as the moisture and fatty materials below it evaporate, causing considerable wrinkling; or it may contract, producing an unequal distortion of the features.

Natural preservations have been achieved most successfully in the hot, dry climates of Egypt, Peru, and Mexico. The hot sterile sand of Egypt produced such satisfactory mummies of unembalmed bodies that during the late nineteenth century European collectors were fraudulently provided with what were supposed to be mummies of Pharaoh times by grave robbers who dug up bodies from relatively new cemeteries and wrapped them in aged, yellowed linen, into which they tucked golden amulets for further deceptive purposes.

Natural mummies are occasionally produced in dry, cold air. A natural mummy was produced in a cave in the highlands of Chile. In February, 1954, the body of an eight or nine-year-old boy was found at 17,712 feet on El Plomo peak. It is believed he was numbed by a narcotic and left to freeze as an Inca sacrifice. The mummified body was brought down with great difficulty and with great caution and is exhibited in a deep-freeze showcase in a Santiago museum. The body is in a sitting position with the arms wrapped around the legs, which were drawn up, permitting the boy's head to rest upon the knees. The death of the youngster, in this position, is thought to have occurred about five hundred years ago.

Bodies of "Iron Age" farmers which have been preserved for nearly three thousand years have been uncovered in the peat bogs of Denmark, Ireland, and Scotland. These bodies are always greatly discolored, due to the chemical reaction of the peat fluids, the bodies ranging from a red color to a dark mahogany. The accidental preservation is attributed to the humic and tannic acid in the peat, which not only inhibits bacterial growth, but also tans the flesh.

A strange and rare condition which permits the body to retain its corporal existence is the formation of a substance called adipocere, which is a waxy, brownish substance produced by the dead body during the chemical changes brought on by the breakdown of the tissues. This material has occurred in bodies which have been interred in soil containing a great deal of decomposed matter or under certain conditions in which moisture plays an important role. These bodies cannot be considered truly incorrupt since the tissues are transformed into another substance. Some of the bodies thus transformed are said to retain the lines of the face, the features and expression, and the hair, but for the most part they are hideous objects. Occasionally this unusual flabby mass—adipocere—is found only in the chest and abdominal cavities, but it is readily recognized by physicians. Since this condition is quite rare, it is not deserving of further attention but is presented here simply as another condition under which a body may retain its existence. It must be noted that this substance was never reported in connection with the bodies of the saints mentioned in this volume, and if the material were actually a part of the bodies, but not recognized by medieval examiners of such relics, it could only have been found in a very few indeed, since its formation is a rarity.

Radiation has been suggested in recent years as the reason for the preservation of the large number of bodies found in Wasserburg Somersdorf Castle in Mittelfranken Province, Germany, where the mummies found were thought to be about two hundred fifty years of age. Strong traces of radioactivity were discovered in the tombs, which is credited with having arrested dissolution. The remains, however, appear to be little more than hair and fragments of flesh covering ghastly skeletal remains.

The Church of St. Antony in Pechersk (also known as Kievo-

Pechersk), Russia, overlooks the Caves of St. Antony, which contain underground chapels in which several rooms were set aside for the tombs of some forty monks who lived during the eleventh century. Their withered skeletal bodies lie in half-opened coffins beneath sheets of glass. Only a small portion of their bodies can be seen since a purple veil covers their skulls and their bodies are clothed in blue robes. Their preservation is attributed to the "special components of the limestone" of the caves.

A curious condition exists in the lead cellar of the Bremen Cathedral (Der Dom Zu Bremen) in West Germany. During the eighteenth century a young man fell into the cellar and succumbed to the injuries he sustained. His body was discovered several years later in an excellent state of preservation. Soon after the discovery, members of the German aristocracy requested burial there and their mummified bodies can now be viewed in their opened caskets. The truly astounding factor of this burial place is that animals or fowl hung there are mummified in due time, the flesh becoming like leather, even though fresh air circulates freely through opened windows. Specialists from time to time perform experiments there, taking bits of flesh for analysis, but as yet the preserving qualities of the place are left unexplained, although radiation could be extended as a contributing agent.

Now that the reasons for the *natural* or *accidental preservations* have been briefly outlined, we will advance to the circumstances under which the incorruptibles have been discovered, the reasons favoring their conservations being, in almost all cases, completely unexplainable.

III

The incorruptibles have been incorrectly classified as natural mummies, but as we have seen, the products of the deliberate and accidental preservations, without exception, have been not more than shriveled specimens, always rigid and extremely dry. Most of the incorruptibles, however, are neither dry nor rigid but quite moist and flexible, even after the passage of centuries. Moreover, their preservations have been accomplished under conditions which would naturally foster and encourage putrefaction, and they have survived circumstances which would have unquestionably necessitated and resulted in the destruction of the others.

As previously noted, if natural mummification is to be accomplished, the process must be done swiftly under ideal drying conditions before various susceptible areas of the body begin the natural processes of deterioration. Nevertheless, the burials of a number of incorruptibles were delayed due to the reluctance of the devout to be separated from the object of their veneration. The body of St. Bernardine of Siena was for this reason left exposed for twenty-six days and St. Angela Merici for thirty days. St. Theresa Margaret of the Sacred Heart was likewise exposed for fifteen days and St. Antoninus for eight days, to name only a few such postponements.

The deliberate and speedy destruction of the bodies of three saints was intended when lime was placed in the caskets of St. Francis Xavier, St. John of the Cross, and St. Pascal Baylon. In the first two cases the hasty destruction of the bodies was anticipated so that their pending translations could be more conveniently and hygenically undertaken by the transference of their bones rather than the removal of their half-decayed corpses. In the case of St. Pascal, the hasty destruction was hoped for so that no offensive odors would be detected by the many visitors to his shrine, a fact which might detract from the devotion lavished on his memory. In all three cases the preservation triumphed. In fact, in the case of St. Francis Xavier, in spite of this initial treatment, various translations, the amputation of his members for relics, and the rough handling the body endured when forced into a grave too small to accommodate its normal length, it was yet so beautiful one hundred forty-two years later that the best description we have of him was recorded at the time of that examination. The body of St. John of the Cross remains even to the present day perfectly flexible.

Moisture is the chief factor which encourages dissolution, yet many of the incorruptibles encountered this condition during their entombments, their preservations being inexplicably maintained in spite of it. We might consider the case of St. Catherine of Genoa, who remained in the grave for eighteen months, but was found perfectly spotless in spite of a damp and decayed shroud. St. Mary Magdalene de' Pazzi was disinterred one year after her death, at which time her religious clothing was found wet, although her body remained completely unaffected. St. Madeleine Sophie Barat remained perfectly preserved for twenty-eight years although she was found in damp and mildewed garments in a casket which was in a state of advanced disintegration. Nine months after her death, St. Teresa of

Avila was found in a coffin, the top of which had rotted away, permitting damp earth to cover her body. Although her remains were clothed in dirty and rotten fragments of fabric, her body was not only fresh and perfectly intact after its cleansing, but was mysteriously fragrant as well.

Such was the excessive moisture in the vault of St. Charles Borromeo in the Cathedral of Milan that it caused the corrosion and rotting of his two coffin lids, causing dampness to penetrate to the body. Considering that the body had been embalmed in the customary manner in vogue at that time, it seems quite likely that the less sainted remains of another would have been either completely destroyed or seriously harmed under similar conditions. As stipulated by the rules of her order, St. Catherine of Bologna was confined to the grave without benefit of a coffin, yet her body remained undamaged after eighteen days. The remains of St. Pacifico of San Severino were similarly entombed for four years; nevertheless, his perfect preservation was maintained.

Fifty-six years following the death of St. Catherine Labouré, her body was found perfectly white and natural looking, even though her triple coffin had been affected in various ways by excessive moisture. So great was the amount of humidity which penetrated through cracks in the caskets that part of her habit faded onto her hand, as observed by the attending physicians. The winding sheet was also found permeated with excessive dampness. The body of St. Catherine of Siena also endured abuses from dampness but was found unaffected after it had been placed in a cemetery where Bl. Raymond of Capua found that "it was much exposed to the rain." Her burial garments were said to have suffered severely from the dampness.

Of the many saintly relics which survived the expected ravages of moisture during their entombments, perhaps the most outstanding is the case of Saint Charbel Makhlouf, who was consigned to the grave without a coffin, as recommended by the rule of his religious order. His body was found floating in mud in a flooded grave during his exhumation, conducted four months after his death—a span of time sufficient to allow at least its partial destruction. His body, which has remained perfectly lifelike and flexible for more than seventy years, constantly emits a blood-like fluid, which has been acknowledged as truly prodigious.

The bodies of three saints endured unusual conditions: that of burial in air, in water, and in a bloody, mutilated condition. The preservation of the body of St. Coloman is quite noteworthy since his body remained suspended from the tree from which he was hanged for such a lengthy period that it was acknowledged by the townspeople as nothing less than miraculous. It must be noted that decomposition of a body exposed to air is eight times more rapid than of those consigned to a tomb because of the activity of the microorganisms in the air.[4]

After the martyrdom of St. Josaphat, his body was thrown into a nearby river, where it remained for almost a week. Upon being retrieved, it was found to have suffered no ill effects and was consigned to a grave, where it was again found undamaged five years later although the place was excessively damp, causing the deterioration of his vestments.

One of the most amazing preservations is that of St. Andrew Bobola. Prior to his martyrdom he was partially flayed alive, his hands were hacked off and his tongue was torn from his head. Splinters of wood were driven under his fingernails, and his face sustained such mutilations that he was scarcely recognizable. After hours of further tortures and mutilations, he was dispatched by a sword's blow to the neck. His body was hastily buried by Catholics in a vault beneath the Jesuit church at Pinsk, where it was found forty years later perfectly preserved, in spite of the open wounds, which would normally foster corruption. Although his grave had been damp, causing his vestments to rot, and in spite of the proximity of decaying corpses, his body was perfectly flexible, his flesh and muscles soft to the touch, and the blood which covered the numerous wounds was found to be like that which is freshly congealed. The preservation was officially recognized by the Congregation of Rites in 1835. Even though the relic was roughly handled during its numerous translations, the body remains after more than three hundred years in a marvelous state of preservation.

Who can explain the reasons for this strange dispensation, which affects so many holy persons who, moreover, represent many nations and who lived in various environmental conditions? Who can explain why these holy relics remained unharmed although buried under diverse situations and frequently in tombs in which the previous occupants had complied with natural laws? Further, who can account for the mysterious exudations of clear, sweet smelling oils which flowed

---

[4]*Ibid.* pp. 284-285.

at one time or another from most of these relics, to the perplexity of examining physicians?

Apart from mysterious perfumes, the transpiration of this unusual liquid is the most frequently reported phenomenon. It has been recorded, to mention only a few of the saints so favored, in the cases of St. Mary Magdalene de' Pazzi, St. Julie Billiart, St. Hugh of Lincoln, St. Agnes of Montepulciano, St. Teresa of Avila, St. Camillus de Lellis, and St. Pascal Baylon. The oil which flowed at various times throughout the centuries from the body of Blessed Matthia Nazzarei of Matelica, who died in 1320, has been flowing continuously from her hands and feet since the year 1920. The phenomenal conservation of Saint Charbel Makhlouf is constantly attended by a perspiration of water and blood, which has flowed since its appearance four months after his death in 1898. In Toledo, Spain, the body of the Venerable Mother Maria of Jesus, a companion of the great St. Teresa of Avila, exudes a perfume described as that of roses and jasmines and additionally transpires an oil which continues to flow in our day. As early as the eighth century, St. John Damascene recognized this phenomenon when he wrote: "Christ gives us the relics of saints as health-giving springs through which flow blessings and healing. This should not be doubted. For if at God's word water gushed from hard rock in the wilderness—yes, and from an ass's jawbone when Samson was thirsty—why should it seem incredible that healing medicine should distill from the relics of saints?" Similar exudations have never been reported with regard to the deliberately or the naturally preserved, nor have they been explained by scientific observers.

The odor of sanctity, which was perceived and deposed by witnesses of unquestionable integrity, is so frequently recorded as to be almost taken for granted.[5] The observers at the exhumation of St. Albert the Great, which was conducted two hundred years after his death, were greatly astonished on detecting a heavenly perfume, which proceeded from the Saint's relics. The body of St. John of the Cross was fragrant many years after his death, and the body of Blessed Angelo of Borgo San Sepolcro was still sweet smelling two

---

[5]The phrase "died in the odor of sancity" is found in countless biographies of the saints and beati, and, whereas it is normally used in a figurative sense to denote "dying a saintly death," the expression has a foundation in fact, as the reader will come to understand as he progresses through the book. Consequently, the term "the odor of sanctity" is used in a literal sense in this work since the research presented here justifies this usage.

hundred seventy-six years after his passing. The mysterious fragrance which was noted about the body of St. Teresa Margaret of the Sacred Heart was found to have attached itself to all the objects she had used during her life. Similarly, the sweetness about the body of St. Lucy of Narni was noticed to cling to objects reverently touched to the relic during its exposition four years after her death. The scent which was often noticed about the body of St. Teresa of Avila during her lifetime was also noticed during the many exhumations and translations of her body and was last observed by the sisters of her convent at Alba de Tormes during the last exhumation of the body in 1914, more than three hundred thirty years after her death. The body of St. Rita of Cascia is also still fragrant after more than five hundred years. The perfume which was noted about the body of St. Vincent Pallotti at the time of his death continued to linger in the room in which he died for one month following his death, in spite of an open window. The same is likewise the case with St. John of God, except that the fragrance which lingered in the death chamber for many days following his passing was renewed there for many years on each Saturday, the day on which his death occurred.

As previously considered, the bodies of natural mummies are hard and rigid. By way of contrast, we must observe that many, if not most, of the incorruptibles never experienced cadaveric rigidity and were flexible for many years after their deaths, many remaining flexible after the lapse of centuries. This departure from the general norm was observed in the cases of Bl. Alphonsus de Orozco whose body was flexible twelve years after his death, St. Andrew Bobola for forty years, and St. Catherine Labouré for fifty-seven years. St. Catherine of Bologna's body was so flexible twelve years after her passing that it was placed in the sitting position in which she is still viewed. The body of Blessed Eustochia Calafato was also placed in that same position one hundred fifty years after her death. The body of St. John of the Cross, who died in 1591, is still perfectly supple as is also the body of St. Clare of Montefalco. This phenomenon is very common and will be mentioned in the chapters covering the particular saints whose bodies were thus exempt from the natural law.

Another condition which defies explanation is the flow of fresh blood that proceeded from a number of these bodies many years after death. This prodigy is carefully analyzed in Fr. Herbert Thurston's *The Physical Phenomena of Mysticism,* in which the reader may find interesting details. This spectacle was observed eighty years after the death of St. Hugh of Lincoln, when the head separated from the neck. Nine months after the death of St. John of the Cross, fresh blood flowed from the wound resulting from an amputated finger. During the solemn exhibition of the body of St. Bernardine of Siena, which lasted twenty-six days following his death, a quantity of bright red blood issued from his nose on the twenty-fourth day, as observed and recorded by St. John Capistran. During the medical examination of the body of St. Francis Xavier one and a half years after his death, one of the physicians inserted his finger into a wound on the body and withdrew from it blood, which was declared to be "fresh and untainted." The mortal wound on the forehead of St. Josaphat bled twenty-seven years following his death. Forty-three years following the passing of St. Germaine de Pibrac, while workmen were preparing the tomb for another occupant, a tool used by them slipped and injured the nose of the corpse; the discovery of the young girl's perfectly preserved and flexible body, coupled with the miraculous flow of blood which came from the wound, set into motion the events which culminated in her canonization. And finally, forty years after the death of St. Nicholas of Tolentino, a lay brother secretly detached the arms of the relic. He was ultimately caught and properly reprimanded when a copious flow of blood signaled the sacrilegious act. The two arms were seen to effuse blood on many occasions during the next four hundred years, an occurrence which was accepted as miraculous by Pope Benedict XIV.

Although having nothing to contribute to the preservation of these relics, the appearance of light about the bodies and tombs of some of these saints signaled, as it were, their heavenly endowment. The sanctity of St. Guthlac was affirmed by the many witnesses who saw the house wherein he died enveloped with a bright light, which proceeded from there into the heavens. The perfume which proceeded from the mouth of St. Louis Bertrand on his deathbed was accompanied by an intense light which brightened his humble cell for several minutes. Many other saints were favored with this illumination, including St. John of the Cross, St. Anthony of Stroncone, and St. Jeanne de Lestonnac. Perhaps the most astounding manifestation occurred at the tomb of Saint Charbel Makhlouf. The light which glowed brightly for forty-five nights at his tomb was witnessed by many villagers and eventually resulted in the exhumation of his body, disclosing phenomena which are still observed.

Even the most persistent and confirmed rationalist must admit, when confronted with these witnessed and avowed marvels, that the incorruptibles cannot be classified with the other preservations, but are, in reality, a unique and exclusive fraternity. The incorruptibles, for the most part, were never embalmed or treated in any manner. The few bodies which were deliberately conditioned will be mentioned when their cases are studied individually. Many of the religious orders of which these saints were members strictly believed and maintained that the natural process of dust returning to its kind should be undertaken without chemical interference. This perhaps accounts for the large percentage of these relics which were unembalmed.

Rarely in these biographies will mention be made of the cause of death since in most instances only vague symptoms were recorded in ancient and medieval records. Some would believe that such maladies might furnish some insight into their preservations; however, we can safely assume that the incorruptibles' final illnesses were nothing unique, but those of a spectrum of infirmities from which millions of others suffered, died, and were buried—never to be seen again.

Pope Benedict XIV included two lengthy chapters entitled *De Cadaverum Incorruptione* in his great work on the beatification and canonization of saints. In these chapters he outlined the Church's position with regard to such preservations. The Pope ruled that the bodies of saintly persons which are found intact, but disintegrated after a few years, could not be considered *miraculous* preservations. The only conservations he was willing to consider extraordinary are those which retain their lifelike flexibility, color, and freshness, without deliberate intervention, for many years following their deaths. These requirements are, of course, magnificently met by most of the incorruptibles included in this volume. That Pope's opinion concerning this phenomenon and the Church's present position is that the Church is reluctant to accept the incorruption of the body of a candidate for sainthood as a miracle supporting proof of his sanctity. Several exceptions have been made, one of which was the preservation of the body of St. Andrew Bobola. Debated by successive Promoters of the Faith and the Postulators of his Cause in both 1739 and 1830, the condition of the body, though mutilated because of the wounds inflicted during his martyrdom, was ultimately accepted by the Congregation of Rites as one of the miracles required for his beatification.

The cause of beatification was well under way in most cases before the tombs were opened for the necessary recognition of the relics, as required by the Sacred Congregation of Rites, the discovery of the preservations contributing only further distinction to their candidacies. The dissolution of some of the relics had no detracting effect whatsoever on their causes, as evidenced by the large number of canonized saints and the relatively small percentage of incorruptibles.

In the individual, present-day descriptions of these relics, it is often reported that their skin is dry or like parchment. This expected condition resulted *after* the bodies were inexplicably moist and lifelike for many years, sometimes for centuries. The darkened condition of some of these specimens can be considered a minor blemish, for we must recall that these relics were constantly exposed to the organisms in the air after their disinterment, were additionally subjected to extensive handling during their numerous translations, and endured in the process sudden changes in temperature and humidity. When we examine the paintings whose origins date from the times of these saints and inspect their surfaces, which time has minutely etched, it seems quite extraordinary that human flesh, so vulnerable to temptation and susceptible to decay, should have survived the initially hazardous circumstances of the tomb, of many scientific examinations, and of years of exposition, without special care or treatment of any nature. In spite of the darkness or dryness of some of these relics, it must be noted that well conserved hearts and other relics were extracted from them without damage, and many of the bodies retained their flexibility in spite of their dry outer flesh.

Various arguments will be presented by the skeptics in an attempt to rationalize these preservations. Perhaps the most frequently forwarded will be that of radioactivity. As explored previously, in the cases where this unseen condition was extended as a cause of preservation, many preserved bodies were found in each such place. With regard to the incorruptibles, only single cases were recorded, and in most instances, the tombs involved had been used previously with normal and expected results. It would seem unlikely for one grave to contain this cosmic element while others immediately adjacent remained unaffected.

One conjecture is that "ascetical diets" and abstinence from foods which would contribute to rapid putrefaction (whichever these may be) aided in these conservations. However, the phenomenon of incorruption was never recorded among victims of famines or in regions where, because of extreme poverty, the inhabitants lived on very "ascetical diets."

The most mercenary of skeptics will argue that such conservations are nothing more than hoaxes perpetrated by the votaries at the shrines or by the religious orders. This opinion is strongly disputed, for when one considers that the members of the religious orders have always striven by a devotion to prayer and the performance of penances for a greater degree of perfection and have withdrawn themselves from the pleasures and comforts of the world to advance in the way of virtue, it would constitute an outrageous discourtesy to accuse them of participating in a deception of any nature. Furthermore, the relics periodically undergo scientific and medical examination, and many are exposed in public shrines and churches for the admiration and examination of visitors.

Those who would question the propriety of exhibiting such relics and criticize those who pay them respect must recall that the tombs of great personages have always been visited. The Russians feel fortunate in visiting and viewing the carefully embalmed body of Nikolai Lenin, which is exposed in the Lenin Mausoleum in Red Square. The body of Joseph Stalin was similarly glass-encased in the same mausoleum from the time of his death in 1953 until 1961 when, during the de-Stalinization program, his body was removed from its position of honor and placed in a plot of ground behind the Lenin shrine.

The presence or absence of faith will undoubtedly determine the viewpoint with which one would accept this phenomenon of incorruption. For those who habitually search for a natural or socioeconomic explanation for everything, there are no arguments which will suffice to satisfy their doubts; therefore, this material is presented to those open-minded readers who would consider the factors involved with patient and respectful consideration.

For those of us who have admired and loved certain of these saints, it is a comfort of sorts to know that they are not just somewhere in the great realms beyond, but that their actual bodies, which will one day be made glorious, are still present among us. Catholics are privileged, indeed, not only to have these unique relics but also to be able to look upon the very faces of these religious paragons who fought a good fight, who finished the course of life in a most edifying manner, and who kept and practiced the Faith to an heroic degree.

Now that the subject of the preservation of human bodies, both saintly and otherwise, has been, it is hoped, adequately, if not briefly, introduced, it is an honor to present the incorruptibles.

SAINT CECILIA

Unknown—177

History indicates that the first saint whose body experienced the phenomenon of incorruption is St. Cecilia, the patroness of musicians. The year of her birth is unknown, but it is believed she died about 177 A.D. Cecilia was a member of a rich and distinguished Roman family, who gave her in marriage to a young nobleman named Valerian, despite her desire to remain a virgin. On their wedding night Cecilia was successful in persuading the new groom to respect her vow of virginity and later converted him to the Faith when he was favored with a vision of Cecilia's guardian angel. Valerian and his brother, Tiburtius, who was also converted by Cecilia, were later called upon by the early Christian persecutors to renounce their religion. When both heroically refused, they were beheaded and buried along the Appian Way. Cecilia was arrested for having buried their bodies and for this "crime" was given the choice of sacrificing to the heathen gods or being put to death. She steadfastly affirmed her faith and chose to die rather than renounce it.

Because of her nobility and youth, her captors decided to execute her in secrecy to avoid the expected criticism of the people. She was subsequently confined to the vapor bath of her home to die of suffocation. She remained a whole day and night in that stifling environment, yet remained unharmed. An experienced executioner was then sent to behead her, but due to a loss of courage at having to kill such a young and beautiful woman, he failed to sever her head with the three blows prescribed by law. He ultimately fled, leaving the Saint on the pavement of her bath, alive and fully conscious, with her head half severed. She was lying on her right side, her hands crossed in prayer before her. She turned her face to the floor and remained praying in that position for three days and nights. The position of her fingers, three extended on her right hand and one on the left, were her final silent profession of faith in the Holy Trinity.

The early Christians clothed the body of the martyr in rich robes of silk and gold and placed it in a cypress coffin in the same position in which she had expired. At her feet were placed the linen cloths and veils which were used to collect her blood. She was laid to rest in the Catacomb of St. Callistus by the future Pope Urban, who had baptized her husband and brother-in-law.

In the year 822, during the time of the restoration of the church dedicated to her memory, Pope Pascal I wished to transfer the remains of the Saint to a place of honor in her cathedral but could not locate her grave. The Saint appeared to him in a remarkable vision while he was at prayer and told him of the location of her body. The relic was found in exactly the place indicated. The Pope then had the body, along with the bones of her husband, her brother-in-law, and the martyr Maximum, placed below the altar of the church.

Seven hundred seventy-seven years later, one of the most documented exhumation of any saint's body occurred in 1599, when Cardinal Sfondrato ordered the restoration of some parts of the basilica. On October 20th of that year, during the course of work being done under and near the high altar, two white marble sarcophagi were discovered, which corresponded with the description left by Pascal I of the caskets containing the relics of the holy martyrs. The Cardinal had the sarcophagi opened in the presence of witnesses of unquestionable integrity. After the marble covering was removed, the original cypress casket was found in a good state of preservation. The Cardinal, with understandable emotion, raised the lid, exposing to view the treasure which had been confided to the grave by Popes Urban and Pascal. The mortal remains were found in the same position in which the Saint had died almost fifteen hundred years before. Through a silk veil which modestly covered the body could be seen the gold embroidered dress of the Saint, the mortal wound in the neck, and the blood-stained clothes. Pope Clement VIII was informed at once of the discovery but was unable to visit the tomb immediately because of a severe attack of the gout, but sent instead Cardinal Baronius, who together with Antonio Bosio, the explorer of subterranean Rome, left us priceless descriptive documents relating to the events of this exhumation.

Peering through the ancient veil which covered the body, they noted that Cecilia was of small stature and that her head was turned downward, but due to a "holy reverence," no further examination was made. Bosio recorded his opinion that the Saint was found in the same position in which she had expired.[1]

Cardinal Sfondrato wished to retain as a memorial of this touching event a small piece of the blood-stained linen, and he distributed tiny pieces of this cloth to many cardinals in Rome. But upon inspecting the last piece, which he had reserved for himself, he discovered adhering to it a small fragment of the Saint's bone, which had been dislodged by the sword and which an early Christian had unknowingly picked up with the cloth while staunching the wound of the holy martyr. Sfondrato preserved this relic as a dear and priceless treasure and placed it and the skulls of SS. Valerian, Tiburtius and Maximum in separate reliquaries for exposition.[2]

The Cardinal also wished to retain a small piece of the Saint's dress and while engaged in securing this, he felt under the virgin's clothing the cords and knots of a hair shirt.[3]

The casket of the Saint was placed in a hall located at the upper extremity of a nave of the basilica where it could be seen through a grated window. The platform and casket were covered with gold-embroidered silk drapery, and the room was magnificently decorated with candelabras, handsome lamps, and flowers of silver and gold. The sanctuary was further enhanced by a mysterious and delightful flower-like odor which proceeded from the coffin.[4]

On the orders of Pope Clement VIII, the relic was left exposed there until the feast of St. Cecilia, November 22, and so great was the outpouring of the Roman faithful who converged on the basilica to view the body that the Pontifical Swiss Guards were called upon to maintain order.[5]

At the end of the one-month period of exposition, the relic, still reposing in the ancient cypress casket, was placed in a silver coffin which had been commissioned by the Pope himself as a symbol of his veneration for the holy martyr. In the presence of forty-two cardinals and diplomatic representatives from several countries, the Pope celebrated the Solemn High Mass during which the body of the Saint was again interred beneath the main altar.

A sculptor of unusual talents, Stefano Maderno (1576-1636), who

---

[1]*The History of the Popes—Drawn from the Secret Archives of the Vatican and other Original Sources.* Ludwig von Pastor. Kegan, Paul, Trench, Trubner & Co., Ltd. London. 1933. Volume XXIV, p. 521.

[2]*Ibid.* p. 522.

[3]*Life of Saint Cecilia, Virgin and Martyr.* Rev. Prosper Guéranger, Abbé de Solesmes. P. J. Kenedy & Sons. New York. p. 283.

[4]*Ibid.* p. 284.

[5]von Pastor. *Op. cit.* p. 523.

it appears was engaged in performing his trade during the restoration of the Basilica, executed a statue of the Saint, which is reputed to be one of the most celebrated and best known Italian works of art and is believed to represent the Saint in the exact posture of her body. This statue is found immediately in front of the high altar in a niche of black marble, which was designed by Maderno to give the appearance of an open sarcophagus. Doing so, Maderno introduced a new altar design which was frequently imitated.[6]

The Basilica of St. Cecilia is believed to have been built on the site of St. Cecilia's family mansion. The second chapel, on the right aisle, is called the Caldarium and is the room where St. Cecilia was condemned to death. Here are found the remains of an ancient Roman bathroom; the conduits are preserved which formerly contained the water which was heated in the lower room. The marble slab on the altar is the one on which Cecilia is believed to have survived the first martyrdom by suffocation and very well may be the slab which marked the place of her death.

---

[6]*Ibid.* p. 525.

A statue of Saint Cecilia (d. 177) executed by Stefano Maderno in 1599 at the time of the second exhumation of her incorrupt body. The position is the same as that of the relic and is believed to be the position in which she expired. Note the wound in the neck. The statue is located in the Basilica of Saint Cecilia in Rome.

— 2 —

SAINT AGATHA

Unknown—251

Saint Agatha, a martyr whose name is mentioned in the Canon of the Mass, has been honored since the most ancient times. Entirely reliable facts, other than those here mentioned, are scarce. The cities of Catania and Palermo dispute the honor of her birth. She is known to have been beautiful and wealthy, spending her life since early childhood in the grace and favor of God.

A magistrate named Quinctianus, whose chief occupation appears to have been the persecution of Christians, was attracted to the young virgin and attempted to seduce her. When she declined his advances, he entrusted her to a matron of a sinful house. When this tactic also failed to destroy her constancy, he had her beaten. Another time she was stretched on a wooden horse while an executioner tore her flesh with iron hooks, and on Quinctianus' direct order, finally amputated her breasts. Although suffering grievously, history records that she was able to address her torturer with these words: "Cruel man, have you forgotten your mother and the breasts that nourished you, that you dare to mutilate me in such a way?" When the third attempt failed to weaken her morals, the magistrate had her rolled naked over hot coals. A violent and sudden earthquake is said to have toppled a nearby hill, causing the torturers to flee in terror. After offering a prayer, the virgin expired.

The holy martyr, having been tortured and having died in Catania, was buried by the Christians of that city, where her body remained until the eleventh century. During an Arab occupation, it was transferred by the Byzantines to Constantinople, and a century later, through historical circumstances little known, it was returned to Catania. At this time, the incorrupt body was divided by the persons who had stolen it.

The body is now preserved in different reliquaries. The arms, legs, and breasts are preserved in a glass case in an incorrupt condition, although rather dried and dark after more than seventeen hundred years. The skull and principal relics are at Catania, enclosed in an ef-

47

figy on which rests a costly jeweled crown. The reliquary consists of the figure of the Saint from the head to the waist and is situated in an upright position. The figure is entirely covered with precious gems, rings, bracelets, pins, chains, and jeweled flowers and crosses donated by her grateful clients whose lives, through her intercession, have been saved from the frequent eruptions of Mount Etna, Europe's largest and most active volcano.

The jeweled reliquary is exposed for public veneration on three occasions during the year: during the three-day solemn festivities commemorating her feast on February 5; on February 12, which is the octave of the feast; and on the 17 of August, the feast of the translation of the relic.

St. Agatha has been designated one of the patronesses of nurses and is invoked against breast diseases and fires.

3

SAINT ETHELDREDA

630—679

King Anna of the East Angles and Queen Hereswide of England have the unique distinction of being the parents of five daughters, all of whom bear the title "Saint." Etheldreda, whose life is under consideration here, was the foundress of Ely Monastery, which she served as abbess for seven years. Her sister, St. Sexburga, entered this monastery after the death of her husband, King Erconbert, and later succeeded her sister as abbess. St. Withburga was a recluse at Dereham in Norfolk, where she founded a religious house, while St. Ethelburga and St. Sethrid each in turn served as abbess of the Monastery at Brie. History also records two brothers of these saintly women, Adlwulf and Adulphus.[1]

Other saints in this illustrious family were their aunt, St. Hilda, the foundress and abbess of Whitby monastery, and their mother, Hereswide, who, though not referred to as "Saint" Hereswide, nevertheless entered the religious life after the death of King Anna and died a holy death in the abbey of St. Clotilde, near Paris.

In spite of her protests, a diplomatic marriage was contracted between Princess Etheldreda and Prince Tonbercht, the ruler of the territory bordering her father's. The bridegroom, however, respected the vow of virginity his bride had made in her youth, and after an alliance of only three years she was left a widow. She then retired to the Isle of Ely, which had been given her as a marriage settlement by her husband, and there devoted herself for the next five years to continual prayer.

When the Saint was thirty years of age, she was coerced into another political marriage, this time with King Egfrid, who was then only sixteen years of age. During their twelve years of marriage she preserved her virginity in spite of the wishes of her husband and the advice of her confessor, St. Wilfrid. Egfrid eventually permitted her to enter the monastery ruled by his aunt, the Abbess Ebba, at

---

[1] *Saint Etheldreda.* Elisabeth Wilcocks. Catholic Truth Society. London. 1961. p. 7.

Coldingham, where the Saint was given the veil by St. Wilfrid in 671. Within a year the King regretted the permission he had reluctantly given his wife, and Etheldreda, with the help of two companions, was forced to flee from the monastery in order to escape the King, who had journeyed to the monastery to reclaim her. In the year 672 she reached her property at Ely, and the following year she secured enough money from her family to begin building, as was the custom at that time, a double monastery for monks and nuns, which she successfully ruled for almost seven years.

History reports that she prophesied her own death from the plague and also the number of those from the community who would fall victim to the disease. In compliance with her wishes, she was buried with all simplicity in a wooden coffin, but sixteen years later her sister, Sexburga, who had succeeded her as abbess, thought it best to take up the bones of the Saint and remove them to the church. It might be well to quote here the events surrounding the exhumation as recorded by St. Bede the Venerable, who carefully questioned those who witnessed the ceremony before reporting the event in his *Ecclesiastical History of the English Nation,* which was written about the year 730. He reports the proceedings in this manner:

> . . . The body of the holy virgin and spouse of Christ, when her grave was opened, being brought into sight, was found as free from corruption as if she had just died and been buried on that very day; as the aforesaid Bishop Wilfrid, and many others that know it, can testify. But the physician, Cynefrid, who was present at her death, and when she was taken up out of the grave, was wont of more certain knowledge to relate, that in her sickness she had a very great swelling under her jaw. "And I was ordered," said he, "to lay open that swelling, to let out the noxious matter in it, which I did, and she seemed to be somewhat more easy for two days, so that many thought she might recover from her distemper; but the third day the former pains returning, she was soon snatched out of the world, and exchanged all pain and death for everlasting life and health. And when so many years after her bones were to be taken out of the grave, a pavilion being spread over it, all the congregation of brothers were on the one side, and of sisters on the other, standing about it singing, and the abbess, with a few, being gone to take up and wash the bones, on a sudden we heard the abbess within loudly cry out. . . . Not long after they called me in, opening the door of the pavilion, where I found the body of the holy virgin taken out of the grave and laid on a bed, as if it had been asleep; then taking off the veil from the face, they also showed the

incision which I had made, healed up; so that, to my great astonishment, instead of the open gaping wound with which she had been buried, there then appeared only an extraordinarily slender scar."

Besides, all the linen cloths in which the body had been buried appeared entire and as fresh as if they had been that very day wrapped about her chaste limbs. . . . They washed the virgin's body, and having clothed it in new garments, brought it into the church, and laid it in the coffin that had been brought, where it is held in great veneration to this day. The coffin was found in a wonderful manner, as fit for the virgin's body as if it had been made purposely for her, and the place for the head particularly cut, exactly fit for her head, and shaped to a nicety.[2]

Etheldreda's body was enshrined in the abbey church, but one hundred years later the edifice was completely destroyed during an invasion by the Danes, who plundered the monastery and killed many of the sisters. The Saint's remains, however, were left undisturbed and remained so for over eight hundred years, until the infamous Reformation, when, on the orders of Henry VIII, her relics were scattered and the shrine so completely destroyed that only a plinth (base) remains. This remnant is still pointed out to visitors to the famous Ely Cathedral, which had developed in architectural perfection about the abbey church.[3]

In spite of the Saint's relics having disappeared during the time of the Reformation, her left hand was discovered about the year 1811 in what was evidently a priest's hiding-hole in penal times. The relic passed from one owner to another until it became the property of the Dominican Sisters of Stone, who have loaned it for an indefinite period to the Parish Church of St. Etheldreda on Egremont Street, Ely, Cambridgeshire, England. The relic rests on a seventeenth-century silver plate on which is engraved "*Manus Sanctae Etheldredae 679*" that is covered by a crystal cylinder, topped by a silver crown.

It is reported that when the relic was first discovered, it was so white it was thought to be carved of ivory, but on exposure to the air it gradually darkened until it is now dark brown and mummified.[4]

---

[2] *The Ecclesiastical History of the English Nation.* St. Bede the Venerable. J. M. Dent & Sons, Ltd. London. 1910 & 1958. Book 4, Chapter XIX.

[3] The relics of Etheldreda's sisters, Sexburga and Withburga, and her niece Ermenilda, were enshrined in the abbey church during the year 1106, and these were also destroyed at the time of the Reformation.

[4] Wilcocks. *Op. cit.* pp. 18-20. The present custodian of the relic related in recent

In 1954 the relic was officially examined in the presence of Cardinal Griffin's delegate, an expert from the Victoria and Albert Museum, and a surgeon, all of whom were very impressed on finding a tendon under the shriveled flesh of the thirteen-hundred-year-old hand.

St. Bede the Venerable composed in Etheldreda's honor a poem praising her virtues, and she remains the most popular of the Anglo-Saxon women saints.

---

correspondence with the author, that he once met some elderly Dominican Sisters who related that when they saw the hand during their youth, the skin of the hand was very white.

4

SAINT CUTHBERT

Unknown—687

Many incidents in the early life of St. Cuthbert illustrate his youthful piety, and it is known that he performed many miracles both before and after his admittance to the abbey of Melrose about the year 651. In addition to the miraculous attainment of food during the prolonged journeys he undertook to teach in various villages, creatures of the land, sea and air paid him homage; and he was at times tormented by devils, many of which he put to flight, both from his own person and from others who were obsessed. He once sowed a field with barley and received a plentiful harvest out of season; he also had the gifts of prophecy and healing.

Cuthbert held various administrative positions in monasteries at Ripon, Melrose, and Lindisfarne, but in the year 676 he resolved to become a hermit and built for himself a small dwelling on a tiny island about nine miles from Lindisfarne, where he lived in great virtue for many years. In view of the many miracles he worked and the degree of sanctity which he manifested, he was elected Bishop of Lindisfarne. Though at first he declined the high position, he finally accepted it, but only after King Egfrid, Bishop Trumwine, and many religious and influential men unanimously pleaded for his consent.

His episcopacy was distinguished by the manifestation of diverse miracles, the practice of extraordinary virtues, and the continued practice of monastic discipline. Feeling that his end was imminent, he resigned his bishopric and returned to his island retreat, where he prepared for death, which occurred in 687. His body was brought back to Lindisfarne and was buried in the cathedral, where it was left undisturbed for eleven years. At that time,

. . . Divine Providence put it into the minds of the brethren to take up his bones, expecting, as is usual with dead bodies, to find all the flesh consumed and reduced to ashes, and the rest dried up, and intending to put the same into a new coffin, and to lay them in the same place, but above the pavement, for the honour due to him. They acquainted Bishop Edbert with their design and he consented to it, and ordered

that the same should be done on the anniversary of his burial. They
did so, and opening the grave, found all the body whole, as if it had
been alive, and the joints pliable, more like one asleep than a dead
person; besides, all the vestments the body had on were not only
found, but wonderful for their freshness and gloss. The brothers seeing this, with much amazement hastened to tell the Bishop what they
had found . . .[1]

The body of the Saint endured various translations throughout the
centuries, one of the most noteworthy being the removal of the
Saint's casket on September 4, 999 into the church which later developed into the magnificent Durham Cathedral. The casket was not
opened at this time, nor was it opened during a visit to the church by
William the Conqueror in 1069 when he requested to see the remains
but was denied the privilege by the Bishop.

In the year 1104, when the Saint had been dead four hundred eighteen years, a dispute arose between certain prelates concerning the
condition of the body. To settle the matter the sepulcher was opened
by the monks, who found the body perfectly preserved, flexible, of a
natural weight and exhaling a heavenly fragrance.

The most noteworthy exhumation occurred during the reign of
Henry VIII when the convents and monasteries were suppressed
throughout England and the tombs of the saints were defaced and
their relics destroyed. The commissioners of the King, namely a Dr.
Lee, Dr. Henley and Mr. Blythman, were sent in the year 1537 to
Durham to destroy the shrine and relics of the Saint. These men, on
approaching the shrine,

. . . found many valuable and goodly jewels, especially one precious
stone which, by the estimate of these three visitors, and their skillful
lapidaries, was of value sufficient to redeem a prince. After the spoil
of his ornaments and jewels, they approached near to his body, expecting nothing but dust and ashes; but, perceiving the chest he lay in
strongly bound with iron, the goldsmith, with a smith's great fore-
hammer, broke it open, when they found him lying whole, uncorrupt,
with his face bare, and his beard as of a fortnight's growth, and all the
vestments about him, as he was accustomed to say Mass, and his met-
wand of gold lying by him. When the goldsmith perceived he had
broken one of his legs, in breaking open the chest, he was sore

---

[1]St. Bede the Venerable. *Op. cit.* Book IV, Chapter XXX. St. Bede is reputed to have
questioned eye witnesses to this event before reporting it in the *Ecclesiastical History*.

troubled at it, and cried, "Alas! I have broken one of his legs"; which Dr. Henley hearing, called to him, and bade him cast down his bones: the other answered he could not get them asunder, for the sinews and skin held them so that they would not separate. Then Dr. Lee stept up to see if they were so, and, turning about, spake in Latin to Dr. Henley that he was entire, though Dr. Henley, not believing his words, called again to have his bones cast down: Dr. Lee answered, "If you will not believe me, come up yourself and see him": then Dr. Henley stept up to him, and handled him, and found he lay whole; then he commanded them to take him down; and so it happened, contrary to their expectation, that not only his body was whole and uncorrupted, but the vestments wherein his body lay, and wherein he was accustomed to say Mass, were fresh, safe, and not consumed. Whereupon the visitors commanded him to be carried into the vestry, till the King's pleasure concerning him was further known; and, upon receipt thereof, the prior and monks buried him in the ground under the place where his shrine was exalted.[2]

The bills for constructing this new grave in 1542 are preserved in the cathedral and bear notations describing the covering stone and other particulars.

This new tomb was opened in the presence of many scientific observers on May 17, 1827, at which time a skeleton swathed in decayed robes, which were once of unquestionable beauty, was found in caskets which matched perfectly the descriptions of the three caskets in which the Saint had been placed during previous exhumations. The designs on the robes also matched the descriptions of those robes in which the Saint had been enveloped in 1104. In the coffins were found various articles: namely, a second skull, that of St. Oswald the king; a tiny oaken and silver altar; a maniple of Old English workmanship; part of a girdle and two bracelets woven of gold and scarlet threads; a gold cross set with garnets, at least as ancient as St. Cuthbert's own time; and pieces of rich robes of Byzantine or Sicilian origin; all of which perfectly matched the descriptions mentioned in ancient documents.

From all this evidence it could be logically presumed that the bones found in 1827 are those of St. Cuthbert; however, there are those who believe that after the 1537 exhumation, the Benedictine monks removed the body of the Saint for safekeeping, put in its stead

---

[2] *The History of St. Cuthbert.* Charles, Archbishop of Glasgow. Burnes & Oates, Ltd. London. and Catholic Publications Society Co. New York. 1887. pp. 337-338.

a skeleton, and hid the incorrupt body of St. Cuthbert in a place known only to three of the monks. As time went on, the location of the secret burial place was passed on to other members until the actual place of interment was either forgotten or misplaced.[3]

In Durham Cathedral, which is considered one of the most perfect, structurally and architecturally, of all the cathedrals of England, still repose the relics of the Saint not far from the remains of St. Bede the Venerable, St. Cuthbert's first biographer.

Disregarding all the arguments for or against the authenticity of the bones of St. Cuthbert, for purposes relating to the interests of this book, we must conclude, from the volume of evidence presented by Archbishop Charles and others, that the body of St. Cuthbert, at the time of the exhumation of 1537, had remained incorrupt for a period of eight hundred fifty years.

---

[3] See Archbishop Charles' *The History of St. Cuthbert,* pages 336-344, for all the arguments concerning the authenticity of these relics.

SAINT WERBURGH

Unknown—699

Werburgh was the daughter of King Wulfhere of Mercia and St. Erminilda and was the granddaughter of St. Sexburga and the grand-niece of St. Etheldreda, the famous Abbess of Ely. Despite her parent's wish that she marry advantageously, she dismissed the suitors, who were attracted by her beauty, and eventually gained the reluctant permission of her father to join her saintly aunt at the monastery of Ely. In 675, after the death of her father, her mother joined her in the same monastery.

St. Werburgh was so highly regarded that her uncle, King Ethelred, entrusted to her the supervision of all the convents in Mercia, which she brought to a state of perfect observance. Additionally, she found favor with him by establishing other houses of prayer throughout his kingdom.

After her saintly death she was buried, as she had requested, at her foundation at Hanbury where her grave became a place of pilgrimage. At the time of the Danish invasions, the incorrupt body of the Saint was removed for safekeeping to what was then a small fishing village named Chester, where pilgrims continued to visit her tomb for centuries.

Various orders of priests served as custodians of her shrine until the year 1050 when the Benedictines were entrusted with its care. Shortly thereafter they began building about it the cathedral and an adjoining monastery. During the reign of Henry the VIII the tomb was completely destroyed, and it is not known if the body was again removed for safety or was destroyed at this time.

SAINT GUTHLAC

667—714

The most reliable source of information concerning St. Guthlac is contained in a biography writted by Felix, an Anglo-Saxon monk, between the years 730 and 740. We are told that at the birth of the Saint a shining hand surrounded with a golden-red brightness descended from Heaven, blessed the front of the house where the pious mother was giving birth to the future Saint, and disappeared into the heavens; meanwhile, people, ". . . seized with uncommon amazement, were rushing up from all sides to see the miracle . . . and all who were present fell prone on the ground at the scene of the holy apparition and, not without some trepidation, humbly praised the Lord of Glory."[1]

We are further told that he joined the army at the age of fifteen, but after nine years considered the course of his life, and after a night spent in contemplation, he resolved to dedicate himself to God and entered the double monastery at Repton. After two years he felt himself called to the life of a hermit and moved to an island in the middle of a desolate region in the Lincolnshire fens. He established residence on the feast of St. Bartholomew and this saint proved to be a source of comfort and assistance by appearing to Guthlac many times when he was tempted and attacked by devils.

Besides his many miracles of healing, he prophesied the future, cast out devils and, like St. Francis of Assisi, had remarkable influence over the birds, fish, and wildlife.

As the reports of his powers and miraculous healings spread throughout the country, many of the faithful journeyed to visit the Saint; among his notable visitors were included Aethelbald of Mercia, whose future kingship was predicted by the Saint, St. Wilfred of York, and Bishop Haedda, who ordained him a priest.

On his deathbed the Saint told for the first time of an angel sent by

[1] *Anglo-Saxon Saints and Heroes.* Clinton Albertson, S.J. Fordham University Press. New York. 1967. p. 173. Words of Felix quoted by Fr. Albertson.

God to be his companion. Felix quotes the Saint as saying:

> From the second year that I began to dwell in this hermitage the Lord has sent an angel to be my consolation and to speak with me every morning and evening. He has revealed mysteries to me which it is not lawful for man to tell, he has softened the harshness of my life with messages from heaven, and he has revealed distant things to me, putting them before me as though done in my presence.[2]

Just as his birth had been heralded by a miracle, so his passing was manifest by another prodigy, for the hut in which he lay was surrounded by an unearthly light, a tower of fire was seen to rise into the heavens, and a scent of "honey-laden flowers" came forth from his mouth and filled the whole house.[3]

The Saint was buried in the ground with all simplicity, according to his wishes, but such was the cultus which developed that his sister, St. Pega, wished to rebury him in a more suitable manner.

> So on the anniversary of his burial, before a number of brothers and priests and other ecclesiastics of various ranks, his coffin was opened and his whole body found to be intact. It was as though he were still alive. The joints of his limbs were so pliant and flexible that he seemed much more like one asleep than dead. And all the garments he was clothed in were not only untainted but still shone with their first newness and original brightness. As soon as all present caught sight of this they shook in their shoes and were so astonished they scarcely could speak; they hardly dared look upon the miracle and knew not what to do.
>
> When Christ's handmaid, Pega, perceived all this, her soul was stirred with joy and, while the hymns and prayers of the Church were chanted in his honor, she wrapped the sacred body again in the cloth which the anchorite Ecgberht had sent for this purpose while Guthlac was still living. However, she did not put the coffin in the earth but rather in a special tomb . . .[4]

King Aethelbald, who had been a close friend of the Saint and who was privileged to have seen him in a vision, had the grave built up and decorated in an appropriate fashion; later, around this grave, the great Abbey of Croyland was built. The tomb was left undisturbed

---

[2]*Ibid.* p. 213.
[3]*Ibid.* p. 214.
[4]*Ibid.* p. 215.

until the time of the devastating Danish invasions and today only the North aisle, which is used as the parish church, and the bell tower are standing. The tomb of St. Guthlac was so completely destroyed that no trace of it or the relics was ever found among the rubble.

— 7 —

SAINT WITHBURGA

Unknown—743

Withburga was the youngest of the five saintly daughters of King Anna of the East Angles. Of her four sisters who were all regarded as saints, the most famous is Etheldreda whose name will forever be associated with England's magnificent Ely Cathedral.

Withburga resolved to become a nun after her father died in battle about the year 650. She proceeded to East Dereham, which was then a very secluded place, and laid the foundation for a church and began the building of a nunnery, which was not completed at the time of her pious death in the year 743.

The remains of the Saint were buried with the usual monastic simplicity in the churchyard at East Dereham where her body was found perfectly incorrupt when it was translated into the church fifty-five years later.[1] In the year 974, Brithnoth, the abbot of the Ely Monastery (which her sister, Etheldreda, had founded) removed the body to Ely and placed it near those of her two sisters, St. Etheldreda and St. Sexburga—and Sexburga's daughter, St. Ermenilda. In 1106 the remains were all interred near the main altar of the new church. At this time it was found that the bodies of Sexburga and Ermenilda had been reduced to bones but the body of Etheldreda was entire and that of St. Withburga was not only perfectly conserved but also flexible as well.[2]

The monk Thomas in his history of Ely, written the year following this discovery, relates that in the place where Withburga had been buried in the churchyard at East Dereham, a fresh spring of water gushed forth, which is still called St. Withburga's Well.[3]

The relics of Withburga, along with those of her saintly sisters, were all destroyed during the Reformation, on the orders of Henry VIII, and no trace of her exists.

[1]*A Book of British Saints.* N. V. Pierce Butler. The Faith Press, Ltd. Westminster. 1957. p. 35.

[2]*Lives of the Saints.* (Complete Edition, 4 Volumes). Butler, Thurston, & Attwater. P. J. Kenedy & Sons. New York. 1956. Vol. III, p. 41.

[3]*Ibid.* p. 41.

— 8 —

SAINT WUNIBALD

702—761

Having renounced the throne in favor of serving God unencumbered by royal duties, St. Richard, prince of the West Saxons in England, no doubt served as an inspiration to his three children, Willibald, Walburga, and Wunibald, since all three entered the religious life and are now recognized as saints. These three, all born and reared in England, were to meet their holy destinies in Bavaria, in and near the ancient city of Eichstätt.

We are told that the two sons, Willibald and Wunibald, were taken by their father on a pilgrimage to Rome and the Holy Land in the year 721. St. Richard, unfortunately, became ill on the way and died in Lucca, where he was buried in the Church of St. Fridian. He is reputed to have possessed miraculous healing powers and was greatly venerated during the Middle Ages. After their father's burial, the young noblemen continued on to Rome and visited other countries before returning again to England. The details of this journey, which lasted seven years, were recorded by an English nun who received the information directly from the Saints. This account is called the *Hodoeporicon* and is the first English travel book.

Their kinsman, St. Boniface, the zealous evangelizer of Germany, sought the assistance of the two young men and both answered the Saint's summons. Wunibald left England in 739, was subsequently ordained in Thuringia, and served many churches both there and in Bavaria. In compliance with what he felt to be the will of God, he founded in Heidenheim, which is about thirty miles from Eichstätt, a Benedictine double monastery for men and women, an arrangement which was customary at that time, particularly in England. He governed the Benedictine monks while his sister, St. Walburga, who had been called from England with other nuns, ruled as the abbess of the Benedictine sisters. Their brother, Willibald, served during this time in Eichstätt as the first bishop of the diocese, which had been founded in 741.

Wunibald is believed to have died after an illness of three years and was buried in a tomb in the Church of Heidenheim, which soon was honored by the display of many miracles. Sixteen years later, on September 24, 777, his tomb was opened in the presence of his sister, St. Walburga. The body was found perfectly entire, to the surprise and holy admiration of all the attendants.

Bishop Willibald assisted his sister in governing the Monastery of Heidenheim after his brother's death, and this monastery and church, which remained so staunchly Catholic through troubled years, was seized by the Lutherans during the Reformation. In 1968 the tomb of the formerly incorrupt St. Wunibald was opened and was found completely empty. It is not known if the relics were removed for safekeeping or if they were destroyed.[1]

The relics of St. Walburga, who ruled the monastery for twenty-five years, are subject to a mysterious, recurring phenomenon which has gone on for centuries. After her holy death in 779, St. Walburga was buried in Heidenheim near the tomb of her saintly brother, but after a hundred years most of her relics were brought to the church dedicated to her in Eichstätt. The other portion was given to the sisters of Monheim, but they were destroyed during the Reformation when the nuns were forced to leave their convent. In 893 the bones in Eichstätt were found beaded with a clear oily liquid, and since the year 1042 this strange, odorless, tasteless fluid, "The Oil of St. Walburga," flows from the bones for four months each year, beginning on the twelfth of October (which is the anniversary of the translation) and ending on the anniversary of her death, February 25.[2] This healing oil is always collected and distributed to the sick.

The relics of Bishop Willibald are enshrined in the Cathedral of Eichstätt and are seen by the people on his feast day, July 7.[3]

---

[1]From the statement of the representative of Bischöfl. Ordinariat of Eichstätt. (Bischöfliches Generalvikariat). See footnote 3 below.

[2]A similar fluid was observed flowing many times from the bones of St. Nicholas of Bari and St. Gerard Majella.

[3]The information contained in this entry is a compilation of data supplied by a representative of the Bischöfl. Ordinariat, Eichstätt; The Abbey of St. Walburga in Eichstätt; and the Convent of St. Walburga, Boulder, Colorado.

SAINT ALPHEGE OF CANTERBURY

954—1012

St. Alphege attained great sanctity in monasteries at Deerhurst near Tewkesbury and Bath, and was chosen Bishop of Winchester when only thirty years of age. After serving in this capacity for twenty-two years, he was elected Archbishop of Canterbury.

In 1011 the Danes invaded Canterbury, plundered the town, killed many religious, robbed churches and took the Archbishop captive in anticipation of a huge ransom. St. Alphege was held prisoner for several months and steadfastly refused to allow his flock to raise the ransom for his release, saying "The treasures of the Church must not be given to the pagans for my freedom." He was severely beaten by his drunken captors until one of them ended his life by a blow with an axe. His body, released to his congregation, was buried in St. Paul's in London, but after ten years it was translated by King Canute to Canterbury, where his relics are still enshrined in the cathedral. During this translation, which occurred ten years after his death, his body was found to be free from every stain of corruption.[1]

Because of his heroic conduct during captivity and the circumstances surrounding his death, he is listed as a martyr in the *Roman Martyrology.*

---

[1] *The History of St. Cuthbert.* Charles, Archbishop of Glasgow. Catholic Publications Society Co. New York. 1887. p. 144.

SAINT ROMUALD

952—1027

St. Romuald, founder of the Camaldolese Order, led a carefree life as a young man until the day he witnessed his father kill a kinsman in a duel. Wanting to do penance on behalf of his father, he entered the monastery of San Apollinare in Classe, where he later became a monk after seeing St. Apollinaris in a vision. Three years later he journeyed to Venice in search of a more austere way of life and there became a disciple of Marinus, a holy hermit who disciplined him harshly for the slightest negligence. In 944 he journeyed to Ravenna to strengthen the vocation of his father, who had become a monk and who was then thinking of re-entering the world.

Emperor Otto III, having recognized the sanctity of Romuald, held him in great esteem and appointed him abbot of San Apollinare. At the end of a year, however, he resigned the office in order to continue the reformation of monasteries and the establishment of hermitages, the most important of these foundations being the one at Camaldoli near Arezzo, which later became the motherhouse of the Camaldolese Order.

This great contemplative died at Val di Castro, in the Marches of Ancona, having lived there for many months in solitude and prayer. When the body of the Saint was exhumed in 1466, it was found to be incorrupt. The condition of the relic is now unknown since the last exhumation of the sacred remains occurred in 1481.

The body of the Saint lies in the crypt of S. Romuald at the Monastery of Saints Biagio and Romuald, Fabriano (Ancona), Italy, enclosed in a medieval stone casket, the front of which was lavishly and artistically embellished during the 18th century.

The holy hermit was canonized in 1595, and his feast is liturgically observed throughout the world on February 7.

SAINT COLOMAN

Unknown—1012

At a time when Austria and the neighboring nations of Moravia and Bohemia were engaged in wars, St. Coloman, on a pilgrimage to Jerusalem, arrived at the town of Stockerau, six miles above Vienna, where he was taken prisoner. Being an Irishman and unfamiliar with the language of his captors, he was unable to give an accounting of himself and was hanged as a spy on July 13, 1012. There is no evidence to substantiate the assumption that he was in the strict sense martyred for the Faith, but it is believed that his patience during his torture and death was proof of his sanctity, and this seems to be confirmed by the number of miracles which attended his incorrupt body.

It is not known for certain how long his body remained hanging from the tree where it was unprotected from the elements, but it remained there for such a lengthy period that the preservation was acknowledged as miraculous.

It is known that he was eventually buried at the Abbey at Melk in 1014 and that his bones were moved to other graves in 1364, 1720, and 1912.

— 12 —

SAINT EDWARD THE CONFESSOR

1004—1066

At the age of forty, St. Edward, son of Ethelred, King of Wessex, and Emma of Normandy, was called from exile in France to serve his country as the first Anglo-Saxon king to rule over a united England. He was crowned in the famous Winchester Cathedral by Archbishop Eadsige, with most of the English bishops in attendance. This ceremony marked the beginning of twenty-five years of peace for England, its strength and well being felt abroad for the first time after many years of turbulent history.

People regarded Edward as a saint even during his lifetime. He won their hearts by his religious and just administration, and he is described by his contemporaries as a chaste and mild man, living the life of an angel in the administration of an empire. Having little inclination to matrimony, he was forced, for reasons of state, to marry Edith, a pious and beautiful woman, with whom he lived in absolute continence. In spite of his monastic austerities, he is known to have been an ardent sportsman who often spent days in the chase, not, however, neglecting his customary prayers or daily attendance at Holy Mass. Because of his devotion to the Church, he was affectionately nicknamed the "Confessor."

Being a strong supporter of the monastic system, and in fulfillment of a vow, he restored the Church of St. Peter in London and restored and enlarged the abbey for the Benedictine Monks situated near the church. This was the beginning of the famous Westminster Abbey. When the new choir was consecrated on the feast of the Holy Innocents in 1066, St. Edward was too ill to be present. He died a week later and was buried the next day in his abbey.

The body of the Saint was first exhumed in 1102, thirty-six years after his death. About the year 1138, Osbert of Clare, Prior of Westminster, wrote of the event based on the accounts of eyewitnesses. He reports that the distinguished persons attending the service were astonished to find the body perfectly incorrupt, with a crown on its head, a costly ring on its finger and a sceptre at its side. He further reports that Gundulf, Bishop of Rochester, tugged gently at the beard of the Saint and merited a rebuke from the abbot.[1]

In 1163, two years after the Saint's canonization, the sacred body was translated to a new tomb, the ceremony being conducted by St. Thomas á Becket and witnessed by King Henry II and numerous archbishops and prelates. In 1269, the body was moved once again; and in 1685, when the coffin was opened, it was discovered that the remains had been reduced to a skeleton.[2]

St. Edward the Confessor's grave is one of the few which was left undisturbed during the Protestant Revolution, and it is still pointed out to visitors to the famous Westminster Abbey. In the shrine which bears the name of the Saint can be found the famous Coronation Chair enclosing the ancient Stone of Scone, which was brought from Scotland and which tradition says was used by Jacob as a pillow.

The relics of St. Edward are the only remains of a saint presently enshrined in Westminster Abbey.

---

[1] *The Life of King Edward, Attributed to a Monk of St. Bertin.* Frank Barlow. Thomas Nelson & Sons, Ltd. London. 1962. pp. 114-117.

[2] *Journal of the British Archaeological Association.* 3rd Series, Vol. XVII, pp. 2-5.

13

SAINT WALTHEOF

Unknown—1159

Waltheof was educated at the court of his stepfather, King David, and while living the cultured life of a member of the higher nobility, he was apparently attracted to the religious life, for about the year 1130 he became a canon regular at the Priory of Nostell (York) and three years later was elected prior of Kirkham. He joined the Cistercian Order at Wardon and was later elected to the prestigious position of second Abbot of Melrose, Scotland. Shortly before his death he refused the Bishopric of Glasgow and died a saintly death on August 3, 1159.

At Waltheof's request his body was buried in the chapter house of Melrose Abbey, where it was discovered perfectly incorrupt on May 2, 1171. The grave was opened in the presence of Ingelram, Bishop of Glasgow, the community of Melrose, and a number of monks and abbots from neighboring monasteries. Not only was the body found perfectly intact, but the robes in which it had been buried had suffered no decay. *The Chronicles of Melrose* relate that:

> Bishop Ingelram, stooping down, touched the garments and different parts of the body, at first gently, and then with a stronger pressure of his hand, to assure himself that every joint and limb was flexible and sound. But Peter the precentor, who was among the bystanders, doubting the propriety of so minute a scrutiny, could not help saying, "In sooth, my lord bishop, begging your pardon, I think you handle the body of the holy man somewhat roughly." When some of the rest murmured their approbation of this remark, the Bishop thus addressed them: "Be not offended, my dear children, that I have scrupulously examined into this matter; but rather praise God, since I have thereby clearly ascertained and made manifest that this is indeed a miracle, which proves that you have now another Saint belonging to you, and that your venerated father Waltheof is become a companion to the holy Cuthbert, who also was a monk of Mailros." At these words many of the brethren shed tears of joy; everybody present uttered some expression of thankfulness; and, at the suggestion of the

Abbot of Kelso, the *Te Deum* was solemnly chanted.[1]

In the year 1206 when a grave adjacent to that of Waltheof's was being prepared for William, the ninth Abbot of Melrose, a mason named Robert seized the opportunity in the course of his work to examine the contents of Waltheof's tomb. The finding of the incorrupt body of Waltheof by this workman is related in the *Official Guide Book of Melrose Abbey.*

The Chronicles of Melrose also record that in 1340, during the transference of the bodies of former abbots from the western to the eastern part of the chapter house, the remains of St. Waltheof were left undisturbed, except for a few small bones, which were removed for relics.

During the 1921 excavations made in the ruins of the Melrose Abbey, which is now a national monument, three stone-lined coffins were found close to the central doorway. It was evident that the coverstone at the foot of one coffin had been disturbed during the making of the adjacent coffin, and the arrangements seemed to comply with the description given by Robert, the mason, during his preparation of the grave for Abbot William. It has not been definitely ascertained whether two of these coffins were those of William and Waltheof, but in the museum within the precincts of Melrose Abbey there is a large fragment of a monumental tomb, finely crafted and still bearing traces of pure gold leaf, which is believed to have formed part of the Saint's shrine.

The lonely but magnificent ruins of the ancient gothic Abbey of Melrose only suggest its former influential position in the Christian development of Scotland and solemnly recall to mind the holy souls who lived and died there and the pious souls who travelled from distant places to visit the shrine of the popular Saint, Waltheof, of whom no trace or relic remains.

---

[1] *The History of St. Cuthbert.* Charles, Archbishop of Glasgow. Burnes & Oates, Ltd. London. Catholic Publications Society Co. New York. 1887. pp 143-144.

14

SAINT UBALD OF GUBBIO

c. 1100—1160

Born of Germanic parents, Ubald was orphaned at an early age and was educated by his uncle in the cathedral school of his birthplace, Gubbio. This city was to be made famous a few years later by St. Francis of Assisi, who tamed a very bad wolf there during one cf his frequent visits. After the completion of his studies he was ordained and was appointed dean of the cathedral, where his fervor and dedication to duty resulted in the reform of the canons among whom irregularities were prevalent.

While repairs were being made in the cathedral, which had burned, Ubald led a delegation to Rome to ask for a successor to the bishop of Gubbio, who had recently died, and was himself chosen for the position. In this capacity he conscientiously fulfilled his duties for thirty-one years in a perfect apostolic spirit.

His mildness and patience were particularly distinguishing characteristics. On one occasion, when he brought to the attention of the foreman who was supervising the repair of a city wall, that the church grape vines were damaged in the process, the workman, not recognizing the ecclesiastic, threw him into a mass of liquid mortar. Without complaint Ubald returned to his house. When the workman was brought to trial by the indignant citizens who had witnessed the offense, Ubald appeared in court, asked for a kiss of peace from the foreman, and immediately requested the dismissal of the case.

After celebrating Mass for his flock on Easter Sunday, 1160, he returned to his sickbed and died on Pentecost Sunday. Many miracles were granted to the people who flocked to the funeral of this pious bishop who was to be canonized three decades later.

Two years after his canonization, the first exhumation of his body took place. During the same year it was translated to Monte Ingino, where it was enshrined in a chapel which is still a place of pilgrimage.

There have been many official examinations of the body during the centuries. The last one took place in 1960 on the occasion of the eighth centennial observance of the Saint's death. The doctors and assistants who conducted the examination found that it had become quite mummified, having brown, dry skin with the texture of leather. The nails of the well-preserved hands were all in place. The only disfigurement was that of the upper lip and the tip of the nose, which were both missing. This was attributed to the natural corrosion of the body that resulted from its interment in an urn which was not hermetically sealed.

The body of the gentle prelate is always exposed under the main altar, where it is frequently visited by the people, who still foster a tender devotion to the Saint. He is popularly invoked against diabolical possession.

SAINT IDESBALD

Unknown—1167

Born into the aristocracy of Flanders, Idesbald had spent thirty years in public service, part of which he served in the court of the Count of Flanders, before applying for admittance at the Cistercian abbey of Our Lady of the Dunes near Dunkirk, France. Having served for a time as a canon of the church of St. Walburga, Idesbald, although no longer a young man, was accepted by the Cistercians as a member and soon won the affectionate esteem of the abbey. The Divine Office was his all-engrossing interest, and he frequently became so absorbed in the performance of his duties as cantor that he became ecstatically oblivious to all about him. During his twenty-year tenure as abbot, the monastery's prestige increased to such proportions that privileges were granted it by the Pope, and outsiders vied with one another in helping the holy abbot in his endeavors.

After Idesbald's death, his brethren, contrary to the dictates of the rule, but in consideration of his sanctity, buried him in a casket in the abbey church. In 1624, more than four hundred fifty years after his death, his body was found intact. A later recognition of the relic occurred on July 23, 1894, which was celebrated by many festivals.

Although the body is no longer conserved, the skeleton of the Saint lies on a mattress of silk in an urn which is kept in the church of Notre Dame de la Poterie in Bruges, Flanders. The left arm of the relic is kept by the bishop of Bruges, and the bone of the right thigh is kept in the church of Notre Dame of the Dunes.

SAINT ISIDORE THE FARMER

1080—1172

High above the main altar of the Cathedral of Madrid is situated, in an impressive setting, an ornate reliquary containing the incorrupt body of St. Isidore the Husbandman, who began life amid tragically poor circumstances.

Isidore was born to very devout parents who instilled in his tender heart a love for his religion and a dread of sin. Because of extreme necessity he was placed at an early age in the employment of John de Vergas, a wealthy land owner of Madrid, for whom he worked the rest of his life. Having married a virtuous girl, he agreed with her to live in perfect continence following the death of their only child, both continuing to live exemplary lives while suffering the trials and hardships of their poor circumstances.

Before reporting to the fields, Isidore attended Mass each morning and is known to have shared with the needy his meager meals, which on many occasions miraculously redoubled in quantity until all were fed to satisfaction. His goodness and kindness toward all did not prevent his detractors from reporting him to his employer for tardiness and periods of inactivity during working hours. John de Vergas, to test the truth of their accusations and to gather sufficient evidence for Isidore's dismissal, hid himself one morning and discovered that while Isidore did indeed report late after lingering in church, his plowing was nevertheless being accomplished by unseen hands who guided snow-white oxen across the fields. John de Vergas and many witnesses, after assuring themselves that angels did in fact perform Isidore's chores while the Saint was rapt in prayer, altered their opinion of him, and he became not only greatly revered by all, but was also placed thereafter in responsible positions of trust.

A miracle supposedly witnessed by his fellow workers involved a sack of grain from which Isidore fed a flock of starving birds one wintry day. Upon reaching the mill, the sack proved to be filled to capacity and after being processed it produced double the usual amount of flour.

After a lengthy life rendered fruitful and glorious by his consistent observance of religious ideals, Isidore died on May 15, 1172, assisted by his virtuous wife, who survived him by several years. Although she is not canonized, she is venerated as Santa Maria de la Cabeza because her head (cabeza) is taken in procession during times of drought.

Throughout the centuries the incorrupt body of the Saint was transferred to six different locations and was each time placed in a different sepulcher. During May 1969 there was observed in Madrid the bicentennial celebration marking the last translation of the body to the Cathedral of Madrid. During this observance, the darkened, rigid, but perfect body of the Saint was exposed for ten days to great throngs of people who passed in solemn files to view the eight-hundred-year old relic. During this celebration the agricultural workers of the city petitioned the Vatican to declare St. Isidore the patron of laborers of all the world.

17

SAINT BENEZET

Unknown—1184

"Little Benedict the Bridge Builder" spent his pious youth tending sheep for his mother in Savoy and reflected often on the perils of people who sought to cross the Rhône. During the Middle Ages the building or repairing of bridges was considered a merciful enterprise, and Benezet is reputed to have had a vision in which he was three times instructed to build a stone bridge at Avignon, where the swiftness of the water had swept away previous endeavors. The smallness of his stature, his complete ignorance of the mechanics of bridge building, and his total lack of funds did not prevent him from presenting himself to the bishop upon his arrival in Avignon. We are told that through the employment of miracles he gained the approval of the bishop and work was begun on the bridge in 1177. For seven years he directed the operations; at the time of his death the main difficulties of the enterprise were overcome, and the bridge was completed four years after his death.

The body of the *"miraculeux constructeur"* was buried upon the bridge itself, and so numerous were the miracles which attended it that the city fathers built upon the bridge a chapel in which the body lay for nearly five hundred years.

In 1669 part of the bridge, which had been weakened with age and the constant pressures of the current, fell into ruin, completely destroying the chapel. Fortunately, the coffin was rescued, and when it was opened the following year, the body was found in a state of perfect preservation, although the iron bars about the coffin were badly damaged with rust, due to the excessive dampness of the situation. The body was again found in an excellent condition in 1674 during its translation into the Church of the Celestines, that order having obtained permission from Louis XIV to keep the relic until such time as the bridge and chapel could be rebuilt.

In this church the relic was reverently guarded until the time of the French Revolution of 1789 when a group of revolutionaries seized the incorrupt body of the Saint, whose miraculous preservation had existed for six hundred years, and sacrilegiously destroyed it. The only parts of the relic remaining are fragments of bone, the skull, and a tibia; these were canonically recognized as authentic in 1854. The treasured relics are in the possession of the Paroisse St. Didier in Avignon.

The Constitution of an Order of Bridge Brothers was approved in 1189, and they regarded Benezet as their founder. He is recognized as the patron saint of Avignon and quite appropriately is regarded as the patron of all bridge builders.

18

SAINT HUGH OF LINCOLN

1140—1200

Hugh was the youngest of the three sons of a knight named William and was born in a castle at Avalon in eastern France. When William's wife died, he joined the Canons Regular of St. Augustine and took with him the eight-year-old Hugh, who said, "I needed no persuasion to renounce pleasure of which I knew nothing, and to follow him as a fellow soldier in the spiritual army." Having been educated by the canons, he became a member of the order at the age of fifteen. Four years later he was made a deacon and was sent to visit the famous Carthusian monastery, the Grande Chartreuse. He was immediately attracted to the austere Carthusian life and after many delays and great difficulties, he secured permission to leave the Augustinians and join the Carthusians, which he did at the age of twenty-three. Ordained a priest at thirty-three, he was made procurator of the Grande Chartreuse and performed the most active duties, although he would have preferred to remain in the solitude of the monastery.

In 1179 he came to the attention of Henry II of England, who appointed him Prior of Witham, a declining Carthusian monastery the King had built in expiation for his part in the murder of St. Thomas a Becket. The Saint improved the monastery, attracted many new recruits and proved to be so competent that the King appointed him Bishop of Lincoln, which was at that time the largest diocese in England. Hugh accepted this position at the insistence of ecclesiastical authorities. He capably restored and expanded the cathedral and, as administrator, engaged in almost continual confrontation with three temperamental kings over royal control of Church affairs and their demands on Church monies. In spite of frequent opposition from them, he was highly regarded by Henry II, his son Richard I (the Lion-hearted), and Richard's brother, John Lackland.

Besides his ecclesiastical duties, he regularly visited and ministered to the lepers in their hospitals, frequently conducted funerals for the abandoned dead, and defended the human rights of the Jews, who were being persecuted.

In 1200 he journeyed through France as the Royal Ambassador of King John and was able to make sentimental visits to the Castle of Avalon, where he was born, and to the monastery of Grande Chartreuse. He returned to England a very sick man and after his death in London on November 16, 1200, he was enbalmed[1] in the usual manner before his body was returned to Lincoln in a triumphal procession.

During the impressive funeral services, which were attended by fourteen bishops and almost a hundred abbots, he was awarded the honor of having his coffin carried by three kings and three archbishops.

On the sixth of October, 1280, the solemn translation of his relics to a worthier shrine was made in the presence of King Edward I of England and Queen Eleanor, four earls, the Countess of Lincoln, many barons and knights, eleven bishops and many abbots. The ceremony was conducted by the Archbishop of Canterbury and the Bishop of Lincoln.

After the recitation of the Office of Matins, all in attendance approached the marble tomb where the body of the Saint had been deposited eighty years before. The body was found incorrupt and almost unchanged, and his Carthusian habit, which he had insisted on wearing during his final illness and in which he was buried in accordance with his wishes, was likewise in an excellent state of preservation.

Then, to the surprise of everyone,

> As soon as the Archbishop laid his hand on the glorious head of the Saint, it separated from the shoulders, leaving the neck fresh and red, just as if death had been recent. Many of those present considered this separation to be miraculous, because the magnificent reliquary which had been prepared to receive the sacred remains was not long enough to have contained both head and body together . . .[2]

The body was then taken out and placed on an elaborate receptacle which had been prepared, and another wonder presented itself, for it was noticed that a great quantity of a pure clear oil had collected in

[1]*Neglected Saints.* E. I. Watkin. Sheed & Ward. New York. 1955. p. 88.

[2]*The Life of St. Hugh of Lincoln.* Herbert Thurston, S.J. Benziger Brothers. New York. 1898. p. 580. This is an eyewitness's account as reported by Fr. Thurston.

the bottom of the tomb.[3]

The body was later taken into the vestry where it and the venerable head were washed and carefully dried.

The following morning, during the conclusion of the solemn ceremony,

> . . . the Bishop of Lincoln took up the head of St. Hugh, and held it for a while reverently before him. As he did this, an abundance of the same pure oil flowed from the jaw over the Bishop's hands, and this notwithstanding that the venerable head had been carefully washed a few hours before, and had been found quite dry in the morning. The oil only ceased to flow when the Bishop had placed his precious burden upon the silver dish upon which this relic was to be carried through the crowd.[4]

The relics were borne in solemn procession to the new shrine, which was richly adorned with gold, silver and precious stones. The Bishop of Lincoln and the canons of the cathedral had the head encased in a coffer of gold, silver, and precious stones, and this was placed close beside the altar of St. John the Baptist, in the same church, not far from the shrine of that saint.

In the year 1364 when England was overrun by bands of ruffians, who went about violating tombs, profaning the relics of the saints, and pillaging churches, the precious reliquary containing the head of St. Hugh was stolen. After dividing the treasure among themselves, the mob discarded the sacred head in a field. According to chroniclers at that time, a raven perched beside the relic and quitted it only after it was recognized and returned to the Cathedral. The thieves, however, were soon punished for the sacrilege. After selling their booty in London, they were themselves robbed, and, struck with remorse, gave themselves up to justice. Being found guilty on their own confessions, they were judiciously hanged at Lincoln.[5]

The relics of the Saint met their destruction during the reign of Henry VIII. Under the guise of protecting the people from superstition and idolatry, Henry ordered the destruction of shrines, relics and ornaments which recalled to mind the saints, and enriched his purse

---

[3]*Ibid.* p. 581.
[4]*Ibid.* p. 581. This is an eyewitness's account as reported by Fr. Thurston.
[5]*Ibid.* pp. 583-584.

with the precious metals and jewels which had adorned the sacred tombs.

On June 6, 1540, a commission was issued by Henry VIII to Dr. George Hennage, Archdeacon of Taunton, his brother, John Hennage, and others, instructing them to dismantle the shrine.

> For as moch as we understand that there ys a certayn shryne and diverse fayned Reliquyes and Juels in the Cathedrall church in Lyncoln, with whych all the simple people be moch deceaved and broughte into greate supersticion and Idolatrye, to the dyshonor of god and greate slander of thys realme and peryll of theire own soules . . .[6]

They were further instructed to,

> . . . take downe, as well the sayd shryne and supersticious reliquyes, as superfluouse Jueles, plate, copes and other suche like as you shall thinke by your wysdoms not mete to contynew and remayne there . . . And to see the sayd reliquyes, Juels and plate safely and surely to be conveyde to owr towre of London in to owr Jewyll house there, chargeing the Master of owr Jewylls with the same . . .[7]

This act of royal piracy proved to be one of the most profitable to the treasury, for it is recorded that the value of the spoil amounted to 2,621 ounces of gold and 4,215 ounces of silver, besides a great number of precious jewels and pearls of tremendous value.[8]

The exact manner in which the body of the Saint was profaned is unknown. It is optimistically hoped by some that the body was taken off secretly and hidden for safekeeping; however, no facts or clues have been discovered concerning the exact end of the relic, and the medieval shrine in Lincoln Cathedral stands sadly devoid of any relics. Fortunately the Grande Chartreuse possesses a fragment of a bone of the Saint and a stole which he frequently wore.[9]

---

[6] *Ibid.* p. 596.
[7] *Ibid.* p. 597.
[8] *Ibid.* p. 597.
[9] *Ibid.* p. 585.

BLESSED BERTRAND OF GARRIGUA

Unknown—1230

As a young child Blessed Bertrand was entrusted to the care of the nuns of the Cistercian Abbey of Notre Dame at Bosquet during a period in history when the south of France was experiencing civil wars caused by the Albigensian Heresy. Having been prepared for Holy Orders by the good sisters, he was ordained some time later and by a happy coincidence became acquainted with St. Dominic, whom he joined in laboring for the conversion of the heretics. From the first day of their acquaintance, he became Dominic's closest associate, participated in the Saint's many apostolic labors, and was his inseparable companion on many journeys. Bertrand also witnessed many of Dominic's miracles, which he kept secret until after the Saint's death, in deference to his wishes.

Bertrand was counted among St. Dominic's original group of followers who formed the nucleus of the Order of Preachers. For a time the group lived in the Priory of St. Romanus in Toulouse, then divided into groups to found new houses where they were needed.

After filling the office of prior at the foundation at Toulouse, Blessed Bertrand was appointed the provincial of Provence, which included at that time the whole of southern France. The Saint died at the Abbey at Bosquet, in the city where he had spent his youth.

Twenty-three years afterwards, his body was found completely incorrupt during the first exhumation, conducted by the nuns at Notre Dame de Bosquet, the same order of sisters who had taught him as a child.

Another exhumation took place at the beginning of the fifteenth century. The body, still perfectly intact, was transferred to the Church of Frères Prêcheurs d' Orange.

What the Lord had preserved miraculously, the Protestants deliberately destroyed during the religious wars of 1561. The church and the body of the Saint were impiously burned and there are unfortunately no relics of this Beatus in existence.

SAINT EDMUND RICH OF CANTERBURY

1180—1240

Having provided handsomely for his wife and four children, Edmund's father, with his wife's consent, retired to the Evesham monastery. Edmund's pious mother, Mabilia, is reputed to have worn a hair shirt and to have attended Matins nightly in the parish church. As a result of his parents' pious example, Edmund was not only prayerful but was also very cheerful and sweet in his disposition and an obedient and avid student. After studying for a time at Oxford, he and his brother Robert were sent by Mabilia to Paris to complete their studies, she giving each of them a hair shirt as a parting gift. His studies were interrupted briefly when he journeyed back to England to console his mother during her last illness. Being asked for a final blessing, his mother replied, "I bless you, and in you I bless my other children, for through you they will share abundantly in the blessings and joys of Heaven." After settling his mother's affairs and placing his sisters in a protective situation, he returned to Paris. Having consecrated himself to God by a perpetual vow of chastity, he wore the hair shirt given him by his mother, fasted frequently, and slept on the floor as an additional penance. He distinguished himself as a teacher and master of theology in both Paris and at the University of Oxford. For a time he served as canon and treasurer of Salisbury Cathedral, having been ordained a priest several years before.

About the year 1227, by order of the Pope, he preached a crusade against the Saracens and was later appointed to the vacant see of Canterbury, being consecrated on the second of April, 1234. Almost immediately he came into conflict with Henry III over the latter's habit of grasping Church money for his own use. King Henry at first had approved the appointment, but after a time he denounced the archbishop, who proved to be inflexible in defense of ecclesiastical immunities. When the chapter of Canterbury, the pontifical legate and many influential religious sided with the sovereign, Edmund was in fact defeated in his efforts to uphold Church rights, and after having served in his episcopal capacity for several years, felt obliged secretly to flee the country for France, where he was received in honor at the court of King St. Louis.

Edmund eventually sought asylum in the Cistercian abbey of Pontigny, where two other archbishops of Canterbury, Stephen Langton and St. Thomas a Becket, had sought refuge from their difficulties with English sovereigns. Bad health necessitated a change in climate, but before departing for Soissy, he promised the monks he would return on the feast of St. Edmund, the martyr king. This vow was fulfilled after his death when his body was brought back to Pontigny on the promised day.

Several years after his death, his body was disinterred in the presence of the French king, St. Louis, and was found to be incorrupt.[1] Numerous miracles attested to his sanctity, and he was canonized by Innocent IV in 1247.

The incorrupt body of the Saint, now brown in color with skin resembling parchment, is clothed in episcopal garments and is enclosed in a reliquary which is kept in the abbey church. It is believed that Edmund's preservation was supernaturally maintained for many years; however, in later years it appears that artificial methods were employed to conserve it.[2]

---

[1] *A Book of British Saints.* N.V. Pierce Butler. The Faith Press, Ltd. Westminster. 1957. p. 16.

[2] This is the opinion of a spokesman for the shrine.

SAINT ROSE OF VITERBO

1235—1252

During an illness when she was eight years of age, Rose had a vision of Our Lady in which she was told to wear the habit of a penitent and to observe a reverential life as a model for her neighbors. When Emperor Frederick II was oppressing the Church and leading many away from allegiance to the Pope, Rose preached throughout Viterbo, calling upon everyone to denounce the opponents of the Church. When threatened by her father, she replied, "If Jesus could be beaten for me, I can be beaten for Him." Eventually the imperial party drove her from the city, but she continued to champion the cause of the Pope at Soriano, Vitorchiano and other towns. After the death of the Emperor in 1250, she returned to Viterbo, where she requested admittance into the Convent of St. Mary of the Roses, but was refused for want of a dowry. "Very well, " she said, "you will not have me now, but perhaps you will be more willing when I am dead." St. Rose returned to her father's house and died on March 6, 1252, when seventeen years of age.

She was buried in the Church of Santa Maria in Podio but was transferred six years later to the church of the Convent of St. Mary of the Roses, as she had predicted. This church was destroyed by fire in 1357, but her body was unharmed and is enshrined in the Monastero Clarisse S. Rosa in Viterbo.

In 1921 her heart, still perfectly incorrupt, was extracted and placed in a reliquary, which is taken in procession through the city every year on the fourth of September, the feast day of this saint who was raised to the honors of the altar in 1457.

The body of the young Saint, who died over seven centuries ago, is dark but perfectly flexible and is exposed in a reliquary for the veneration and edification of the faithful.

SAINT SPERANDIA

1216—1276

Sperandia's fervent parents instilled in her tender heart a fervent love of God, and even as a young child she was attracted by their excellent example to prayer and the practice of virtue. Later she was inspired to lead a life of extreme penance, and finding the comforts and geniality of her home a hindrance, she left all for the sake of God and retired to the solitude of a cave on a nearby mountain, enduring the hardships thereof for the sake of sinners. After a time she felt compelled to make a pilgrimage to the Holy Land; the next ten years were spent visiting the holy places there and the shrines throughout Italy and in Rome. During her travels, Sperandia taught in the villages through which she passed and exhorted her audiences to the practice of penance. On completing her travels, she applied for admission to the Benedictine convent at Cingoli. The abbess immediately recognized her saintliness and accepted her as a member. After distinguishing herself by the strict observance of charity, penance, and the conscientious practice of the ascetical life, she was elected abbess and served in that capacity for many years. Fortified with the prayers of her devoted community, she passed from this world in a most edifying manner, surrounded by the odor of sanctity, which pervaded the whole convent. Shortly after her death, the grateful populace, who had benefited by her prayers and penances, accepted her as the patron saint of the city.

The body of the saint was first examined two years after her death. At that time it was found so perfect, fresh, and beautiful that it was put into a new coffin and enshrined beneath the major altar of the convent church. In 1482 the still remarkably preserved body was examined in the presence of the bishop, and in 1525 it was transferred to the special chapel which had been erected to enshrine her remains. Other examinations took place in 1635, 1768, 1834, and 1870.[1]

---

[1]*Un Fiore di Santita Benedettina S. Sperandia, Vergine.* D. Guglielmo, Can. Co. Malazampa. Cingoli. 1952. pp. 46-47.

The body of the Saint was last examined in 1952 when it was found to be still perfectly intact, flexible, and "exhaling a suave fragrance."[2] Although the skin is dry, it has maintained a natural color, with only a slight tendency to darken. The excellent condition and suppleness of the body has existed for over seven centuries and for that reason is reverently esteemed by the devoted pilgrims to the shrine as a "Miracolo Permanente."

---

[2]*Ibid.* p. 57.

The incorrupt body of St. Sperandia (d. 1276) in the Benedictine convent church of Cingoli, Italy. Exhumed eight different times, the last in 1952, it is still incorrupt and exudes a sweet fragrance.

23

ST. ZITA

1218—1278

The future patroness of domestic workers was reared by poor but devout parents in the village of Monte Sagrati. At the age of twelve she was sent to Lucca, eight miles away, where she was placed in the employ of a wealthy merchant family, whom she served for the next forty-eight years of her life.

She performed her duties faithfully, reserving to herself the most menial tasks. She led a very prayerful and penitential life, and in addition to other penances, arose during the night to pray, often gave up her bed to homeless women, attended daily Mass, and frequently fasted in order to give a greater portion of her food to the poor. For a number of years she patiently withstood the abuse of her employers and fellow workers, who ridiculed her religious habits. By her patience and charity she eventually overcame opposition and became the advisor and dearest friend of the whole household. Towards the end of her life she was relieved of her duties so that she could spend more time in her favorite occupation, that of caring for the poor and sick of the district.

At the age of sixty, St. Zita died a holy death and was buried in a simple manner in the Church of St. Frediano in Lucca, where she is now magnificently enshrined. Her casket, opened in 1446, 1581, and 1652, revealed her perfectly incorrupt body. The relic, as seen through the glass-sided walls of her reliquary, appears somewhat dark and dry, but still perfectly entire, a condition quite remarkable, considering that the death of the Saint occurred almost seven hundred years ago.

Blessed is that servant, whom when his lord shall come, he shall find so doing. Verily I say unto you, He shall set him over all that he possesseth.

Luke 12:43.

The incorrupt body of St. Zita, Patroness of Domestic Workers (d. 1278), enshrined in a glass reliquary in the Basilica of St. Frediano in Lucca, Italy.

24

SAINT ALBERT THE GREAT

1206—1280

Albert was born in Lauingen on the Danube, and against the wishes of his noble family became a Dominican friar while a student at the University of Padua. He excelled particularly in the natural sciences, in which his knowledge was described as encyclopedic. He correlated the findings of this science with philosophy and laid the foundation for the proper use of reason in matters of faith, which was further developed by his illustrious pupil, St. Thomas Aquinas. He taught at many European colleges, particularly those of Ratisbon, Freiburg, Cologne, and Paris. He was for a time provincial of his order in Germany and in 1260 accepted, under obedience, the bishopric of Ratisbon, from which he resigned after two years. His holiness and knowledge were so highly regarded that he was dubbed "The Great" by his contemporaries and also "Universal Doctor." He was described as "a man no less than godlike in all knowledge, so that he may fitly be called the wonder and miracle of our age."

The last two years of his life were undoubtedly very trying and humiliating, for his strength of mind failed him, and he was frequently afflicted with loss of memory. He died peacefully at Cologne without illness, sitting in his chair amid his confreres. His body, clothed in pontifical robes, was consigned to a wooden coffin, which was placed in a temporary vault in the conventual church near the high altar. There is some evidence that the body was given more than the usual preparation for burial, since it is recorded that the church of Ratisbon, which Albert had served as bishop, requested the removal of the remains of the Saint to their city, but when this was refused them, there was sent instead a relic, a piece of intestines, "which had been buried behind the high altar."[1]

After approximately three years, when the permanent tomb was

---

[1] *Albert the Great of the Order of Friar Preacher—His Life and Scholastic Labours from Original Documents.* Doctor Joachim Sighart. Trans. from the French by Rev. Fr. T.A. Dixon, O.P. R.Washbourne, London. 1876. and Wm. C. Brown Reprint Library. Dubuque, Iowa. pp. 418-419.

completed in the choir, the transfer of the remains took place, and the body was found at this time in a state of perfect preservation and exhaling a delightful fragrance.[2] The remains were carefully replaced in the old coffin, and this was deposited in the new vault, where it remained for two centuries.

After the University of Cologne grew to impressive proportions and the number of Albert's devotees increased in equal measure, the tomb of the Saint in the Dominican Church of Cologne no longer seemed suitable for his holy relics, so an elaborate mausoleum was constructed. During the transfer of the relic to this worthy tomb in the year 1483, the body was again examined in the presence of many ecclesiastics, the prior of the convent of Cologne, the rector of the university, many professors, doctors and students. The records of the Church of St. Andrew, which now possesses the relics of the Saint, indicate that the body at this disinterment was reduced to a skeleton, and so it might be considered, for the descriptions of the findings as found from other sources are carefully worded. They relate that the head was almost intact, the eyes still were found in their sockets, the chin was found to be covered with flesh and part of the beard, one ear was seen and the feet were still attached to the legs, indicating of course, that the major part of the relic was not conserved.[3] The witnesses, however, were astonished to discover a delightful perfume about the body, which had been consigned to the grave for over two hundred years. The relics were placed in a glass case at this time and remained in it for many years. After this translation, miracles of healing were accorded to many of the sick who visited the tomb, and many visions were recorded.

Over three hundred years later, in 1804, the relics of the Saint were removed from the damaged Dominican Church and taken to St. Andrew's Church, but this was done without ceremony since Cologne was then occupied by Napoleonic troops.

The remains of the Saint, which consist only of bones, are wrapped in silk and rest in two cases which bear the seals of the Archbishop of Cologne. These are kept in a stone sarcophagus in the crypt of St. Andrew's Church.

The heroic quality of Albert's virtues was recognized by Pope Gregory XV during his beautification in 1622. Throughout the cen-

---

[2]*Ibid.* p. 422.
[3]*Ibid.* pp. 429-430.

turies St. Albert the Great was regarded as a Doctor of the Church, and this title was officially conferred on him in 1931 by Pope Pius XI, who, by doing so, equivalently declared him to be a saint of the universal Church.[4]

---

[4]*A Dictionary of Saints.* Donald Attwater. P.J. Kenedy & Sons. New York. 1958. p. 9.

25

SAINT MARGARET OF CORTONA

1247—1297

This "Magdalen of the Seraphic Order," as she is called in the Benedictus of the office of the Saint, was the daughter of a poor farmer in Tuscany. When Margaret was seven years old, she lost her pious mother, and the stepmother her father brought home two years later treated her harshly, constantly finding fault with the child's high-spirited, pleasure-loving nature. Thirsting for the affection denied her as a child, she fell a willing victim to a young and wealthy cavalier who persuaded her to live with him, always holding out the prospect of a marriage but never bending to the entreaties of his paramour. The illicit romance endured for nine years, during which a son, who later became a member of the Franciscan Order, was born to her. She gave great scandal by living openly as the cavalier's mistress, and by riding about the countryside on a fine horse, wearing costly clothes and flaunting her sin before the people.

One day, when the cavalier failed to return home, his faithful dog led Margaret to a wooded area where she found his mangled body in a shallow grave, covered with leaves. Seeing in this the judgment of God, she immediately turned over all their possessions to the gentleman's family and left Montepulciano with her young son. Dressed as a penitent, she presented herself to her father, but, persuaded by the stepmother, he refused to take them in. She then went to Cortona to seek the aid of the Franciscans, who thereafter became her spiritual fathers. She advanced rapidly under the direction of two friars, one of whom, Giunta Bevegnati, later wrote her "legend." On more than one occasion she is known to have publicly asked pardon for the scandal she had given.

Margaret earned her living by nursing the ladies of the city, later giving this up to live on alms so that she could spend more time in prayer and helping the poor. After three years, when they saw that her conversion was sincere, the Franciscans accepted her as a tertiary of their order, and she advanced to an even higher plane of spirituality, being in direct communion with her Redeemer, experiencing frequent ecstasies, and severely mortifying her body to expiate for her sins. She is known to have suffered for a time from the unfounded suspicions of the townspeople, who later forgot their doubts and turned to her for prayers and counsel.

With the sanction of the bishop and with the financial aid of the city, she established a hospital called the Spedale di Santa Maria della Misericordia, the nursing staff consisting of fellow tertiaries, formed into a congregation by the Saint and called the Poverelle.

Her last years were sanctified by many miracles of healing and the conversion of hardened sinners who traveled from neighboring countries seeking her help. She died on the day revealed to her, at the age of fifty, twenty-three years of which were spent in penance.

The sacred body of the Saint lies incorrupt in a glass-sided reliquary which exposes her to view, under the main altar of the Basilica of Cortona, named in her honor. The red velvet background of the reliquary is studded with precious gems and valuable ornaments donated by her grateful clients. The body is light in color and dry, but completely whole. Even the eyes are full and all the nails of the feet and hands are still in place—truly a miraculous preservation which has existed for almost seven hundred years.

Thou art the third light granted to the order of my beloved Francis.
He was the first, among the Friars Minor: Clare was the second,
among the nuns: thou shalt be the third, in the Order of Penance.
(Words of Our Lord to St. Margaret of Cortona).

26

BLESSED JAMES DE BLANCONIBUS

(Blessed James of Bevagna)

1220—1301

At the age of sixteen, James attended the Lenten services in Bevagna, which were conducted by two visiting Dominicans, and was immediately inspired by their words to seek Christian perfection in the religious life. After reflecting for several days on the possibility of such a vocation, one of the friars advised him to spend the night in prayer before the Blessed Sacrament. During the night of Holy Saturday, he was favored with a vision in which St. Dominic told him, "Do it! According to God's will I choose you, and will be ever with you." His vocation thus determined, he joined the order at Spoleto. After completing his studies, in which he excelled in philosophy and theology, he was ordained and was assigned to preaching. Throughout his life he struggled to combat heresies, especially that of Nicolaitanism, which defended a married clergy.

Perhaps the incident most often recorded of this holy friar is the vision which was accorded him while praying before a crucifix. After experiencing a great dryness of spirit and fearing the loss of his soul, he was comforted by the words, "Behold the sign of your salvation!" and was immediately drenched with blood which spurted from the crucifix.

Warned by a vision of his approaching death, he prepared for his departure, and died eight days later on August 22, 1301.

The body which had been bathed in the Redeemer's blood is still incorrupt and well kept. Except for the left foot which was stolen as a relic, it is perfectly entire, the best parts being the face, hands, and right foot.

Pope Boniface IX sanctioned the cultus of Bl. James on January 7, 1400, and his feast is solemnly celebrated on August 23, his body being reverently displayed on that day in the Sanctuary of the Beatus in Bevagna.

— 27 —

ST. NICHOLAS OF TOLENTINO

1245—1305

The Bishop of Fermo was so impressed with Nicholas' piety and intelligence that he admitted him to minor orders while Nicholas was still in early boyhood. Born in Sant' Angelo in Pontano, he entered the Augustinian monastery in that city and proved from the beginning to be an outstanding religious. Ordained in 1271 at Cinguli, he served various houses of the Order for four years before being assigned to the monastery at Tolentino where he stayed for his remaining thirty years on earth. Nicholas' apostolate included daily preaching in the streets, administering the Sacraments in homes, hospitals, and prisons, spending long hours in the confessional, and performing countless miracles to which he would charge the recipients, "Say nothing of this. Give thanks to God, not to me." Not only were the faithful impressed with his persuasive powers and advanced spirituality, but they also placed great trust in his intercession in relieving the sufferings of the souls in Purgatory, a confidence which was confirmed many years after his death when he was officially designated the "Patron of the Holy Souls."

In the latter years of his life when he was enduring a prolonged illness, his superiors, with no success, urged him to partake of more strengthening foods than his customary meager rations. The Blessed Virgin appeared to him one night, instructed him to ask for a small piece of bread, to dip it in water and then to eat it, promising that he would be cured by his obedience. In grateful memory of his immediate restoration to health, Nicholas began blessing similar pieces of bread and distributing them to the sick, a practice which produced numerous favors and marvels of healing. In commemoration of these miracles, the shrine of the Saint continues to distribute worldwide St. Nicholas Breads, which are blessed and which continue to provide for his clients many favors and graces.

After an illness of one year, the Saint died on September 10, the day on which his feast is liturgically commemorated each year.

Immediately after his passing, a commission was appointed to collect reports of his miracles and evidence of his heroic virtues. His canonization, which was requested twenty years after his death, was delayed because of the troubles of the Avignon Papacy and the Western Schism, but was eventually proclaimed in 1446. During the fortieth year following his death, his incorrupt body was exposed to the faithful in the wooden urn in which it was first consigned. During this exhibition, the arms of the Saint were detached, thus beginning the strange, six-hundred-year history of the bleeding arms, verified by an unusual, documented record. The rest of the body was subjected to circumstances of another nature.

The shrine of the Saint has no documented proof concerning the identity of the amputator, although legend has adopted the report that a German monk, Teodoro, detached his arms, intending to take them to his native country. A stupendous flow of blood signaled the sacrilegious act and resulted in his apprehension.[1] A century after their detachment they were found perfectly intact and imbued with blood, although the body of the Saint had completely decomposed. The remains of the Saint were again placed beneath the pavement of the "Cappellone," a chapel adjoining the church, where the body had first been buried. The arms were kept apart, in precious and beautifully crafted silver cases.

Toward the end of the fifteenth century, fresh blood spilled from the arms of the Saint, an occurrence that was repeated twenty times. The most noteworthy seepage occurred in 1699 when the flow began on May 29 and continued until September 1. The Augustinian monastery and the archives of the Bishop of Camarino possess many reliable and authoritative documents concerning these effusions.[2]

A number of years after the finding of his relics, the community of Tolentino discovered the disappearance of his bones. The books in the Tolentino City Hall contain reports of the many meetings that were conducted between 1475 and 1515 regarding this mysterious disappearance, but the motive and the place of concealment were never discovered. It was not until five centuries later, in 1926, that the bones were located, buried far beneath the pavement of the Cappellone. The bishop immediately petitioned the Vatican for an examination and recognition of the findings, and on March 2, 1929, the

---

[1] *Un Asceta e un Apostolo, S. Nicolo da Tolentino.* P. Domenico Gentili, Agostiniano. Editrice Ancora. Milan. 1966. pp. 154-156.

[2] Taken from a statement prepared by representatives of the shrine.

Pope issued a Papal decree declaring the authenticity of the relics. The fourteenth century Basilica of St. Nicholas is a veritable treasury of relics and medieval art. Three of the chapels are of particular interest. The Cappellone, where the Saint was first buried and where his remains were secretely hidden, contains fourteenth century frescoes which cover the walls from the floor to the vaulted ceiling. These depict, in addition to biblical subjects, scenes of the Saint's life and some of his most noteworthy miracles. In one corner of the room can be found the miraculous well which the Saint dug before his death. The Chapel of the Holy Arms, built in the sixteenth century, contains in the coffer situated above the silver altar, many notable relics of the Saint's blood which issued from the arms. A fifteenth century silver chalice contains a quantity of the blood, and a gem-studded seventeenth century urn displays behind a glass panel the blood-stained linen which is said to be the cloth used to staunch the flow which occurred at the amputation.

The crypt was built between 1926 and 1932 as a fitting place for the reliquary of the Saint. Here are found his remains, arranged in a simulated figure that is covered by an Augustinian habit. The skull of the Saint was covered with silver, and the incorrupt, but mummified arms, still contained in their fifteenth century silver casings, can be seen in their normal positions beside the figure. The silver and crystal urn which houses the relics was personally blessed by Pope Pius XI.

BLESSED PETER GHIGENZI

(Blessed Peter of Gubbio)

Unknown—1306

Peter Ghigenzi was a practicing attorney in Paris before he returned to his native Gubbio where he joined the hermits who professed the rule of St. Augustine. He distinguished himself as an exemplary religious, and his administrative abilities were so greatly respected by the officials of the order that he was sent to Rome, where the governing body of the order maintained its headquarters, and was promptly nominated the vicar general. In this capacity he visited with great zeal many of their religious houses and gave helpful counsels and an edifying example by his perfect religious conduct. His great sanctity was manifest in the miracles he performed both before and after his holy death, which occurred at the Monastery of St. Augustine, which had been built upon his recommendations and which has for many centuries enshrined his incorrupt body. Attention was drawn to Bl. Peter in a unique fashion shortly after his death when his voice was heard chanting with the hermits the alternate verses of the night office. The community traced the recurring nocturnal voice to Peter's tomb, and many years later his incorrupt body was found in a kneeling position with mouth open and hands joined in an attitude of prayer.

The Monastery of St. Augustine in Gubbio, Italy, can prove by a great collection of documents contained in its archives that the voice of the Beatus was heard emanating from his tomb many years after his death, as testified and sworn to by many distinguished authorities of the Augustinian Order and many reliable witnesses.[1]

The incorrupt body of Bl. Peter was conserved whole and entire in the hollow of the main altar of the monastery chapel until the year 1957 when it was almost completely destroyed during a fire which gutted the church, completely ruining the reliquary and the high

---

[1]Taken from a statement to the author by the present superior of the monastery.

altar. Only a few bones were spared destruction, and these are kept in a smaller urn, which is reverently displayed to the public every year on October 29, the day on which Bl. Peter's feast is liturgically celebrated.

The voice of this blessed hermit has long since ceased to be heard, but a similar vocal phenomenon is being repeated in modern times in the convents and institutions of the Order of Suore Minime dell' Addolorata, where the voice of Bl. Clelia Barbiere is frequently heard accompanying the sisters in prayer, speaking to them and predicting future events.

A Similar Case

Blessed Clelia was born on the thirteenth of February, 1847 in Le Budrie near Bologna, Italy, to poor parents who were never able to provide her with a formal education. Throughout her brief life she edified everyone by her fervent religious conduct, and by the time she was twenty-one she had inspired three young ladies of similar religious attributes to join her in the performance of good works. After acquiring a small house near a church in Le Budrie they began living a community life but retained their secular status throughout Clelia's lifetime. They devoted their energies to the teaching of Christian doctrine, to sewing, to aiding the sick, and to performing every manner of charitable assistance to those in need. Many years after Clelia's death, this small devout group developed into the religious order which was placed under the protection of St. Francis of Paola and was given the name Suore Minime dell' Addolorata. This flourishing order, which maintains over thirty-five institutions throughout Italy, proudly claims Clelia as its founding mother.

During the past one hundred years, Clelia's heavenly voice has been periodically heard in these houses. Especially at Le Budrie, the voice is heard accompanying the sisters in their hymns, in religious readings and in their conversations. It is also heard accompanying the priest during the celebration of Holy Mass and during the sermons. Even in the parish churches it is heard lingering among the faithful.[2]

The vocal manifestations confirm the protective promise made by

---

[2]This information is taken from a statement dated February 18, 1970, which was prepared for the author by the present Mother Superior of the order who further stated: ". . . . this prodigious gift stimulates us to do well, increases our faith, is a relief to the trials of life, and gives us a great desire for heaven."

Clelia to her companions before her death: "Be of good heart because I am going to Paradise, but I will all the time be with you just the same; I will never abandon you."[3]

The voice has been described as one unlike any of this earth. Always sweet and gentle, it is sometimes sad, and not only is it frequently accompanied by angelic strains but is itself often transformed into the purest celestial music. Many witnesses of unquestionable integrity including her original companions, various superiors and sisters of the order, priests and lay hospital workers, have adequately testified that they have heard the voice.[4] Moreover many witnesses have given sworn testimony before ecclesiastical tribunals who investigated the prodigy prior to Clelia's solemn beatification on October 27, 1968.

In addition to these vocal manifestations, Clelia also frequently makes her presence known by "knocks"[5] which are variously interpreted by the sisters.

Needless to say, many of those who were privileged to hear Clelia's celestial voice became converts to the faith and many miracles have resulted through contact with her relics.[6]

---

[3]*"State di buon animo perche io me ne vado in Paradiso, ma saro sempre con voi egualmente e non vi abbandonero mai."*

[4]*Beata Clelia Barbiere, Fondatrice delle Minime dell' Addolorata.* Giorgio Cardinal Gusmini. Casa Generalizia, Suore Minime dell' Addolorata. Bologna. 1968. pp. 159-184.

[5]See entry of St. Paschal Baylon and Bl. Antony of Stroncone for reports of a similar phenomenon. Also see the entry of the Venerable Maria Vela whose voice was also heard after her death.

[6]The body of Beata Clelia was never found incorrupt. The information concerning her is given here to present to the reader another, more detailed instance and a present-day example in which the voice of a chosen soul was and is still heard after death.

BLESSED ANGELO OF BORGO SAN SEPOLCRO

Unknown—1306

What was considered the most authoritative biography of Bl. Angelo, written by John of St. William, has unfortunately perished, and as a consequence we are ill-informed concerning particulars of his life and career. In the decree written by the Congregation of Sacred Rites in 1921, which confirmed the cultus of the Augustinian hermit, a few facts are mentioned with certainty, including, of course, that Angelo practiced the theological and cardinal virtues in an heroic manner and that the faithful adherence to his holy rule and his pure and holy way of life merited recognition by the Church.

Angelo was born of a family named Scarpetti in Borgo San Sepolcro and took the Augustinian habit about the same time as the famous St. Nicholas of Tolentino. Many legends are told regarding his miracles and it is known for a certainty that in the year 1583 his still incorrupt body exhaled a sweet fragrance. The Convento S. Maria dei Servi of San Sepolcro relates that the body of this holy hermit is still admirably preserved.

SAINT CLARE OF MONTEFALCO

1268—1308

In addition to the conserved body of St. Clare, the Augustinian Monastery of the Saint possesses other relics of exceptional interest: her heart, in which are clearly imprinted the symbols of the Redeemer's Passion, and three pellets, which in a unique fashion represent the mystery of the Trinity, a devotion of which the Saint was particularly fond.

Displaying from early childhood signs of infused knowledge and an unusual sanctity, Clare was permitted at the age of seven to join a group of recluses. After six years she received the permission of the Bishop of Spoleto to join her sister, Joan, in a community which was later given the Rule of the Augustinian Order. With great reluctance, Clare accepted the office of abbess on the death of her sister, and the austerities which she had performed were then increased on behalf of her charges, who, inspired by her mystical gifts and saintly life, sought more diligently to imitate the virtues which Clare practiced to such perfection.

Her life, which was distinguished by the performance of miracles, the spirit of prophecy, and a singular understanding of divine mysteries, came to its earthly end during the Saint's fortieth year, on August 17, 1308. After Clare's death, her sisters remembered the words she had once uttered, "If you seek the cross of Christ, take my heart; there you will find the suffering Lord." These words were taken literally and her larger than average heart revealed, upon its extraction, clearly distinguishable symbols of the Lord's Passion, composed of cardiac tissue. These figures are: The crucifix, which is about the size of one's thumb. The head of the Crucified inclined toward the right arm. The clearly formed corpus is a pallid white, save for the tiny aperture in the right side, which is of a livid reddish color. White tissue covers the loins of the Crucified as a loin-cloth. The scourge is formed of a hard whitish nerve, the knobbed ends of which represent the tongues of that cruel instrument of torture. The column is formed of a round white nerve, hard as stone, and entwined by a nerve denoting the cord with which Christ was fastened to the pillar during the scourging. The Crown of Thorns is of tiny sharp nerves resembling thorns. The three nails are formed of dark fibrous tissue and are exceedingly sharp. The largest of these was attached to the inner wall of the heart by a thread of flesh. The lance is represented by a nerve which has every likeness to the shape of that instrument. The sponge is formed of a single nerve resembling a reed, with a tiny cluster of nerve endings resembling the sponge at its tip.[1]

These symbols are believed to have been imprinted on her heart during a vision in which she heard from the lips of the Lord: "I have sought a place in the world where I might plant My cross, and have found no better site than your heart." The iconography of the Saint often depicts a figure of Christ or the Saint holding a crucifix, the bottom of which penetrates her heart.

One part of the incorrupt heart is enclosed in a bust of the Saint and can be viewed under a square crystal covering in the chest portion of the figure.

The three pellets previously mentioned were found in the gall of the Saint at the time of the extraction of her heart. These pellets, about the size of hazel nuts, ". . . were judged by theologians to be symbols of the Trinity, as it was found that any one of them was as heavy as the other two, and any one of them equalled the weight of all three together."[2] These pellets can be seen under circular crystal coverings in the jeweled cross which encloses, under a similar but larger crystal covering, the other half of the Saint's incorrupt heart, on which are still seen, after six hundred years, the distinct figures representing the instruments of the Passion.

The incorrupt body of the Saint can be seen in her shrine in the Church of the Holy Cross in Montefalco. It was here that John Addington Symonds, the scholarly English author and historian, viewed the remains, after which he wrote in the *Cornhill Magazine* of October, 1881:

> "Only her hands and the exquisitely beautiful pale outline of her face (forehead, nose, mouth and chin, modelled in purest outline, as though the injury of death had never touched her) were visible. Her closed eyes seemed to sleep."[3]

---

[1]The preceding is quoted directly from literature supplied to the author by the Sanctuario S. Chiara da Montefalco.

[2]Taken from literature supplied by the shrine.

[3]*Lives of the Saints.* (Complete Edition, 4 Volumes.) Butler, Thurston, & Attwater. P.J. Kenedy & Sons. New York. 1956. Vol. III, p. 341.

Clad in exquisitely decorated robes with a veil covering the face and a crown adorning the head, the relic was found during its last examination in 1968 to be dry but perfectly flexible. The exposed hands of the Saint, only slightly darker than normal, appear perfectly formed.

Clare's canonization occurred in 1881 and during the year, Montefalco and the Augustinian order prayerfully observed the seventh centennial celebration of the Saint's birth.

SAINT AGNES OF MONTEPULCIANO

1268—1317

Possessing wisdom beyond her years, St. Agnes, at the age of nine prevailed upon her parents for permission to join a group of holy nuns in Montepulciano who were called the Sisters of the Sack because of the coarse garments they wore. Her intelligence and holiness so impressed the sisters that they elected her bursar at the age of fourteen. The following year she joined a group of the sisters who were founding a new convent of the order at Proceno, and she was soon elected their abbess. Before assuming her position, a special dispensation was obtained from Pope Martin IV, who authorized the appointment of the fifteen-year-old girl. From that time on she increased her austerities, slept on the earth, and ate only bread and water.

Many extraordinary graces were bestowed on Mother Agnes: in a vision she was once permitted to hold the Infant Jesus; several times she was privileged to receive Holy Communion from an angel, and she was often seen in ecstasy levitating from the floor. One of the most extraordinary occurrences recorded concerning her is the formation of white cross-shaped particles, described as manna, which frequently fell on her and the area where she was kneeling in prayer. She had the gift of prophecy, performed many miracles and is known to have mysteriously supplied food for the convent.

Wanting the return of their Saint, the people of Montepulciano built for her a new convent in their city on grounds which formerly had belonged to houses of ill repute. After the convent was placed under the rule of St. Dominic, it flourished under the guidance of the Saint, who served as its abbess until her death at the age of forty-nine.

Bl. Raymond of Capua,[1] one of St. Agnes' first biographers, served for many years as confessor of the monastery in which the body of Agnes was conserved, and in this capacity he was able to

---

[1] He was for many years the confessor of St. Catherine of Siena and was also her first biographer.

study at length the documents in the archives relating to her. Several years after her death, he wrote of the Saint's miracles and prodigies, that

> . . . there is one ever subsisting; her virginal body has never been interred and is miraculously and entirely preserved. It was intended to embalm her body on account of the admirable deeds she had accomplished during her life, but from the extremities of her feet and hands, a precious liquor issued drop by drop and the Convent sisterhood collected it in a vase of crystal and still preserve it: this liquor is similar to balm in color, but it is without doubt more precious. God designed thereby to show that her pure flesh that distilled the balm of Grace had no need of earthly embalmment.[2]

Among the countless pilgrims who visited the incorrupt remains of the Saint can be numbered Emperor Charles IV and St. Catherine of Siena, who was especially devoted to her memory. Bl. Raymond, in writing of St. Catherine's visit to the shrine, relates an incident which is frequently depicted in Agnes' iconography.

> ". . . she had entered the cloister and approached the body of St. Agnes, with almost all the nuns of the Convent and the Sisters of Penance of St. Dominic who had accompanied her: she knelt at her feet and prostrated to embrace them piously; but the holy body that she intended honoring, unwilling that she should stoop to kiss it, raised its foot, in the presence of the whole assembly. At this sight Catharine, much troubled, prostrated profoundly and gradually restored the foot of Agnes to its usual position.[3]

On hearing the report of this miracle, Bl. Raymond, who had received authority over the monastery from the prior provincial, further reports:

> . . . I assembled all the sisters in conference according to the Rule of the Order, and made a minute examination of this miracle under a precept of holy obedience. All present declared positively that they had seen it perfectly . . . [4]

---

[2]*Life of Saint Catherine of Siena.* Blessed Raymond of Capua. P. J. Kenedy & Sons. New York. pp. 239-240.

[3]*Ibid.* p. 240.

[4]*Ibid.* p. 241.

Another remarkable miracle occurred during a later visit to the shrine by St. Catherine, who had traveled there in the company of her two nieces and their mother, Lysa. Not wanting a repetition of the miracle which had occurred during her first visit, Catherine remained at the head of the Saint for a long time in prayer and then said smiling:

> "What, do you not observe the present that heaven sends us: do not be ungrateful!" At these words, Lysa and the others lifted their eyes and saw a very fine and very white manna falling like heavenly dews and covering not only Agnes and Catherine, but also all the persons present, and with such abundance that Lysa filled her hands with it.[5]

This manna recalled to mind the mysterious cross-shaped particles which frequently fell upon Agnes during her ecstasies. Bl. Raymond again questioned the witnesses, all of whom affirmed that the occurrence took place as reported.

> . . . several nuns belonging to the convent have equally affirmed before me and before the Friars who were with me, that thus the occurrences took place. Many are now dead; but myself and my Brethren recall perfectly their depositions: further, Lysa collected the manna which fell, showed it frequently, and gave it to several persons.[6]

The body of St. Agnes remained whole and incorrupt until the sixteenth century, when it was placed inside the walls of the main altar of the church. Unfortunately the tomb retained an excessive amount of humidity and this provoked the decomposition of most of the body. Parts of it, however, remained unharmed and are still preserved, including the arms, hands, legs, feet, and the brain.[7]

Today her bones, pieces of her flesh, and her brain are enclosed in a figure representing the body of the Saint, the incorrupt hands and feet occupying their normal positions on the model.

The relic has been in the possession of the Dominican Fathers since 1435 and can be seen by pilgrims who visit the Sanctuary of St. Agnes in Montepulciano, Italy.

---

[5]*Ibid.* p. 242.
[6]*Ibid.* p. 243.
[7]*Sant'Agnese Segni Domenicana, Patrona di Chianciano Terme.* P. Timoteo M. Centi, O.P. Santuario S. Agnese, Montepulciano. 1966. p. 49.

32

BLESSED MATTIA NAZZAREI OF MATELICA

1252—1319

Mattia was the only child of noble parents, Count Guarniero and Sibilla Nazzarei. Spurning the vanity and pomp of her position, she preferred instead to live a life of simplicity and prayer and dedicated herself to God by a vow of virginity. When her father insisted that she marry, she could only escape his arguments by fleeing to the Poor Clare convent which had, by coincidence, been established around the time of her birth. The abbess of the convent of Santa Maria Maddalena was related to the Count and refused to accept her without her father's permission. According to tradition, Mattia entered the convent chapel, cut off her hair, and donned a cast-off habit. Her father, finding her in this condition, sadly relented and gave his permission for her entrance. Only vague generalities are known of her life from this time, but it can safely be assumed that she was patient, intelligent, understanding, and virtuous, having been elected by the community to serve as its abbess for a period of forty years.

The holy abbess died on December 28, 1319, an event she had previously predicted, surrounded by a heavenly fragrance and a mysteriously bright light.[1] Many miracles were performed during the solemn exhibition of her relic, and it was noted on the eighteenth day that the body was still flexible and fragrant.[2] Interment was in an elegant urn deposited near the major altar.

The body was carefully examined in 1536, two hundred seventeen years after Mattia's death. At that time, when it was removed from the casket, the community was astonished to see it sweat profusely. The sisters found it necessary to dry it with linen towels and duly recorded the incident in the documents pertaining to the cult of the Beata.[3]

When repairs were being made in the chapel during the year 1756,

[1]*Breve Vita della B. Mattia Nazzarei, Abbadessa Delle Clarisse in Matelica.* P. Ferdinando Diotallevi, O.F.M., Arti Grafiche-Gentile-Fabriano. 1962. p. 25.

[2]*Ibid.* p. 38.

[3]*Ibid.* p. 39.

the tomb was disturbed and the bishop seized the opportunity to examine the relic, which was found perfectly incorrupt, flexible, and emitting a sweet fragrance. Miracles continued to occur after the body was reinterred in a new urn beneath the altar of St. Cecilia.

Two years later, in December, 1758, a "blood-fluid" was seen proceeding from the corpse, to the amazement of the many witnesses and the physicians summoned to the scene. Throughout the years the miraculous flow was witnessed and affirmed by numerous doctors and ecclesiastical authorities.[4] It has been noticed to commence at various times, especially prior to the deaths of members of the community or before the outbreak of wars, plagues, or events of epic proportions. In 1920 the linens kept under the Beata's hands and feet were changed, and today, after fifty years, the pads are saturated with this miraculous fluid.[5]

The monastery and church were renamed in the Beata's honor in 1758 and her cultus was confirmed in 1765. Her body, which was never embalmed, is still perfectly incorrupt. The flesh is rather dark, but it is reported as being soft and "spongy." The relic is solemnly displayed three times during the year: March 1, the anniversary of her birth; December 28, the anniversary of her death; and January 1, which commemorates the return of her body from Macerata, where it was taken for safekeeping during the Napoleonic revolution of 1810-1811.

The inexplicably incorrupt body of Mattia Nazzarei, with its mystifying issue of "blood-fluid," has miraculously existed for over six hundred fifty years.

Within the last few years, however, a slight deterioration of the body has been noted. After a recent official recognition and examination, the relic was enclosed in plastic.

---

[4]*Ibid.* pp. 44-56.

[5]This information was supplied by the Monastery Beata Mattia, Matelica, Italy, in a statement dated November 9, 1969.

33

BLESSED MARGARET OF METOLA

(Blessed Margaret of Citta-di-Castello)

1287—1320

Because she was dwarfed, blind, hunchbacked and lame, Bl. Margaret was kept hidden by her parents throughout her childhood. When she was sixteen, she was taken from Metola to the miraculous shrine at Citta-di-Castello, where a cure was anticipated. Unfortunately, no miracle occurred, and it is recorded that the child was left abandoned. She was cared for by various families of the city and earned money for her board by attending small children. Her cheerfulness, based on trust and love of God, endeared her to everyone. She became a Dominican tertiary and devoted herself to the sick and dying, but she showed special solicitude toward prisoners. Her holy death occurred on April 13, 1320, when she was thirty-three years of age. After her death, more than two hundred miracles occurred in confirmation of her heroic sanctity.

The preliminary steps toward the cause of her beatification were undertaken by the Dominican Order, but at various times it languished, until it was almost forgotten. During the sixteenth century, interest in her cause was rekindled after the discovery of her incorrupt body. On June 9, 1558, the bishop authorized the transfer of the Beata's remains to a new coffin after it was noticed that the original one was rotting away.

The exhumation was undertaken in the presence of a number of official witnesses who were awe-stricken when the coffin was opened. While the clothing on the body had crumbled to dust, the body itself was found to be perfectly preserved, as though Margaret had just died. It was obvious that she had been a dwarf, her body measuring only four feet long. Her head was rather large in proportion to the rest of the thin figure. The forehead was broad, with the face tapering to the chin. Her nose was quite prominent, and her small, even teeth were serrated at the edges. The witnesses noticed that the hands and feet were small, that the right leg was an inch and a half shorter than the left (which had caused her to walk with a limp) and that the arms were crossed in front of the body, with the left arm and hand being slightly raised without support. The body was thoroughly examined by physicians, who declared that no chemicals had been used to preserve it. The body was reclothed in a fresh habit and was placed in a new coffin.[1]

Many miracles followed this ceremony, and the cause, which was undertaken with renewed interest, came to a successful conclusion on October 19, 1609, when the Church officially recognized Margaret's sanctity, pronouncing her a beata and designating April 13 as her feast day.

The body of Bl. Margaret, which has never been embalmed, is dressed in a Dominican habit, and lies under the high altar of the Church of St. Domenico at Citta-di-Castello, Italy. The arms of the body are still flexible, the eyelashes are present, and the nails are in place on the hands and feet. The coloring of the body has darkened slightly and the skin is dry and somewhat hardened, but by all standards the preservation can be considered a remarkable condition, having endured for over six hundred fifty years.

For my father and my mother have left me: but the Lord hath taken me up.

Psalm 26:10

---

[1] *The Story of Margaret of Metola.* William R. Bonniwell, O.P. P.J. Kenedy & Sons. New York, 1952. pp. 172-173.

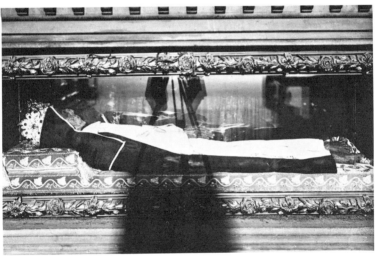

The dwarfed, malformed body of Bl. Margaret of Metola (Citta-di-Castello), a Dominican tertiary who died in 1320 and was discovered incorrupt in 1558.

BLESSED JOHN OF CHIARAMONTE

(Blessed John of Caramola)

Unknown—1339

A native of Toulouse, Bl. John led an austere life as a hermit in the wilderness of Mt. Caramola in Lucania, Italy, where he stopped while on his way to join the Crusades. There he lived in close communion with his Creator. He is believed to have possessed the gift of prophecy and to have practiced extreme dietary mortifications. Following a severe illness, he sought assistance from the Cistercian monastery of Santa Maria of Sagittario at Chiaramonte, where he is believed to have continued his former austerities as a lay brother. His companions testified that his diet consisted of meager portions of bread and water and that they had never seen him sleep. They were greatly edified by his consistent practice of penance, his strict observance of silence and his love and frequent practice of mental prayer.

At Chiaramonte, legend reports that while he was spending some time in contemplation on a mountain, hunters entrusted to his keeping a small goat. On their return, they became enraged upon finding that the monk had returned it to its bleating mother, who had led it away. In consequence, they threw the holy man into the valley below. Three trees are said to have sprouted on the spot where his body fell and the place is fondly pointed out by the villagers, who regard him as a saint.[1]

After his death, many miracles were performed through his intercession, and many of those suffering bodily afflictions were cured by touching his incorrupt body.

The relic has suffered a little during the lapse of some six centuries. The face has especially been ravaged by time, and the legs are missing from the knees down, but are believed to have been given to Toulouse, his hometown, as relics.

The parish church at Chiaramonte has possession of the remains, which are kept under the altar in an ancient urn. The relic is not exposed, but the urn can be opened for those who request to view it.

---

[1]This legend was supplied by the pastor of Chiaramonte.

SAINT PEREGRINE LAZIOSI

1265—1345

Known throughout the world as "The Cancer Saint," Peregrine was born in Forli, Italy. His father belonged to a political faction named the Ghibellines, which was loyal to the German Emperor and in conflict with the defenders of the Pope; whereas, his mother was steadfastly loyal to her religion and to the Papacy. From her he learned his first prayers and the rules of the Church, but the future Saint preferred to side with his father against the Pope and soon displayed the qualities of a natural leader.

Once when Pope Martin IV sent St. Philip Benizi, the Prior General of the Servite Order to Forli as peacemaker, Peregrine separated himself from the crowd which had been listening to the Saint, approached St. Philip and slapped him soundly in the face. Peregrine and his followers succeeded in chasing St. Philip from the town, but on his return, through the grace of God, Peregrine was struck with repentence.

In a vision, the Blessed Mother reportedly requested his entrance into the Servite Order, and he was accompanied on a trip to Siena by his guardian angel, who appeared in the guise of a young man. As a Servite, Peregrine performed the duties of a lay brother for twelve years and was then ordered by his superiors to prepare for ordination. He returned to Forli as a newly ordained priest and founded there a new monastery for his order. He was called the "Angel of Good Counsel" for the wise and prudent advice he gave to people of all walks of life who visited the monastery seeking his aid, and it is known that he cured many who were afflicted with various diseases, that he frequently multiplied wheat and wine for the poor during a famine, and that, on more than one occasion, he raised the dead to life.

During the plague of 1323-1328, when he was risking his own health to help the sick, he was stricken with cancer in his right leg. He was then sixty years of age. After suffering for a number of years, he was at last almost completely incapacitated when an excellent surgeon recommended an amputation. He spent the night before the scheduled operation in prayer before a picture of a crucifix and beheld Our Lord in a vision, descending from the cross with an outstretched hand. This vision is most often depicted in the Saint's iconography. The next morning he was found perfectly cured, with no trace of the former disease. Because of this miracle and those which followed after his death, he became known as the "Universal Patron of Cancer Victims." Following this miraculous cure he spent his remaining twenty years ministering to the sick, preaching, and fulfilling various duties of his monastery. He died on May 1, his eightieth birthday, after having spent sixty-two years in the service of Mary.

The cultus of the Saint began immediately after his death. The process of beatification, which was entrusted to St. Robert Cardinal Bellarmine, was brought to a successful conclusion and the canonization ceremonies followed in the year 1726. We are told that during the thirty-two years prior to his canonization there were over three hundred miracles attributed to him and authenticated by Church officials.

After the erection in 1639 of a new, more splendid shrine in the chapel of the monastery at Forli, the body of the Saint was removed there and was found to be incorrupt. The relic, now reclothed in silk, is always exposed for the veneration of the faithful, who may approach the shrine and touch the glass of the urn. The relic was last officially viewed on April 16, 1958. Although some of the bones are exposed, the lower legs and feet, the arms, skull, neck and chest are well covered with flesh, which is of a predominately black color.

36

BLESSED SIBYLLINA BISCOSSI

1287—1367

Orphaned at an early age, Sibyllina was forced to work as a servant until, as the result of a severe illness, she completely lost her sight at the age of twelve. The Sisters of the Third Order of Saint Dominic charitably took charge of the pious child and clothed her in their habit. Blindness was a heavy trial for the young girl, and she earnestly prayed to St. Dominic for a cure. After a vision in which the holy Patriarch appeared to her, she accepted the burden with perfect resignation, seeing in her trial the holy will of God.

At the age of fifteen she began to live the life of a recluse in a cell adjoining the church of the Dominicans and remained in her contemplative seclusion for the remaining sixty-four years of her life. She is known to have practiced severe austerities and to have had the gift of prophecy. She was divinely inspired concerning matters of faith and was the recipient of many visions and revelations. Unable because of her blindness to assist her neighbors in other ways, she communicated through a small window of her cell with those who sought her counsel. Though lacking in formal education, she spoke with such fluency, intelligence and theological precision that she capably assisted those who sought her advice and succeeded in converting many to the Faith. Sibyllina was especially devoted to the Holy Eucharist and the Holy Spirit, and she considered Pentecost the greatest feast in the Church.

During the eightieth year of her life, Sibyllina passed to her eternal reward, and many were the miracles which marked her blessed departure. The cult of this holy tertiary was officially confirmed in 1853 with her beatification by Pope Pius IX.

During the year of her beatification the body was exhumed in order to be placed in a more appropriate and convenient location, and it was at this time found perfectly entire. It is now enshrined in the Cathedral of Pavia under the altar of the Chapel of St. Lucy. The body is dry and hard and the skin is like parchment, through which the bones of the skull are quite visible. In the mouth of the relic, which is arched in a delicate smile, the lower teeth are visible, the upper teeth having been extracted, probably as relics. The hands of the relic hold a rosary and beautiful artificial flowers, and the head is covered with a garland of blossoms. The relic, clothed in the black and white habit of a Dominican tertiary, is reverently displayed three times during the year: on March 19, the Feast of St. Joseph, which is also the anniversary of her death; on March 20, the day on which her feast is observed in Pavia; and on the Feast of All Saints, November 1.

Bl. Sibyllina Biscossi is held in great veneration by the people of Pavia and is regarded as the patroness of Italian servant girls.

37

SAINT CATHERINE OF SIENA

1347—1380

Twenty-five children were born to Jacomo and Lapa Benincasa, of whom Catherine was the twenty-third and her twin sister, Jane, who died in infancy, was the twenty-fourth. Being very pious as a child and possessing wisdom beyond her years, Catherine made a vow of virginity at a tender age and was favored with a number of visions. During her sixth year, while on an errand with her brother Stephen, she saw a vision of Our Lord near the church of the Friar Preachers in the Valle Piatta. The vision was clothed in pontifical ornaments, a tiara was upon His head, and He was seated upon a throne around which stood St. Peter, St. Paul and St. John the Evangelist. After Stephen succeeded in rousing her from the ecstasy, she cried and said, "O, did you but see what I saw, you would never have disturbed me in such a sweet vision." It was from this time that she seemed to be no longer a child, and her thoughts, her conduct and her virtues were those of one superior to her age. It was shortly after this experience that she determined to join the Order of St. Dominic. Over the vigorous opposition of her mother, she eventually succeeded, at the age of seventeen, in becoming a tertiary in the Third Order of that illustrious company. She remained in the house of her parents dressed in the habit of the Sisters of Penance and spent three years in seclusion and contemplation. Later, however, she devoted herself to the active apostolate, caring for the sick, visiting and converting prisoners, distributing alms, and attracting to herself disciples and friends who were later to bear her name.

Catherine experienced possibly all the mystical gifts. She is known to have delivered many from diabolical possession, to have performed many miracles of healing, to have levitated frequently during prayer, to have enjoyed an extraordinary intimacy with Our Lord and His Mother, and to have experienced the mystical espousal in which Our Lord, in a vision, gave her a golden ring, set with four precious stones, in the center of which blazed a superb diamond. The ring was visible only to Catherine, and she acknowledged that it was always with her and that she never tired of viewing it.[1]

These mystical favors were the result of years of severe penances. From her childhood she sacrificed and mortified herself and wore a hair shirt. Her prolonged fasts were divinely transformed into a complete abstinence, and while she subsisted only on the Holy Eucharist, her strength and vitality were spiritually maintained. During the plague of 1372-1373 she cared for the repulsive sick, prepared numerous people for death, and buried many of the victims with her own hands.

Catherine also bore the stigmata on her body, but at her request, Our Lord made the marks visible only to herself, and, as also happened in the case of Bl. Osanna of Mantua, the marks became quite pronounced after her death, as verified by her incorrupt hands and feet.

St. Catherine is known to have labored tirelessly for the interests of the Church and Apostolic See. She is credited with having persuaded Gregory XI to return the Papacy from Avignon to Rome and—as a result of her exhaustive travels—with having brought back to obedience to the Holy See many rebellious Italian cities. She corresponded with kings and queens for the causes of the Church and prayed and pleaded for Church unity.

Distressed over the terrible schism which afflicted the Church, she offered herself as a victim to God and died in Rome after a painful seizure on April 29, 1380, being at the time of her death only thirty-three years of age.

Blessed Raymond of Capua, her confessor, tells us that immense crowds visited her remains, "and those who succeeded in touching them, considered themselves highly favored." During the three days her body was left exposed to the veneration of her devotees, her arms, neck and legs remained as flexible as though she were still alive.[2]

She was buried in the cemetery adjoining the Church of Santa Maria Sopra Minerva, but was shortly thereafter removed by Bl. Raymond, who placed the casket at the foot of a column facing the Rosary Chapel, where it remained until 1430. During this translation from the cemetery, Raymond had the casket opened, " . . . a thing easily done, as in point of fact it was not actually buried beneath the ground and found that the clothes had suffered somewhat from the

---

[1]*Life of Saint Catherine of Siena.* Blessed Raymond of Capua. P. J. Kenedy & Sons. New York. p. 76.

[2]*Ibid.* pp. 371-372.

dampness of the place where the body was deposited, and where it was much exposed to the rain.["3]

Raymond felt that a major relic of the Saint should be entrusted to the church of Siena, the city of her birth and the scene of her many miracles, so after securing the necessary permission from the Sovereign Pontiff, Bl. Raymond had the sacred head separated from the body, enclosed it in a reliquary of gilded copper and gave it to the keeping of two friars of the Order for removal to Siena. In 1385 it was taken in secret to the convent at the Campo Reggio and placed in the sacristy, until such time as the Church might accord her the honors of the altar. Plans for the solemn translation of the head of the Saint were subsequently made by Bl. Raymond, the bishop, and officials of the city. Following several days of preparation and religious activities, the head was taken outside the town to the Hospital of St. Lazarus, where the Saint had often ministered to the sick and from whence the solemn procession was to begin for its triumphal reception into the city. The most notable personage attending this function was the aged mother of the Saint, Lapa, then an octogenarian, who walked behind the relic, dressed in the habit of the Sisters of Penance.[4]

During the same year of the translation of the head, 1385, other relics were taken from the body, namely an arm, which was given to Siena, and three fingers, which were given to Venice. During the year 1430, St. Antoninus, the prior of the church containing the Saint's relics, ordered that the body be placed in a more appropriate manner in a new stone sarcophagus, artistically embellished and surmounted by a statue of the Saint dressed in the habit of her order. This sarcophagus has been opened at intervals during the centuries and relics taken from it to enrich the churches of the Order throughout Europe. So it was that in 1487 a hand was given to the Dominican Sisters of the Monastery of S. Domenico e Sisto in Rome, and the left foot was given to the Church of SS. John and Paul at Venice. The stigmata on this foot was carefully examined during its official recognition in 1597.[5] In 1501 one rib was given to the convent of St. Mark in Florence, and in 1575 a shoulder blade was entrusted to the Dominican Sisters of Magnanapoli in Rome.

[3]*The History of St. Catherine of Siena and Her Companions.* Augusta Theodosia Drane. Longmans, Green and Co. London. 1899. Vol. II, p. 282.

[4]*Ibid.* p. 287.

[5]Bl. Raymond of Capua. *Op. cit.* p. 412.

During the time that the church was undergoing restoration, the tomb was again opened in April, 1855, in the presence of the general of the Order and many ecclesiastics and a

> . . . considerable portion of the sacred relics was taken out by the General and sent to the Convent of St. Dominic's, Stone, the Mother-house of the English congregation of the Sisters of Penance, which bears the name of St. Catherine. These relics, which fill two silver and crystal reliquaries each three and a half inches long, consist of portions of bone and skin representing the appearance of grey ashes, among which appear mingled threads of gold, the remains, probably, of the cloth of gold in which the holy body was wrapped. One of these reliquaries is preserved at St. Dominic's, Stone; the other at the convent of St. Catherine, at Bow, near London.[6]

The finger which received the mystical ring denoting the Saint's heavenly espousal is in the keeping of the Chartreuse of Pontiniano near Florence. Many other small relics were distributed to the churches dedicated to her memory.

After the restoration of the church was completed on August 3, 1855, the relics, still reposing in their ancient sarcophagus, were deposited beneath the main altar on August 4, the Feast of St. Dominic. The day following this feast, the shrine was visited by the Roman Senate and the relics were borne in solemn procession through Rome, followed by a large number of sisters of the Dominican Third Order. This event was henceforth known as the Translation of the Relics of St. Catherine, which feast is yearly commemorated on the Thursday after Sexagesima Sunday and which had previously been kept as the commemoration of the Mystical Espousal. After the relics were returned to the high altar, the sarcophagus was so securely replaced (it has recently been described as being "walled-in") that it has not been opened since that time. However, the gilded, artistic monument housing the ancient statue is exposed for the admiration and consideration of her devotees. To the left of the altar containing her body is Michelangelo's "Christ with the Cross," and near the sacristy is a room decorated by Perugino called the Room of St. Catherine, whose walls are actually those of the convent cell which she occupied during her stays in Rome.

St. Catherine ranks among the greatest mystics and spiritual writers

---

[6]Drane. *Op. cit.* p. 292.

the Church has produced, and she has been the inspiration and model for many of the saints who followed her. Venerated as a saint even during her lifetime, she was solemnly canonized by Pope Pius II in 1461, and in 1939 Pope Pius XII gave to Italy, as its chief patron saints, St. Francis of Assisi and St. Catherine of Siena. The importance of her writings and spiritual doctrine was officially recognized by the Apostolic See during the solemn ceremonies conducted by Pope Paul VI on October 4, 1970, during which she was declared a Doctor of the Church, the second woman to bear such an illustrious title.

BLESSED ANDREW FRANCHI

1335—1401

Born of a noble family, Bl. Andrew embraced a Dominican vocation about the year 1351 and soon earned a doctor of theology degree at Rome. Renowned as a teacher, spiritual director and preacher, his great administrative abilities were likewise extolled, and he was made prior of several houses of the Order in Pistoia, Orvieto, and Lucca. For twenty years he served the Church as the Bishop of Pistoia and continued to observe the same rules to which he was bound as a Dominican friar. It is recorded that he spent his income on the needy and for pious endeavors. A year before his death he retired from the episcopal throne to prepare for his death, which occurred on May 26, 1401.

The body of the holy bishop was buried in San Domenico in Pistoia, where it was found incorrupt during its first recognition in 1911. A second exhumation occurred in 1944 and the last in 1966. The medical report composed during this last exhumation described it as being completely mummified. The head is without hair and is detached from the body, while the upper lip, the point of the nose, all the toes, and parts of the fingers are missing.

The relic reposes in a glass-fronted reliquary beneath a side altar of the same church in which it was first interred. The body is clad in episcopal garments, the head is crowned with a bishop's mitre, while a silk veil covers the full length of the relic.

In 1921 the virtues of the saintly bishop were recognized by Pope Benedict XV, who sanctioned his cultus.

SAINT FRANCES OF ROME

1384—1440

The Roman family into which Frances was born and the one into which she married were both illustrious and wealthy. Wed at the age of twelve, she bore three children. Her husband, who had become increasingly dear to her, left her a widow after forty years of marriage. Always a paragon of the perfect wife and mother, she complied with her husband's request and wore rich fabrics and jewels, as befitted one of her rank. Beneath these external trappings she is reported to have worn a hair shirt next to her skin and to have practiced secret austerities. She is known to have helped the sick in the hospitals of Rome and to have given generously to the needy.

St. Frances left many reports of the visions with which she was favored, most notable of which are the graphic portrayals of her guardian angel, whom she was permitted to see uninterruptedly.

Four years before her death she joined the Olivetan Benedictine Oblates, which she had founded previously, according to the guidelines set by St. Benedict. Frances died on March 9, 1440, not among her sisters in religion, but in the home of her ailing son. Her death was mourned by a grateful and devoted populace, and her sanctity was extolled by many ecclesiastics, who boldly foretold her eventual canonization, which after many unfortunate and unavoidable delays, was finally culminated May 29, 1608.

Several months after her death, her tomb was opened to transport the corpse into a monument which Baptista, Mobilia and several Roman noblemen had erected in her honor. It was found in a state of perfect preservation and exhaling the same fragrance which had been noted before her death.[1] Two centuries later, in 1638, the tomb was opened in conjunction with alterations being performed in the Basilica Maria Nuova, which has since been renamed in honor of the Saint. Only the bones were found at this time, and these are contained

[1] *The Life of St. Frances of Rome, of Blessed Lucy of Narni, of Dominica of Paradiso and of Anne de Montmorency.* Lady Georgiana Fullerton. D. & J. Sadlier & Co. New York. 1855. pp. 134-135.

in a crystal repository above the altar of her crypt, which was erected at the expense of Agatha Pamphili, a sister of Pope Innocent X, who was also an oblate of the Saint's order. The skeletal remains are clothed in the religious habit of her order, which permits the skull to be viewed by the countless wives and widows who pray before the remains of the saint they regard as their model and patroness.

40

SAINT BERNARDINE OF SIENA

1380—1444

Orphaned at the age of six, Bernadine was brought by paternal relatives to Siena where he received an excellent education. After completing university studies, he distributed his goods among the poor and joined the Friars Minor when twenty-two years of age. Ordained in 1404, he was commissioned to preach, and he labored in this apostolic work for the rest of his life. He is especially remembered for his zeal in promoting devotion to the name of Jesus, and he popularized, with the help of St. John Capistran, a symbol representing the Holy Name. The Gothic letters for the name of Jesus, "IHS," were set in a blazing sun to whose tongues of fire and spreading rays he attributed mystical significance. For a time the Saint was denounced as a heretic and the symbol regarded as idolatrous, but his vindication was effected and the symbol has remained in popular use since its innovation over five hundred years ago. The Saint was a prolific writer, and his extant sermons are said to be as applicable today as they were when first delivered. The Saint died at L'Aquila in a convent of his order, but his funeral was repeatedly postponed, owing to the crowds of mourners who visited his bier.

St. John Capistran, who had journeyed to L'Aquila to visit the tomb of his friend, was astonished to find that the funeral of the deceased had been so long delayed, and he was an eyewitness to an inexplicable wonder to which he frequently referred in his letters and sermons. On the twenty-fourth day following Bernardine's death, a flow of blood was seen to issue from his temporarily closed casket. The flow originated from the nose, and his habit and pillow were saturated with blood, which appeared as normal as that of a living person. The people reverently gathered it up with cloths, which were cut up and distributed as relics.[1]

On the twenty-sixth day following his death, the city of L'Aquila honored the Saint by solemnizing an unprecedented funeral service

---

[1] *St. John Capistran, Reformer.* Rev. John Hofer. Translated by Rev. Patrick Commins, O.S.B. B. Herder Book Co. St. Louis, Mo. 1943. p. 146.

for the illustrious churchman it jealously claimed as its own. He was buried in the Church of St. Francis, where his body remained until 1471, when it was moved to the newly erected church dedicated to him. It was during this translation that his body, which had been consigned to the grave twenty-seven years before, was found perfectly preserved. His body was put into a crystal reliquary, which was later placed inside a silver sarcophagus, a gift of the king of France.

The body has been examined several times during the years, the last examination occurring in August, 1968. The body at that time was found wrapped in tobacco leaves, and it was determined that preservatives had been used during a previous exhumation. Parts of the body are held together by various means, and chemicals were applied to the relic to maintain its condition.[2]

The body of the Saint, who is considered the foremost Italian missionary of the 15th century and the greatest preacher of his time, reposes in an artistic sarcophagus, which is situated in a sculptured marble shrine in the Basilica of S. Bernardino, L'Aquila, Italy.

---

[2]*Ricognizione Canonica delle Venerate Spoglie di S. Bernardino da Siena. L'Aquila, 20-22 Agosto 1968, Estratto da: Acta Provinciae Aprutinae, Santi Bernardini Senensis, Ordinis Fratrum Minorum.* Tipografia Labor, Sulmona. 1968. XXII, Fascicola 1.

SAINT HERCULANUS OF PIEGARO

Unknown—1451

Regarded as one of the most prominent preachers of his time, Herculanus led a life of solitude and prayer after his entrance into the Franciscan Convent of the Strict Observance at Sarteano. Following his ordination, he was sent forth to preach and did so with such eloquence that many were reduced to tears and reformed their lives, while others experienced an increase of devotion.

While he was preaching a Lenten service in the Cathedral of Lucca during the year 1430, the town was besieged by Florentines. Herculanus encouraged the people, during this hazardous and painful time, to resist surrendering, promising if they trusted in the Lord that food would be sent by Easter to replenish their diminishing supplies. His prophecy was fulfilled, for the town was delivered at the time of the Paschal feast.

The penances which he recommended to others he practiced most severely and persistently himself, his fasts being so prolonged that it seemed at times that he subsisted entirely on the Holy Eucharist.

Herculanus died on May 28, 1451 at Castronovo in Tuscany. Five years later, when his body was being transferred to the Franciscan Church for enshrinement, it was found perfectly entire although the grave had been exceedingly damp.

SAINT RITA OF CASCIA

1381—1457

St. Rita was given the name of Margherita at her baptism, but the name of the future Augustinian saint was affectionately abbreviated to that by which she is now known throughout the world—to which has been added the Miracle Worker of Cascia and Saint of the Impossible. At the tender age of twelve, the pious girl was married to Paolo Ferdinando—against her natural inclinations, but in obedience to her elderly parents, who were fearful, so some have recorded, that their death would leave her alone in the world. The eighteen years of her marriage produced two sons and a veritable martyrdom for Rita, resulting from Paolo's violent and quarrelsome nature and the physical abuse he frequently awarded his refined and prayerful wife. Shortly before his politically motivated assassination, his disposition was completely transformed, and for a time the household was an ideal one, a fact credited to Rita's patient long-suffering and persistent prayers. After the murder of her husband, another serious trial presented itself when her two young sons came of age and vowed to avenge his death. When Rita's pleadings failed to alter their intentions, she prayed for their deaths rather than have them commit such a dreadful crime. In due time her prayers were answered and both died with the consolations of the Church, forgiving their father's murderers.

Shortly after this loss, she applied for entrance into the convent of the Augustinians in Cascia, to which she had been attracted before her untimely marriage, but her admittance was denied because of stipulations in the rule of the order which barred the acceptance of widows. Again her prayers were answered when her patron saints, Augustine, Nicholas of Tolentino, and John the Baptist appeared to her one night and accompanied her to the Augustinian convent, Santa Maria Maddalena; bolted gates and locked doors miraculously opened to permit her entrance into the chapel, where the astonished sisters discovered her the next morning. Seeing in her unusual entry the holy will of God, Rita was at last admitted into the convent, which was to be renamed in her honor during subsequent ages. Inspired by a sermon preached by St. James of the Marches, she implored God for some participation in Christ's sufferings and was divinely accorded a thorn wound in her forehead, which festered and produced such an offensive odor that the next fifteen years of her life were spent in reverential seclusion.

Three days before her death at the age of seventy-six, Rita was blessed with a vision of Our Lord and His Holy Mother. At the time of her entrance into Heaven, the cell wherein she lay was filled with an extraordinary perfume; an astounding light emanated from the wound on her forehead; and the bells of the city are said to have been joyously pealed by angels.

The numerous miracles which occurred after her death and her sweetly perfumed body, which scented the entire church where she lay exposed, induced the civil and ecclesiastical authorities to install her remains in a place accessible to the pilgrims who constantly visited the bier. It was subsequently placed in the inner oratory where it was enshrined beneath an altar. In this position between the cloister and the church, the wooden sarcophagus could easily be seen and its precious contents venerated by both the pilgrims and the cloistered nuns.

Rita's beatification was pronounced on July 16, 1627, in ceremonies conducted by Pope Urban VIII. Immediately prior to this declaration, the body was carefully examined and found to be as perfect as it had been on the day of her death, with the flesh still of a natural color.[1] The excellent condition of her body after the lapse of over one hundred fifty years seems quite extraordinary since it was never properly entombed.

About the time of the solemn beatification, the eyes of the relic are reported to have opened unaided, the miraculous occurrence of which is reported to have quelled a riot.[2] The eyes seem to have remained open for some time as paintings executed during that time indicate. The body at times was also seen to move to one side and after a lapse of some years to have changed position to the other side. The elevation of the entire body to the top of the sarcophagus was also observed, a circumstance which was carefully recorded by the eyewitnesses to this prodigy. The documents pertaining to these occur-

---

[1]*Saint Rita.* Willy De Spens. Hanover House. Garden City. New York. 1960. p. 140.

[2]*Ibid.* p. 140.

rences are preserved in the archives of the Archdiocese of Spoleto and it would seem likely that the convent of the Saint would likewise possess copies of such important and unusual declarations.[3]

At the time of Rita's canonization in 1900, the devotion to "The Saint of Impossible and Desperate Cases" had spread beyond Italy into Europe and across the seas. In 1946 a church was built in her honor in Cascia, which was elevated to the dignity of a basilica in 1955. In this impressive edifice is located the golden shrine which houses the Saint's crystal reliquary.[4]

St. Rita's body, as viewed by countless pilgrims, appears only slightly discolored and is perfect in all its members, except for one eyebrow, which moved in its position about the year 1650, and a right cheek bone, which became dislodged. These were repaired with wax and string as the two medical examinations of 1743 and 1892 indicate.

The distinguishable sweetness, which in past ages was recognized by the most reputable persons, who also gave sworn testimony to its presence about the body, is still frequently noticed at the shrine. Although it is not continuous, it is observed on the occasion of some miracles.[5]

The convent of the Saint possesses several interesting relics which figured in an important manner in Rita's life. Besides the cell of the Saint in which is kept her first decorated sarcophagus, the oratory where she received the thorn of the Crucified, the wedding ring, and other mementos, there is still growing in the courtyard the five hundred-year-old vine, which owes its existence to an incident in the Saint's early religious life. To test her obedience, her superior ordered Rita to plant a certain piece of dry wood and to water it each

---

[3]*Our Own St. Rita, A Life of the Saint of the Impossible.* Rev. M. J. Corcoran, O.S.A. Benziger Bros. New York. 1919. pp. 155-161. The sisters of the Convent of St. Rita at Cascia declared that the levitations did occur in past times, but they consider the reports in other works incorrect which state that the elevations occurred on the feast days of the Saint or during the various visits of bishops.

[4]The reports which state that the religious habit in which the body is presently clothed is the same one she received at the beginning of her religious life is totally incorrect according to the sisters of Cascia. The garments on the body were changed several times during the ages, the old ones being used for relics. The habit in which the relic is presently clothed was made in 1947 for the translation of the body into the new church. Moreover, during her forty-four years of religious life, her worn habits were replaced as necessity demanded.

[5]Taken from a statement made by the Sisters of Cascia dated May 13, 1970.

day. The stick eventually sprouted into a healthy grape vine, which still bears fruit. Each year the harvest is distributed among high ranking ecclesiastics, while the leaves are dried, made into a powder, and sent to the sick around the world.[6]

The bees of St. Rita are another curiosity. When she was an infant, tiny white bees were once seen swarming about Rita's mouth, attracted no doubt by something sweet which she had been fed. This unusual incident is always mentioned in Rita's biographies and is usually given a miraculous connotation. Bees still play a part in the Saint's history. About two hundred years after her death, a strange variety of bees[7] took up residence in a fifteenth century wall of the monastery and have lived there continuously since that time. They remain in hibernation for ten months of the year and emerge during Holy Week of each year. They are never seen to leave the convent enclosure, and after a few weeks of activity about the gardens and rooms of the convent, they return to the ancient wall after the feast of St. Rita, May 22, and seal themselves into holes which they make themselves. Contrary to some opinions, the members of the Order and the sisters of the convent of Cascia do not consider their presence or behavior to be in any way of a miraculous nature. It is regarded as a purely natural phenomenon which, by an unusual coincidence, occurs in the walls of their convent.

St. Rita has taken her rightful position among the great saints who served in turn as wives, mothers, widows, and nuns, providentially given to us for our edification. She is still overwhelmingly and affectionately regarded by her many satisfied devotees around the world as the "Guardian Saint of Desperate and Impossible Cases."

---

[6]*The Life of Saint Rita of Cascia.* Fr. Atanasio Angelini, O.S.A. Poligrafico Alterocca. Terni, Italy. pp. 146-147. This vine recalls the thorny rose bushes of Assisi into which St. Francis threw himself to combat a temptation against purity. The bushes were thereafter transformed into thornless ones, which are still growing since those ancient times. Their leaves also are distributed.

[7]According to one professor of biology, the bees might well be flies which mimic bees since they never sting and do not gather pollen. Another authority considers them a mutation. They have not as yet been examined or classified by entomologists.

The intact body of St. Rita of Cascia, "Saint of Impossible and Desperate Cases," displayed in a glass case in the Basilica of St. Rita in Cascia, Italy. She died in 1457; her body has shifted positions several times, plus the eyes have opened and closed unaided.

SAINT ANTONINUS

1389—1459

Having been professed a Dominican in 1406, Antoninus was ordained in 1413 and served as prior of many houses of the Order including that of S. Maria sopra Minerva in Rome. During his administration of that magnificent church, he had the incorrupt remains of St. Catherine of Siena enshrined in the artistic golden sarcophagus which has been admired by succeeding generations of her clients.

After serving for a number of years as vicar-general of the Dominican convents of the strict observance, he returned to his native Florence and established the Convent of San Marco, the interior of which was glorified with many admirable frescoes executed by his dear friend, Blessed Fra Angelico. As a token of esteem, Pope Eugene IV and the entire college of cardinals assisted at the consecration of this church, which has always been considered one of the artistic glories of Florence. The library of San Marco, which the Saint made accessible to scholars, is thought to have been the first public library in Europe.

Antoninus has been likened to St. Thomas Aquinas and St. Alphonsus Liguori because of his writings on canon law and moral and ascetical theology, but he has also been widely acclaimed as a counsellor, preacher, reformer, economist, sociologist and historian.

After his consecration as the Archbishop of Florence, a position he was through humility reluctant to accept, he was soon regarded, "the people's prelate" and the "father of the poor," for he promptly divested the episcopal palace of all that suggested pomp or luxury. In the simplified surroundings, which he felt were more befitting a poor friar, he was able to reduce his household staff in order to distribute more funds to the poor.

The Saint died a most holy death on May 2, 1459. Pope Pius II presided at the obsequies, which were delayed for eight days. During that time the body of the pious Dominican remained not only flexible but also intensely fragrant.[1]

Because of the great services he had performed for the Church and in recognition of the heroic nature of his virtues, he was declared a saint of the Universal Church in 1523.

The body was found perfectly entire in the year 1589, and so it remains today in the Dominican church of San Marco.

.

[1]*The Physical Phenomena of Mysticism.* Herbert J. Thurston, S.J. Henry Regnery Co. Chicago. 1952. p. 248.

— 44 —

BLESSED ANTONIO VICI

(Blessed Anthony of Stroncone)

1381—1461

Anthony's noble parents were both members of the Franciscan Third Order and at the age of twelve, feeling also attracted to the Franciscan way of life, he applied to the monastery in Stroncone for admittance. Three times he was refused acceptance because of his youth and delicate constitution, but the superior at last relented and clothed him in the garb of a postulant. Because of his many talents, the superiors intended to educate him for the priesthood, but he begged to be allowed to remain a humble lay brother. After a year's probation, Anthony was sent to Fiesole for his novitiate and was trained there by his uncle, Friar John of Stroncone who was the guardian of the monastery, and by Blessed Thomas of Florence. So rapidly did Anthony advance in virtue that he was assigned to assist in the training of novices, although he was only a lay brother. In 1428 he was sent to the island of Corsica to help in the establishment of a new monastery and after several years was sent back to his native country, to the hermitage of the Carceri near Assisi, where he spent the next thirty years in prayer, fasting, and begging alms for his order.

He was transferred to the monastery of San Damiano in 1460 and died there the following year at the age of eighty, after spending sixty-eight years in the religious life.

The body of the holy friar was buried in the common sepulcher beneath the flooring in the sanctuary of the church of San Damiano. A year minus one day after his death, a flame was seen burning brightly on the slab, which was accepted by St. James of the Marches as "a sign from Heaven" and resulted in an almost immediate exhumation. St. James assisted at the undertaking, which brought to light the perfectly intact and sweetly perfumed body of the humble religious.[1] The devotion of the brethren and the populace would not permit its

[1]*Antonio Vici, Principe Conteso.* Luciano Canonici, O.F.M. Edizioni Porziuncola. Assisi. 1961. p. 155.

being returned to the subterranean sepulcher, and it was instead consigned to a vault in the wall of the church on the Gospel side of the main altar.

A second exhumation and examination were undertaken on June 28, 1599, with the permission of Cardinal Mattei and in the presence of the Bishop of Assisi. After this solemn function, the body was placed above a side altar in a crystal urn. Before this shrine astounding miracles took place. One of these marvels consisted of distinct knockings emanating from the urn, which were heard by many priestly witnesses immediately prior to the deaths of various religious in the community. The monastery of S. Francesco in Stroncone contains, in its archives, the documents drawn up by these observers.[2]

In 1649 another unusual manifestation was noted. The body, which was always prone, with the right hand resting against the left, raised itself when a girl possessed by the devil was brought before the shrine. The head and shoulders were elevated twenty centimeters, and the right hand was raised several inches above the other.[3] Both positions are still maintained by the relic. One hundred sixty years after this occurrence, in 1809, at the time of its solemn processional transference to Stroncone, the body was found perfectly flexible in its members although the shoulders, head, and right hand remained elevated without support. It was also observed that the relic was perfectly entire, the flesh marvelously preserved and still of a natural color.[4]

The tomb of the holy friar has been the destination of many pilgrimages and the scene of astounding miracles of healing and the bestowal of divine graces. In consideration of these marvels and in confirmation of the degree of sanctity which Anthony had attained during his lifetime, Pope Innocent XI declared him a Beatus on June 28, 1687.

The fifth centennial of Anthony's death was joyfully celebrated in Stroncone in 1961 at the Sanctuary of Blessed Antonio Vici in the Church of St. Francesco. Here and in Franciscan churches around the world, the feast of the blessed friar is liturgically commemorated each February seventh.

---

[2]*Ibid.* p. 160. On this page are listed the names of those priests who heard these sounds and the names of those religious who died shortly afterwards. See also the entries of St. Pascal Baylon for reports of similar knockings.

[3]*Ibid.* p. 161.

[4]*Ibid.* p. 155.

45

SAINT DIDACUS OF ALCALA

(San Diego de Alcala)

1400—1463

During early manhood, Didacus joined the Third Order of St. Francis and served God for a time as a hermit. Desiring greater perfection, he entered the Franciscan monastery at Arizafa in Castile and was later admitted to solemn vows as a lay brother. His rapid advancement in virtue made him a model for his fellow religious, and his divinely infused knowledge of the mysteries of the Faith attracted many learned theologians, who listened with amazement at the discourses of the unschooled religious.

His desire was to save souls in the missionary field; thus, his superior sent him to evangelize and convert the wild infidels of the Canary Islands, where he uncomplainingly endured many hardships for eight years. Having returned to Spain in 1450, he was summoned to Rome by St. John Capistran to attend the canonization ceremonies of St. Bernardine of Siena. During his visit at the monastery of Aracoeli an epidemic spread among the friars, and in spite of the scarcity of supplies in the city, Didacus somehow maintained a sufficient amount for the needs of the religious he was attending. Returning to his native Spain in 1456, he was assigned to the monastery in Alcala where he was revered for his many miracles. Knowing instinctively of his approaching death, he donned a worn-out habit and died while gazing upon a crucifix, a true son of St. Francis.

Great crowds converged on the monastery to venerate his body before it was buried in the common grave of the religious. During the burial service the witnesses marveled at the complete flexibility and intense fragrance of the body, a condition which was again noted five days later when it was exhumed on the inspiration of the guardian of the monastery. Because of the extraordinary manifestation of its incorruption six months after his death, the relic was placed in a wooden urn and exposed for the many people who were drawn to the monastery by the rumors of its incorruption. During this time the right hand was amputated and placed in a reliquary for consignment to the infirmary where Didacus had cared for the sick with saintly solicitude.[1]

The King of Castille, Don Enrique IV, was himself a pilgrim to the shrine amid much ceremonial pageantry, having visited there with all of his court. As a result of the miraculous cure of his afflicted arm and the miraculous cure of his daughter, Doña Juana, of a serious malady of the mouth, the King built a splendid chapel in the room of the Porteria where Didacus had lived.[2]

Perhaps the most frequently recorded miracle of St. Didacus occurred in 1562 when the body of the Saint was removed from the urn and taken in solemn procession to the bedside of Don Carlos, son of King Philip II, where an immediate and dramatic restoration to health was miraculously accomplished.[3] Shortly after this miracle and with the approval of the Archbishop, the King, various distinguished political and ecclesiastical personages, and the whole of the Franciscan Order petitioned the Pope for the canonization of the humble religious. Pope Sixtus V, himself a Franciscan, presided at the canonization ceremonies of St. Didacus on July 2, 1588.

Except for parts of its extremities, which were detached for relics, the body is clothed in a costly Franciscan habit made of golden tissue and lies in an incorrupt state in the Santa e Insigne Iglesia Magistral of Alcala de Henares, which is the second cathedral of the archdiocese. The urn which encloses the body was a gift of the royal house of Austria, to which many kings of Spain were related. Made of wood, the urn is covered with precious metals, much of which was removed during the War of Independence in 1808 and the recent War of Liberation. For the celebration of the fifth centenary of the death of the Saint the urn was rebuilt and restored to its original artistry.

When the Franciscan Order was establishing missions throughout the western United States and blessing its foundations by placing them under the protection of various Franciscan saints, the mission entrusted to the heavenly patronage of St. Didacus of Alcala was San Diego, California.

The body was once seized during a violent political situation (which included very cruel and bitter persecutions) and taken in a

---

[1]*Brevisimo Compendio de la Vida del Insigne Lego Franciscano, San Diego de Alcala,* Alcala De Henares. 1955. p. 11.

[2]*Ibid.* pp. 12-13.

[3]*Ibid.* p. 13.

sacrilegious procession amid much abuse and mockery. After being left abandoned in the chapel of a cemetery, it was discovered later and returned to the church where it was enshrined in a devotional manner worthy of the venerated body which housed the soul of a saint.[4]

---

[4]*Ibid.* p. 18.

46

SAINT CATHERINE OF BOLOGNA

1413—1463

Catherine was born on the feast of the Annunciation of the Blessed Virgin in the year 1413. As the daughter of John of Vigri, she was a member of the nobility and while still very young was sent to the court of a relative, the Marquis of Este, who resided in Ferrara, to be educated with the Marquis' daughter, Margaret, in all matters important to the culture of young women of rank. She was greatly admired for her beauty, intelligence, and purity of soul, but eventually she lost interest in the splendors of the court, rejected a number of suitors, and at the age of seventeen joined a group of Franciscan tertiaries in Ferrara who later adopted the rule of St. Clare.

At first she assumed the duties of the bakers, then those of novice mistress. It was during this time that she wrote an important treatise, *The Seven Spiritual Weapons,* which reflects the mystical quality of her spiritual life. Among her other works are many books of sermons, devotions and verses. Her extant artistic works include a number of miniatures and paintings, notably her illustrated breviary.

She was favored with a number of remarkable visions. According to her own statements, she was visited one Christmas Eve by Our Lady, who placed the newborn Christ Child in her arms. On another occasion she was permitted to hear the angelic choirs singing after the Elevation of the Mass and from that time on was relieved of the constant temptation to slumber during religious exercises.

After spending twenty-four years in the convent at Ferrara, she was sent to her native Bologna with fifteen sisters to establish a similar convent, which she served as abbess for the rest of her life. The Saint died on March 9, 1463, causing great sorrow to the community which she had lovingly served for many years. Johann Joseph von Gorres, the great German Catholic philosopher and writer, described as follows certain miraculous occurrences involving the Saint:

> When she died and the grave was dug, the sisters carried her body
> to be buried without a casket. As the body of the saint was lowered

into the grave an incredibly sweet fragrance emanated from it, filling the entire cemetery and regions beyond. After several days, when the sisters visited the tomb, the fragrance was still there. There were no trees, flowers or herbs on the grave or in the vicinity, and it was safely established that the scent came from the grave. Soon, eighteen days after the interment, miracles began to happen at the grave. Persons incurably sick were cured. The sisters suddenly felt guilty because they had buried the body without a casket and that as a result masses of earth might have fallen on her face. They thought the body should be exhumed and placed in a casket. The sisters went for advice to the confessor of the convent, who was quite surprised to learn that after eighteen days the body had not yet started to decay. And when the nuns told him of the fragrance still emanating from the grave, he gave his consent for the exhumation. The face was only slightly distorted because of the pressure of earth. The body had remained white and fragrant, without any sign of decay. The fragrance became even sweeter, pervading the church and immediate neighborhood.[1]

After the body was examined by doctors and ecclesiastical authorities, it was enclosed in a crypt beneath an altar, where it remained for several months. When it was again exhumed, it was arranged on a wooden stretcher and brought to the cell which the Saint had used during life. When the faithful asked to view the sacred remains, four nuns reverently carried the stretcher from the cell to the choir, where it was placed by the narrow window through which the nuns received Holy Communion. The passages and narrow stairs made the effort very difficult, necessitating a change in the arrangements. A special chest was then constructed in which the Saint was placed, seated on a chair. This chest was thereafter kept in the choir and was rolled to the window and opened upon request. The body, in this elevated position, could be more easily viewed through the narrow window between the chapel and the choir. These arrangements were made twelve years after the Saint's death.[2]

The Saint appeared in a vision to one of the nuns, Leonora Poggi, at the end of the year 1500, and requested that her body be placed in a special chapel, the location and layout being specified by the Saint, who also requested that her body be kept in its sitting position. The

---

[1]*Christliche Mystik*. (In *Collected Works of Görrës*). Johann Joseph von Görrës. Bachem Verlag. Cologne. 1936.

[2]The information contained herein was taken from data supplied by the shrine of the Saint, Monastero del Corpus Domini, Detto Della Santa, Bologna.

chapel was immediately provided and the Saint, taken from the wooden reliquary, was enshrined in a location easily accessible to the pilgrims, many of whom kissed the feet of the relic with reverence and devotion.

During the early part of the year 1688, a larger and more beautiful chapel adjacent to this one was made available and was artistically decorated with frescoes by Franceschini, Affener, and Quaini. On August 11, 1688, the relic was moved with great solemnity to this chapel, where it is still enshrined.

For over four and one-half centuries the relic remained without a protective covering; however, now it is surrounded by a glass urn that was constructed in 1953. During the last World War the hands and feet of the relic became somewhat chapped and these were covered with a light coat of wax for protection. The face and body are still normal, but the color of the flesh is black, a condition blamed for the most part on the oil lamps used throughout the centuries in the chapel and the many votive candles which burned near the unprotected relic.

The Saint's canonization ceremonies were conducted by Pope Clement XI on May 22, 1712, and she has been designated the Patroness of Artists.

The darkened but incorrupt body of St. Catherine of Bologna, Patroness of Artists (d. 1463), seated in an upright position since the year 1475, more than 500 years. Exposure to burning candles and votive lights is believed to have darkened her skin.

BLESSED MARGARET OF SAVOY

Unknown—1464

Margaret came from an illustrious family which claimed alliance by blood with the principal royal houses of Europe. In 1403 she married Theodore Palaeologus, Marquis of Montferrat, a widower with two children, a soldier by profession, and a good Christian. Margaret had no children of her own but devoted herself to the care of her stepchildren. During a plague and famine in Genoa, she worked selflessly among the stricken and endeared herself to all. In 1418 the Marquis of Montferrat died, and Margaret completed the rearing and education of his children before she retired to her estate at Alba in Piedmont, where she made a vow to remain a widow. Her beauty and political station attracted Philip Visconti of Milan, but his proposal of marriage was graciously declined.

Through the influence of St. Vincent Ferrer, she took the habit of the Third Order of St. Dominic and with a small group of ladies formed a community at Alba where they led a retired life of study, prayer, and charitable work. Later she founded the Monastery of St. Mary Magdalen, made solemn vows as a nun of the Dominican Second Order, and served the community as abbess until her death.

She was favored during her life with many ecstasies and numerous miracles. During one of her visions she beheld Our Lord offering her three arrows, each of which was marked with a word: *Sickness, Slander, Persecution.* This vision is frequently depicted in her iconography. It has been established that at one time or another during her life she had been wounded by all three arrows. The Saint died on November 23, 1464, having been strengthened by a vision of St. Catherine of Siena, which was seen by all those assisting at her deathbed.

Pope St. Pius V authorized her cult in 1566, and Clement IX confirmed it in 1669.

The sacred body of the Saint, clothed in the Dominican habit, lies exposed to view in a glass-sided reliquary on the lateral altar of the Church of St. Magdalen in Alba, Italy. The body is rather brown, but after five hundred years it still retains its softness and flexibility.

BLESSED EUSTOCHIA OF PADUA

1444—1469

Eustochia was the unfortunate daughter of a seduced nun and was actually born in the same convent in which she died. The misruled community, which tolerated such irregularities, was dispersed by the bishop and replaced with that of a more observant foundation.

As an infant, Eustochia was placed by her father in the care of a nurse, but after four years she was taken to live with his wife and legitimate children where she was greatly disliked and barely tolerated by her stepmother. When she began to show signs of diabolical possession, she was sent back to live with her mother in the convent, but after the dispersal of the convent she stayed and sought admission into the new community. Because of the circumstances surrounding her birth, the sisters at first refused, but with the sanction of the bishop, they finally and reluctantly gave their permission for her entrance. Her profession, however, was delayed for several years. Sometime after her acceptance, she exhibited signs of her former diabolical symptoms. Normally gentle and obedient, her character would undergo a complete transformation, and she would display rude and violent outbursts of temper. When the abbess was ill of a mysterious ailment, Eustochia was suspected of poisoning her and, as a consequence, was in danger of being burned as a witch by the townspeople. A learned confessor intervened, and under his direction Eustochia returned to normalcy, was permitted to make her vows, and eventually won the love and respect of the community.

The Beata's last days were spent in great physical suffering, her death occurring on February 13, 1469, when she was twenty-five years old. When her body was being prepared for burial, the sisters found mysteriously imprinted on her breast the name of Jesus. Many miracles and apparitions followed her death and the odor of sanctity was noticed about her tomb, located in the convent chapel.

Three years and nine months after her death, on November 16, 1472, the bishop ordered the removal of the body to a more honorable resting place. Although it had been buried without a coffin, it was found perfectly preserved. After being reclothed, the corpse was placed in a wooden casket and interred in the main hall of the monastery, until November 14, 1475, when it was transferred to the cathedral near the main altar.[1]

During this time a fresh spring of water appeared in the place where the Saint had first been buried. Many afflictions were cured or relieved for those who drank of it and great numbers of people journeyed there on pilgrimages. The water possessed the strange property of never overflowing the tub which had been built up around it.[2] (Its abundance and peculiar behavior were comparable to that of the spring near Rome which St. Peter caused to appear while he was in prison, so that he could baptize his guards, who later became martyrs for the Faith.) A record of the miracles which occurred at the spring was kept by Dr. Padre Giammatteo Giberti of the Augustinian Order and was later published as a book in Venice in 1672.[3]

The body of the Saint was still in a state of preservation in 1633, but at this time only the skeleton remains. This is dressed in a Benedictine habit and lies exposed in a glassy urn in the former Benedictine church of St. Peter in Padua.

---

[1] *Vita, Virtu e Miracoli della Beata Eustochia.* Dal P. Giulio Cordara. Goi Tipi della Minerva. Padova. 1836. pp. 96-97.

[2] *Ibid.* pp. 97-101 & 108-116.

[3] *Ibid.* p. 99.

BLESSED ANTHONY BONFADINI

1402—1482

Blessed Anthony was a member of a noble family of Ferrara, Italy, and spent the early part of his life enjoying the leisure and amusements of court life. At the age of thirty-nine, he abandoned his comfortable existence to join the Franciscan Order and, having obtained his doctorate in theology, was ordained a priest. He became a renowned preacher throughout Italy and a zealous missionary in the Holy Land, his labors being crowned with innumerable conversions and miracles. On his return from the Holy Land he stopped at Cotignola to preach, took violently ill, and died at a pilgrims' inn. Many miracles were attributed to him after his death, and Cotignola, spared from calamities in 1630, 1688, and 1696, credits these favors to his intercession.

In 1495 his body was transferred to the Church of the Observant Friary founded by Bl. Angelo Carletti di Chivasso, where a special chapel was erected for him in 1666. Pope Leo XIII confirmed his cult in 1901, and in the following year the recognition of his incorrupt body took place.

The sacred relic was last officially examined in 1945, and the body is still well preserved, even though the glass case that contained it was destroyed during the aerial bombardments of World War II.[1] The body of the Beatus is exposed for the veneration of his clients at Cotignola during the week following Easter.

---

[1]Statement is based on correspondence between the author and the Reverend Father of the Tempio Del Santo, Cotignola.

BLESSED EUSTOCHIA CALAFATO

1434—1485

Born Esmeralda Calafato, this Beata was benevolently favored with a virtuous and pious mother and as a small child is known to have imitated her mother's holy example and to have given every indication of being further blessed with a religious vocation. As the beautiful, rich and nobly born daughter of Count Calafato, Esmeralda was sought in marriage by several distinguished gentlemen, whose proposals were graciously declined. After the death of her father, who had opposed her entrance into the religious life, she joined the Poor Clares at S. Maria de Basico and was given the name Eustochia. After eleven years spent in this convent, she was inspired to found a new convent where the original rule of St. Clare was to be observed in greater strictness and in absolute poverty. With the permission of Pope Callistus III, she took with her two of the nuns, a young niece, and her own sister and established the Convent of Accomandata amid persecution, intense sufferings, and difficulties. Because of the poor condition of the buildings, the sisters were forced to move five years later to Montevergine (Maiden's Hill) in northeast Sicily, which, in 1964, observed the fifth centenary of its founding.

In the biography written by Sister Pollicino, one of the Beata's original companions in the new community, there are many testimonials to the heroic nature of the virtues practiced by Eustochia, and numerous miracles are recorded of her concerning the multiplication of food. It is said that on many occasions when the treasury of the convent was insufficient to buy provisions, Eustochia made the Sign of the Cross over two or three little pieces of bread, and there was miraculously enough to satisfy the appetites of the ten sisters who comprised the community.

After fifty-one years spent in the performance of God's Will, Eustochia died a saintly death on January 20, 1485, after having borne in her flesh for many years the stigmatic wounds of Our Lord's Passion.

Perhaps the most dramatic miracle performed by the Beata, who had so often protected the city from damaging earthquakes, occurred in 1615, when the city was shaken day and night by almost constant vibrations. The senate and people of the city petitioned the sisters to pray to Bl. Eustochia for protection. The sisters removed the perfectly preserved body from the oratory where it had been conserved for almost a hundred fifty years and placed it in an upright position in her old choir stall. After they had charged Eustochia to pray for the protection of the city, the lips of the obedient Beata opened and her voice was heard chanting the first verse of the Psalm of the Night Office. The sisters, completely terrified, nevertheless joined in the recitation and bowed their heads during the Gloria in unison with the Blessed. The earthquake is reported to have ceased at that moment.[1]

Still preserved at the Monastero Montevergine is the perfectly preserved body of the Beata. Although darkened after the lapse of five centuries, the body is nonetheless perfect in every respect, with the two fingers of the right hand poised in an attitude of perpetual blessing. A golden crown adorns the head and the relic is dressed in beautiful white robes delicately and artistically embroidered with gold. Undoubtedly the most magnificent adornments on this blessed relic are the marks of the stigmata, which are clearly visible on the darkened hands of this holy foundress.

---

[1]This miracle is related in papers composed by Monastero Montevergine in 1964 at the time of the observance of the fifth centenary of the founding of the Monastery.

51

BLESSED BERNARD SCAMMACCA

Unknown—1486

Born of a noble family at Catania in Sicily, Bernard spent his youth in sinful pursuits until his leg became seriously injured in a brawl. During his lengthy convalescence, he considered the dangers to which he had subjected his soul, and turning to God, renounced his evil habits and resolved to enter the religious life. He was received into the Dominican Order at Catania and spent the rest of his life practicing severe penances to expiate for the sins of his youth.

It is reported that he was favored with the gift of prophecy and was seen levitating in ecstasy before a crucifix. On another occasion his fellow religious found his cell flooded with light, which emanated from a torch held by a child of heavenly beauty who stood beside the enraptured Saint.

After his death on February 9, 1486, he was buried with the customary religious simplicity, but many extraordinary events were soon reported. After a lapse of fifteen years, the Saint appeared to the prior of the monastery and requested that his body be removed to a more honorable resting place. His remains were exhumed and found to be perfectly preserved. During the translation of the body, the church bells are said to have rung unaided, and numerous miracles are reported to have taken place.

A nobleman who had been cured through Blessed Bernard's intercession plotted secretly to remove the relic to his castle. Accompanied by a group of raiders, he entered the monastery at night, and while he was engaged in opening the shrine, the Saint is reported to have awakened the sleeping friars and instructed them to hurry to the church. The raiders were found at the door of the church vainly trying to lift from the floor the sacred relic, which had become mysteriously weighted. After the raiders were put to flight, the friars, with no difficulty, raised the body from the floor and restored it to its shrine.

The sacred relic, still incorrupt after a period of almost five hundred years, is exposed to view in the parish church of S. Biagio in

S. Domenico, Catania, where the faithful still marvel at the preservation of the remains of the Beatus which, though somewhat dry, are still tender and light in color.

Always greatly revered throughout Sicily, the cultus of Bl. Bernard Scammacca was confirmed by Pope Leo XII in 1825.

52

BLESSED ARCANGELA GIRLANI

1460—1495

In the company of family and friends, Eleanora (Arcangela) prepared to set out upon the journey to the Benedictine convent of Rocca delle Donne, where solemn ceremonies had been planned for her reception into that order. When the horse upon which she was riding refused to advance, the company gradually dispersed and Eleanora returned to her home after the uncommon behavior of the animal was accepted as a heavenly intervention. Soon afterwards a Carmelite friar introduced her to the life led by the nuns of his order and she immediately saw in this the holy will of God that she join them. On her seventeenth birthday, Eleanora joined the Carmelites at Parma and received the name Arcangela. The following year she pronounced her vows, and as was customary during those times, Arcangela, being a member of a distinguished family, was soon placed in a position of responsibility, in spite of her tender age. She was later sent to Mantua to found a new convent there, which, under her saintly administration, received a reputation for fostering great holiness. The saintly abbess spent several fruitful years in that convent, the recipient of extraordinary mystical favors. On many occasions she was found by the sisters enraptured in a position several feet above the floor, and one notable ecstasy is said to have lasted more than twenty-four hours.

After her holy death at the age of thirty-four, she was buried with all simplicity in the common sepulcher within the cloister. Three years later, when the tomb was opened to receive the remains of another nun, the body of Arcangela was found as perfect as it was on the day of its burial. Not only was the body entire in every respect, but it had also retained its natural color and was, moreover, perfectly flexible.[1]

The miracles and thus the clients of the holy nun increased in such astounding numbers that it seemed appropriate to enshrine the pre-

---

[1] *Vita e Miracoli della Beata Arcangela Girlani.* Distributed by the Church of S. Lorenzo in Trino Vercellese, the shrine of the Beata. 1960. p. 30.

cious relic in a beautifully decorated urn, which was placed above an altar composed of precious marble.

Almost three hundred years after Arcangela's death, on September 24, 1782, the incorrupt body was taken from Mantua to Trino, the place of her birth, amid unbounded rejoicing. It was later placed in the Church of S. Lorenzo in Trino Vercellese, where it is still visited by her countless devotees.

In 1932 it was carefully examined prior to its placement in a new urn, but unfortunately the skin of the face was injured at this time by the faulty application of a chemical, which stripped away part of the flesh.[2]

A few months before the solemn festivities of 1960, which marked the fifth centenary observance of the Beata's birth, the relic was once again taken from the urn for an official recognition and examination. It was again found perfectly entire, with the flesh and muscles completely flexible.[3] A facial mask was ordered to conceal the wound caused by the disfiguring chemical treatment of 1932, and a matching covering was also placed upon the perfectly conserved hands.

The cult of Blessed Arcangela was officially confirmed by Pope Pius IX on October 1, 1864. Her body, dressed in the habit of a Discalced Carmelite, reposes in a beautifully decorated crystal urn.

---

[2] Taken from a statement of the chaplain of the shrine.

[3] The author is indebted to the shrine for the first-class relic it so generously gave her, which consists of a piece of flesh *(Ex carne)*. While the color of the body is not explicitly stated by the shrine, the flesh in the small reliquary is of a definite dark brown color.

— 53 —

BLESSED OSANNA OF MANTUA

1449—1505

At an early age Osanna, desiring to dedicate herself wholly to God's service, applied to a number of convents for admission but did not meet with success, undoubtedly because of her youth. It is known that she was inspired, instead of entering a cloister, to join the Third Order of St. Dominic, which she did at the age of fourteen. After being clothed in the habit, she was not permitted to make her solemn profession for many years. She saw the will of God in the obstacles which constantly prevented her from realizing her ambition, and she used her time well in the practice of virtue and the performance of good works.

The obstacles which constantly delayed her profession consisted of the ecstasies and raptures she experienced in prayer, which she was unable to hide from the other tertiaries, who frequently persecuted and reproved her for what they were convinced was pretense and sanctimonious affection. They were also disquieted by the fact that she was widely acclaimed for her sanctity, and people of rank and distinction flocked to her for guidance. So it was that her spiritual progress actually proved to be a barrier to her solemn profession, which, though for long not permitted on earth, nevertheless took place mystically in the presence of the Mother of God and the angels of heaven.[1] The event was eventually celebrated on earth during the last year of her life when she was fifty-five years of age.

Ardently desiring to participate in the sufferings of Our Lord's Passion, for two years she persistently requested some share in His sacrificial agony. Her prayers were answered, first by the imprinting of the crown of thorns, and secondly by the marks of the stigmata. The agonies she endured never satisfied her insatiable thirst to suffer for sinners and for the souls in Purgatory.

Knowing prophetically the date of her own death, she prepared herself with joyful submission for her entrance into Heaven, which

---

[1]*Short Lives of the Dominican Saints.* A Sister of the Congregation of St. Catherine of Siena (Stone). Kegan Paul, Trench, Trubner & Co., Ltd. London, 1901. p. 177.

occurred on June 18, 1505. After her death, the stigmata which were scarcely visible during life became quite pronounced, as also occurred in the case of St. Catherine of Siena. The visible appearance of these mysterious markings, after all apparent signs of life had left the body, completely refutes the opinion of those who attribute the stigmata to autosuggestion, since, quite understandably, a dead body has no control over what happens to it.[2]

Sometime after the burial in the Church of S. Domenico, the incorrupt body was translated to the Cathedral of Mantua, where it still reposes in a crystal shrine beneath the altar of Our Lady of the Rosary. The sacred relic is solemnly displayed three times during the year: on June 20, when a special Mass is said in her honor; on November 1, which is the Feast of All Saints; and on the Sunday following November 11, when the faithful honor the patroness of Mantua.

The popular cultus which spontaneously sprang up after her death was authorized by Pope Leo X in 1515, and was later confirmed by Pope Innocent XII in 1694. Her feast day was designated as June 20.

During the summer of 1965 the sacred relic was examined in the presence of the vice chancellor of the episcopal curia of Mantua, the chief physician of the department of anatomy at the hospital at Mantua, and two witnesses, all of whom testified that the body, which is hazel brown in color, is dried and darkened and wrinkled with age, but still admirably preserved.

---

[2]*Neglected Saints.* E. I. Watkins, Sheed & Ward. New York. 1955. p. 164.

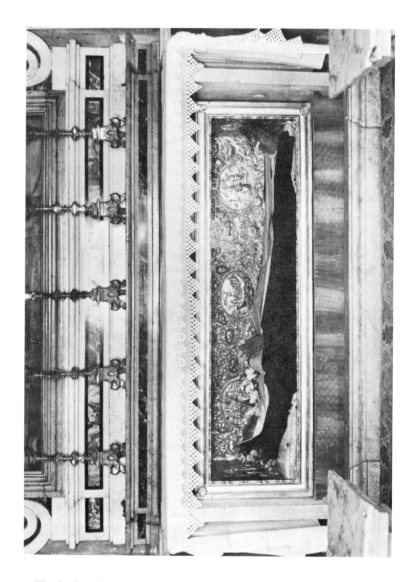

The body of Blessed Osanna of Manua (d. 1505) reposes in a crystal shrine beneath the altar of Our Lady of the Rosary in the Cathedral of Mantua, Italy. After her death, the stigmata appeared on her body.

SAINT CATHERINE OF GENOA

1447—1510

Reliable details concerning the early life of St. Catherine of Genoa are scarce; however, it is known that she was the youngest of five children of the Fieschi family, a powerful and distinguished family of Genoa. At the age of thirteen she tried unsuccessfully to enter a convent and was married three years later to Giuliano Adorno, a man of low standards to whom she was unsuited both in ideals and in temperament. The first ten years of her married life were marked by neglect from her husband, great emotional distress, and a certain fascination with the frivolities of the world. Once, during Confession, she was overwhelmed with the grace of God and was favored later with a vision in which she saw Our Lord carrying His cross. From His shoulders ran rivers of blood, which seemed to fill the whole house. In sorrow for her sins, which she felt had caused the Lord's sufferings, she disposed of her jewelry and fashionable clothing and began to live a life of severe penance and prolonged fasts. During the next twenty-five years she received personal spiritual direction from Our Lord Himself by means of visions, ecstasies, and mystical experiences.

Her prayers and heroic patience caused the conversion of her husband, who became a member of the Franciscan Third Order. Together, and without financial compensation, they worked in the hospital of the Pammatone, near which they lived, and in addition did charitable work among the poor and sick of the district. After Giuliano's holy death in 1497, Catherine continued to work as a nurse and later as administrator of the hospital.

Catherine of Genoa has left us three literary works of great theological value: the *Spiritual Dialogues,* the *Vita e Dottrina,* and the *Treatise on Purgatory,* in which she describes the suffering, disposition and happiness of the souls bathed in the purgatorial fire of divine love.

In 1510 the Saint died a holy death at the hospital of the Pammatone, her sanctity recognized and known throughout the district. She

was buried in the hospital chapel, where her remains were left undisturbed for eighteen months, after which time it was discovered that a
conduit of water ran under the wall near the tomb. Damage to the
casket and the body was feared, and the tomb was opened to ascertain
their condition. Due to the excessive dampness, the casket was found
in a deplorable condition; however, the body of the saint remained
perfectly incorrupt and spotless despite the moistness of the shroud
which enveloped it.[1] Many miracles were recorded as having taken
place at this time, and a popular cultus began.

After the body was cleansed and appropriately attired, it was left
exposed for eight days to accommodate the large crowds of pilgrims
who converged on the chapel to view the miraculous preservation.
The relic was then placed in a marble sarcophagus, which was installed in a higher position in the same chapel. In the years 1551,
1593, and 1642, the sarcophagus was again moved to various locations. In 1694 the body was placed in a shrine having glass sides, and
it is in this reliquary that it still reposes high above the main altar of
the church dedicated to her in the Quarter of Portoria, in Genoa.

The Saint's body was carefully examined by physicians in 1837 and
again on May 10, 1960, when it was ascertained that the relic, which
is brown and somewhat dry and rigid, was never embalmed nor had
any treatment administered to it in order to preserve it. After this
most recent examination, the scientific inspector recorded: "The
conservation is truly exceptional and surprising and deserves an analysis of the cause. The surprise of the faithful is justified when they attribute this to a supernatural cause."[2]

---

[1] *The Mystical Element of Religion as Studied in Saint Catherine of Genoa and Her
Friends.* Baron Friedrich von Hügel. J. D. Dent & Sons. London. And E. P. Dutton &
Co. New York. 1923. Vol. I, p. 300.

[2] *"La conservazione appare veramente eccezionale, sorprendente e degna di analisi
alla ricerca delle cause; appare giustificata le meraviglia quindi dei fedeli che attribuis-
cono volentieri al fatto una significazione soprannaturale."* This statement was furnished by the St. Catherine Cultural Center, Genoa, Italy.

The incorrupt body of St. Catherine of Genoa (d. 1510) exposed in a glass reliquary high above the main altar of the church built in her honor in Genoa, Italy.

BLESSED MARGARET OF LORRAINE

1463—1521

At the age of twenty-five the nobly born Margaret of Lorraine married René, Duke of Alençon, and was four years later left a widow with three small children. During the minority of her son, she ruled the duchy so capably that when her children came of age their inheritance had increased over and above what had been left at the time of their father's death. During the early part of her widowhood, she came under the influence of St. Francis of Paola and began leading the life of an ascetic. When her responsibilities to her children were discharged, she joined the Franciscan Third Order and retired to Montagne, where she devoted herself to the care of the sick and poor. In 1513 she founded a convent at Argentan for the Poor Clare nuns, and after joining them in the strict enclosure in 1519, she humbly refused to accept the office of abbess. It was here that she died two years later on November 2, 1521, and was buried in the convent where her body was preserved for over two hundred fifty years.

In 1792 the relic was exhumed and the thin, skeletal body was wrapped in cloth and transferred to the Church of St. Germain in Argentan. In the casket was found a small reliquary which contained the heart of the Saint. The following year a group of revolutionaries, described as Jacobins, seized the relic and after profaning it (in what manner it is not definitely known) placed it in a common grave situated in the wall of a cemetery.

The only relics surviving are a few bones and the heart, which is reverently treasured by the Monastère des Clarisses at Alençon.

SAINT ANTHONY MARIA ZACCARIA

1502—1539

Anthony's mother, widowed at the age of eighteen, gave her whole attention to providing an excellent education for her young son, and he subsequently obtained a doctorate in medicine at Padua in 1524. While exercising his skills among the poor of Cremona, he felt attracted to the religious life and was ordained a priest in 1528. Angels are said to have appeared during the celebration of his first Holy Mass. With the help of two friends he laid the foundations of the Congregation of Clerks Regular of St. Paul, more commonly known as the Barnabites, which was approved in 1533 by Clement VII. Two years later he founded an order for women which was called the Angelicals of St. Paul.

During his ministry he introduced many innovations which renewed devotion and inspired the people to the performance of good works. Anthony became ill while laboring to restore peace in Guastalla, which was under pontifical interdict, and died when only thirty-six years of age in Cremona where he had retired for a final visit with his mother.

Although his body was kept above ground, it remained perfectly entire until 1566, when it was buried in damp soil. In 1664 only his skeleton was found.[1] The skull of the saint and the rest of the bones are arranged in a simulated manner to suggest a body, and this is attired in priestly vestments and is exposed in a crystal case in the crypt beneath the main altar of the Church of St. Barnaba in Milan.

---

[1]Thurston. *The Physical Phenomena of Mysticism.* p. 249.

SAINT ANGELA MERICI
1474—1540

The future foundress of the Ursuline Order was favored at the age of thirty-two with a prophetic vision in which she saw on a staircase which reached into the heavens, a number of young women and some angels. One of the young ladies detached herself from the celestial group and advanced to where Angela knelt in ecstasy and delivered this message: "Know, Angela, that our Divine Lord has sent you this vision to teach you that before you die, you are to found in Brescia, a company of young virgins like these. This is His will for you." Angela waited in Desenzano for a providential action which would lead her to that city, and she received it a few years later in the form of an invitation from a family in Brescia who wanted her to live with them after the recent death of their two sons.

It was not until 1531 that a group of young ladies began helping her in the catechetical work she had begun among young children. Four years later, the group, numbering twenty-eight members, became known as the Company of St. Ursula. Each member of the company continued to live in her own home, took no vows and only joined the others for prayer and teaching assignments. The original group, in reality a secular organization, was reorganized after Angela's death by St. Charles Borromeo, Bishop of Milan, and they were later known as the Ursulines, the first teaching order of the Church.

Immediately after Angela's death, she was acclaimed a saint by the people of the city, who visited the remains in such numbers that her burial was delayed for thirty days. The relic, exhumed several times throughout the centuries, always retained its flexibility. On May 28, 1907, ". . . when the venerated remains of St. Angela Merici were taken out from the urn, the venerated body presented itself admirably preserved and intact, without any chemical aid . . ."[1] At that time Doctor Vittorio Gallia extracted a piece of bone with which to make

---

[1]This quotation was taken from the *Verbals of Recognition* which was signed by the Rev. Bishop's Chancellor and Monsignor Gaffuri and many witnesses. This information was supplied by the Casa S. Angela in Brescia.

relics, and to his surprise he found it well preserved, as if the saint had died a few months before.[2]

In 1930 a priest of the Catholic University of the Sacred Heart in Milan made a chemical treatment of the relic with natural resin to preserve it. Today the body is rather dark in color but still in a state of preservation. Visitors to the Casa S. Angela in Brescia, Italy, may view the relic, which is enclosed in a beautiful reliquary situated above the main altar.

On her deathbed, she had given this thought-provoking counsel: "Whatever you would wish at your dying hour to have done in health, that do now while you may."

St. Angela Merici was canonized on May 24, 1807.

[2]*Ibid.*

The body of St. Angela Merici, foundress of the Ursulines (d. 1540), shown in a glass case in the Casa S. Angela in Brescia, Italy.

58

BLESSED LUCY OF NARNI

1476—1544

Lucy was the oldest of the eleven children of the treasurer of the community of Narni in Italy. At an early age she resolved to consecrate herself to God, but after the death of her father, marital arrangements were made, despite her objections. She steadfastly refused to marry the young man, but a year later she consented to marry a certain Count Peter, after being advised to do so by her confessor and encouraged by the Blessed Virgin herself. After three years the Count gave her the freedom she undoubtedly requested and she retired to her mother's house, received the habit of the Dominican Third Order, and joined a community of these tertiaries in Rome. After spending a year in this convent, she was sent to found a similar convent of the Order at Viterbo, and three years later, after her twenty-third birthday, the Pope commanded her to proceed to Ferrara and establish yet another convent in that city.

After being favored with many miraculous visions and favors, including the gift of prophecy, she was visibly marked with the sacred stigmata and participated in the sufferings of the Passion every Wednesday and Friday. Her condition was examined by many physicians, among them the physician of Pope Alexander VI, and a Franciscan bishop, all of whom were convinced of the genuineness of the prodigy. It is believed that Count Peter also viewed the signs of the Passion and in consequence joined the Friars Minor.

To the sufferings of the Passion were added the bitter pains of persecution from members of her own community. After the death of the Duke of Ferrara, the patron of the convent, some of the sisters whom Lucy had to reprove on occasion, conspired against her and she, the foundress of the community, was deposed as abbess and made to take the lowest position in the community. Denied the privileges of the house, continually mistreated and cruelly neglected during serious illnesses, the Beata was never heard to complain. So completely was she effaced during these thirty-nine years of persecution that when she died, the people of Ferrara were astonished to learn that she had been alive all those years; they had thought her dead years before.

At the time of her entrance into Heaven, angelic voices were heard singing in her cell and the whole house was filled with an extraordinary perfume. The wound in her side was examined at this time and was found dripping with fresh blood. Small cloths soaked with this blood were distributed, and these occasioned many miracles.

The sisters, largely deceived by a few in authority, were amazed at the wonders which attended the sacred body, and regretting their behavior toward their former prioress, undoubtedly prayed with fervent contrition for her blessing and forgiveness.

The stigmatic was accorded a most reverential and solemn funeral, and four years later, for reasons unknown, the body was exhumed and found in exactly the same condition as when it was first consigned to the grave. The faithful who paid it honor were amazed that the odor of flowers which surrounded the body attached itself to objects touched to the relic. In 1710, the year of her beatification, the body was again disinterred and found in the same excellent condition with the marks of the stigmata clearly visible.[1]

The body was eventually translated to Narni in May, 1935, where it still reposes in a glass reliquary in the cathedral of that city under an altar dedicated to her.

---

[1] *The Life of St. Frances of Rome, of Blessed Lucy of Narni, of Dominica of Paradiso and of Anne De Montmorency.* Lady Georgiana Fullerton. D. & J. Sadlier & Co. New York. 1855. p. 157.

59

SAINT JOHN OF GOD

1495—1550

Born in Montemor Novo, Portugal, John left home while still a child, tended sheep and cattle for a time in Spain and, after reaching an acceptable age, joined the Spanish army. Military life completely undermined his morals, and he pursued a sinful life until his military discharge at the age of forty. After returning to his former occupation of tending sheep, he experienced a renewal of faith and a rekindling of fervor. To atone for his sins, John attempted to enter Africa, where he thought his work among the captives would result in his martyrdom for the Faith. Assured by a confessor that his wish to die for his sins was not God's will for him, he returned to Spain and in 1538 opened a store in Granada for the purpose of selling religious books and objects at modest prices. After hearing a sermon by St. John of Avila, he became excessively remorseful over his past sins and became so extreme in his fervor and behavior that he was confined for a time to a lunatic asylum. Through the counseling of St. John of Avila, he returned to normalcy and devoted himself to the care of the sick, an endeavor which was to associate his name with that of St. Camillus de Lellis, his Italian counterpart, who by coincidence, was born two months after John's death.

The Saint rented a house in Granada in which he housed the neglected sick and soon attracted others into the service of nursing these unfortunates. The Archbishop of Granada, greatly impressed with John's charitable and able administration of this hospital, approved his endeavors, became his patron, and referred to him those in other parts of the country who wished to open similar houses of mercy.

Although the founding of a religious community was not John's intention, the Bishop of Tuy, who gave him the name John of God, recommended a habit for the dedicated man. A rule which bears the Saint's name was drawn up and approved after his death. The group became known as the Brothers Hospitallers and are sometimes called the Brothers of St. John of God.

The manner in which the saint passed from this life is quite unusual, for he died while kneeling before the altar in his sickroom, his body remaining unsupported in that prayerful attitude for some time. The archbishop, on being informed of the Saint's death early in the day, hastened to pay his respects and was astonished to find the body in that position. He was greatly surprised that the heavenly fragrance which proceeded from it had scented not only the room of his death, but the whole house as well.[1] At the time of this episcopal visit, another unusual manifestation was noted, for the bells of the city rang of their own accord, a repetition of the prodigy which is said to have occurred at the time of his birth.[2]

To satisfy the demands of those who wished to pray before the precious remains, the body was carried down and placed on a platform before the house, in the same kneeling position in which the Saint had died.[3]

Since the chapel in the Saint's hospital was not adaptable for his interment, the remains were buried in the vault in the church of the Minims, Our Lady of Victory. The body was conveyed there, being in turn carried by the Franciscans and the Minims and followed by a huge procession of the rich and poor alike—the homeless girls and women he had sheltered and cared for, representatives of many religious communities, and the archbishop of Granada. On arriving at the church, the body was placed in a position where it could be viewed and was left exposed there for nine days.[4]

The wonderful perfume that was perceived about the body at the time of the Saint's death was attested to in depositions made by order of the Holy See and was also recognized on many occasions in the room in which he had died. During the nine days before his burial, the perfume in the death chamber was ". . . looked upon as a sure mark of sanctity by the judges of the city, who came with the archbishop's deputies to make an inventory of the things that belonged to him, which they wished to preserve as relics."[5]

Because of this prodigy, Doña Anna Ossorio, who owned the house in which the Saint had died, with the cooperation and assistance of the archbishop, converted the room into a chapel, where

---

[1] *Life of St. John of God, Founder of the Order of Hospitallers (The Saints & Servants of God—Second Series).* R. Washbourne. London. 1876. p. 282.
[2] *Ibid.* p. 282.
[3] *Ibid.* p. 283.
[4] *Ibid.* p. 285.
[5] *Ibid.* p. 291.

every Friday at midnight the same fragrance was renewed until Saturday evening—Saturday having been the day on which he died.

Concerning this fragrance, a certain Doña Ursula Romos testified fifty years after the Saint's death that she visited Mary, the daughter of the aforementioned Doña Anna Ossorio, on a Saturday afternoon and upon reaching the door of the chapel where the family was at prayer, perceived the sweet fragrance which permeated the air and inquired about it. Mary asked Doña Ursula, ". . . Do you not know that this oratory was the room in which St. John of God died? Though it is now more than fifty years since his death, the odour you speak of is still renewed by him, but it is on Saturdays chiefly that we perceive it . . . This which seems to you so surprising a favor is a common thing with us; we enjoy it every Saturday."[6]

Many miracles and similar prodigies were manifested at the Saint's birthplace in Portugal, which resulted in the building of a magnificent church over the spot where he was born.

In 1570 the fragrant body of the Saint was found entire, except for the tip of the nose,[7] but at a later date only the bones were found. Many of these were distributed in small reliquaries to churches on the five continents, but especially to those churches and hospitals of the Brothers Hospitallers. The skull and principal bones are enshrined in the Basilica of St. John of God in Granada in a golden setting that challenges description.

The relics are kept in a chest of beautiful wood, which is upholstered inside and out with costly fabrics and bears the seal of the Archbishop of Granada.[8] This chest is kept inside an exquisitely crafted silver urn which in 1757 was placed atop a golden altar. This is located in a small room called a *camarin,* which is actually itself a reliquary, since its walls contain, in artistic groupings surrounded with golden embellishments, the small crystal cases containing the relics of almost two hundred saints. The unusual feature of this camarin is that it is situated approximately halfway up the main altar, which almost touches the lofty ceiling. Since the camarin opens into the basilica and extends back toward the sacristy, the magnificent shrine of the saint, surrounded by its bright golden altar, can be

---

[6]*Ibid.* p. 292. This quotation is taken from a sworn statement made by Doña Ursula Romos, as quoted in *Life of St. John of God.*

[7]Thurston, *Op. cit.* p. 247.

[8]This chest was last opened on November 28, 1951, and the bones found in an excellent condition.

viewed by those fortunate enough to visit this magnificent structure. The craftsmanship of this golden, sculptured altar and its artistic surroundings makes one wonder at such beauty.

Several Pontiffs have recognized the sanctity of St. John of God: Pope St. Pius V, who approved his religious congregation in 1571; Pope Sixtus V, who gave it final approval in 1596; Pope Alexander VIII, who canonized him in 1690; and Pope Innocent XII, who issued the bull of canonization the year following its pronouncement. In 1886, Leo XIII declared this saint, with St. Camillus de Lellis, the patron of hospitals and the sick, and in 1930, Pope Pius XI extended the patronage to include nurses. He is also honored as the patron of booksellers.

SAINT FRANCIS XAVIER

1506—1552

One of the Church's most illustrious missionaries is St. Francis Xavier, who was born of noble parents and was by nature refined, aristocratic and ambitious. He was for a time professor of philosophy at the University of Paris, where he met St. Ignatius Loyola and became one of that saint's original seven followers. His missionary career began in 1540, when he set out on his first journey to the East Indies. Within ten years, he had made successful visits to Ceylon, India, Malaya and Japan. He performed many miracles, was granted the gift of tongues, foretold the future, healed countless persons, established churches in remote areas, and is reported to have raised several persons from the dead.

His dream of evangelizing China was never realized. This great apostle fell ill of a fever within sight of Canton and after suffering for two weeks of a strange and painful illness, which was marked by periods of delirium, died recollected on December 3, 1552, at the age of forty-six.

The Saint's young Chinese companion and interpreter, Antonio, in writing to the Jesuit Manuel Teixeira at Goa, India, described the lonely burial and told of their efforts to hasten the decomposition of the body by the application of lime, so that when the opportunity arose to transfer the Saint's remains, the bones could more easily be transported. He described the proceedings in this manner:

> . . . In death the blessed Father looked so happy and so fair that one might have thought him still alive. . . . I went at once to the ship (the *Santa Cruz*, still riding at anchor off Sancian) to obtain the vestments and all else necessary for his burial. . . . Some of those on the ship returned with me . . . and we made a wooden coffin in which we placed the body clothed in sacerdotal vestments. We then took it in a boat to another part of the island opposite to where the ship and its people lay. . . . It was very cold, so most of them stayed aboard and there were only four of us at the burial, a Portuguese, two slaves and a Chinaman. . . . Having dug a deep grave we lowered the coffin into it

and were about to cover it with earth when one of the company suggested to me that it might be a good idea to pack the coffin with lime above and below the body, as it would consume the flesh and leave only the bare bones, in case anyone in time to come should wish to take them to India. This seemed to us an excellent suggestion, so we withdrew the coffin, obtained four sacks of lime (from the ship) and poured two underneath the body and two above it. Then we nailed on the lid again and filled in the grave. . . . I put some stones around it as markers, so that if I or any member of the Society happened to come to the lonely spot in the future and desired to see where the body of the blessed Father rested, we would be able to find it. Thus did we bury him, full of bitter sorrow, on the afternoon, of Sunday, December 4, the day following his death.[1]

Ten weeks after the burial, a ship bound for Malacca, where the Saint was greatly revered, gave permission for the casket to be placed on board, so on February 17, 1553, the coffin was raised and the body found to be perfectly preserved under the layer of lime. The body, still packed in this destructive agent, was left in the same casket and shipped to Malacca, where it was taken to the Church of Our Lady. A grave which had been prepared near the high altar proved to be too short and could not be lengthened, so the body, still dressed in priestly vestments, was taken from the casket and pressed into the grave in such a way that the head was forced over the chest, causing the neck to break. The body, in this position, lay under and in full contact with the earth for nearly five months until a friend of the Saint, Jaun de Beira, visiting the city on business, had the remains secretly exhumed. The body was found in exactly the same condition as before, except that the nose was injured and bruises were on the face, owing to the pressure of the mud and the position of the body in the inadequate grave. It was decided that such a treasure should be taken to Goa, then considered the Rome of the East, where the Saint had so successfully evangelized. Upon arriving at that port some months later, the body was met by throngs of people, who for four days visited the remains, which were left exposed in the Basilica of the Bom Jesus where the relic is still enshrined.

During this time, when the preservation of the body was widely acclaimed as miraculous, a number of skeptics suggested that the body had been carefully embalmed; so, to settle the issue, the Viceroy had

---

[1]*Monumenta Xaveriana,* ii, 897-898. As quoted in *St. Francis Xavier.* James Brodrick, S.J. The Wicklow Press. New York. 1952. p. 527.

the body examined by the chief medical authority in Goa, who testified as follows:

> I, Doctor Cosmas Saraiva, physician to the Senhor Viceroy, have been to examine the body of Father Master Francis, brought to this city of Goa. I felt and pressed all the members of the body with my fingers, but paid special attention to the abdominal region and made certain that the intestines were in their natural position. There had been no embalming of any kind nor had any artificial preservative agents been used. I observed a wound in the left near the heart and asked one of the Society who was with me to put his fingers into it. When he withdrew them they were covered with blood which I smelt and found to be absolutely untainted. The limbs and other parts of the body were entire and clothed in their flesh in such a way that, according to the laws of medicine, they could not possibly have been preserved by any natural or artificial means, seeing that Father Francis had been dead and buried for about a year and a half. I affirm on oath that what I have written above is the truth. Signed: Doctor Cosmas de Saraiva.[2]

In 1614 the body was again found "beautiful and whole." The right eye was open and was as fresh as in life. The legs and fingers were also fresh, but the body for the most part was dry with the skin still entire. During this same year the right forearm of the Saint was amputated and taken to Rome, where it was enshrined in the Jesuit church of Il Gesu, which also contains the relics of the founder of the Jesuit Order, St. Ignatius Loyola. In 1949 this mummified arm was taken on a pilgrimage around the world and through Japan in observance of the four-hundredth anniversary of the Saint's arrival in that country. After a triumphal tour of Japan, it was taken to the United States, where it was met and venerated by crowds in every city it visited on its three-month tour. The arm was returned to Il Gesu, where it remains a treasured possession.

One hundred forty-two years after the Saint's death, his still perfectly preserved body was carefully examined by Bishop Espinola and a French Jesuit, Père Joseph Simon Bayard, and officials of the shrine, who exhumed the body in secret to avoid the crowds who had flocked to the church on previous occasions. Their report contains the following description of the Saint:

---

[2]*Ibid.* ii, pp. 910-911.

The Saint's hair is black and slightly curling. The forehead is broad and high, with two rather large veins, soft and of a purple tint, running down the middle, as is often seen in talented persons who concentrate a great deal. The eyes are black, lively and sweet, with so penetrating a glance that he would seem to be alive and breathing. The lips are of a bright reddish colour and the beard is thick. In the cheeks there is a very delicate vermillion tint. The tongue is quite flexible, red and moist, and the chin is beautifully proportioned. In a word, the body has all the appearance of being that of a living man. The blood is fluid, the lips flexible, the flesh solid, the colour lively, the feet straight and the nails well formed. The loss of two toes left a darkish trace on the right leg. But for this, there can be found no other body so clean and sound as the body of the Apostle of the Indies. It is so great a marvel that on seeing it, while I was present, the Commissary of the Dutch East India Company, Mynheer Vandryers, became at once a convert to the Catholic Faith.[3]

The sacred body of the Saint has endured countless examinations and many mutilations throughout the centuries. At the time of the first exhumation of the body at Sancian, a piece of flesh, a finger's length, was taken from the knee and shown to the captain of the ship as proof of the excellent condition of the body. It was on the basis of this evidence that the captain permitted the body to be placed on board for removal to Malacca. A number of toes are missing, one of them having been bitten off in 1544 by a Portuguese lady named Donna Isabel de Carom, who refused to return the relic. One toe was sent to the Castle of Xavier, Spain, in 1902, and after the exposition in 1890, another, which fell off, was placed in a reliquary, which is kept in the Basilica of the Bom Jesus in Goa; the other toes are unaccounted for.

In 1619, when Japan was suffering from persecution and an epidemic, the Jesuits in that country asked for a relic of the Saint, so the upper part of the right arm was amputated and given to them, after permission had been received from Rome. A few years later the upper part of the left hand was divided into two parts; one part was given to Cochin, and the other part, along with the shoulder blade which became detached from the right shoulder at the time of the amputation of that arm, was given to the College of Malacca.

In 1636, in order to satisfy the many demands for relics from around the world, the internal organs were used as relics and official

---

[3]*Ibid.* ii, pp. 776-778.

records speak of them as coming *"ex praecordies," "ex intestinis," "ex carne," "ex visceribus."* Without the support of the interior organs, the bones became loose and were braced with wires. Because of the condition of the relic, the authorities in Rome ordered in 1798 that the body be enclosed in such a way that it could be seen through a glass case but never directly touched. This order was executed, and it has ever since been protected in a glass-sided reliquary.

The relic at the present time is dry and shrunken in size, but there is no corruption and some hairs of the beard are still seen on the dried cheek flesh.

At the time of the 1952 exposition, His Excellency, D. Costa Nunes, then the Patriarch of the East Indies and Archbishop of Goa, for the first time referred to what remains of the body of the Saint as the "relic of the body of St. Francis Xavier."

The present condition of the body in no way detracts from the inexplicable preservation which was miraculously maintained for one hundred fifty years, as confirmed by numerous medical reports and countless eyewitness accounts.

In what was described as its "last" exhibition, the body of the Saint was viewed for a six-week period, from November, 1974 until January 5, 1975. During the first three weeks 200,000 visitors are said to have visited the relic; 15,000 paid their respects during the last morning of the exhibition alone, and an estimated 50,000 people lined the path of the outdoor procession before the glass coffin was again placed in its artistically crafted silver reliquary in the 17th century Basilica of Bom Jesus.

In its December 30, 1974 issue, *Newsweek* magazine described the body of the Saint as being "surprisingly well-preserved," and quoted one of the priests as claiming that four decades ago, "the body was fresh as though the saint was only sleeping."

Although it was described by officials of the shrine as perhaps the last exhibition of the relic, it is hoped by the Saint's devotees and the people of Goa that the body will again be viewed within a few years.

St. Francis Xavier was canonized by Pope Gregory XV on March 12, 1622, and was proclaimed by Pope St. Pius X as the "Patron of Missions," a title he shares with St. Thérèse of Lisieux. He is considered the greatest individual missionary to the heathens since St. Paul.

The remains of the body of St. Francis Xavier (d. 1552) being borne in procession to the Basilica of Bom Jesus in Goa, India, after its last exhibition, which closed on January 5, 1975. The right arm, several toes, and other parts of the body are missing, having been removed for relics.

A painting on wooden panels depicting an earlier exposition of St. Francis Xavier's incorrupt body. The painting is from the Basilica of Bom Jesus in Goa, India.

The arrival of St. Francis Xavier at Yamaguchi, Japan, depicted by a modern artist.

The beautiful silver reliquary in the Basilica of Bom Jesus in Goa, India, where the body of St. Francis Xavier reposes.

61

SAINT STANISLAUS KOSTKA

1550—1568

Born into the Polish nobility, Stanislaus was one of seven children and received a firm and exacting secular and religious training. At the age of fourteen he and his brother Paul enrolled in the Jesuit college in Vienna, where his desire for holiness intensified and his penances and prayers were followed by certain spiritual favors. Once when seriously sick, he received Holy Communion from St. Barbara, the patroness of his sodality at school, who appeared surrounded by angels. On another occasion the Blessed Virgin appeared and advised him to enter the Society of Jesus, but he encountered many difficulties in fulfilling her wishes. In Vienna, the Jesuit superior was reluctant to accept him, fearing the possible violent reactions of his father. In Germany, where he again applied, he met St. Peter Canisius, the German provincial of the Order, who advised him to enter the novitiate at Rome, which was governed by St. Francis Borgia. The ten remaining months of his life were spent in the practice of great virtue, and he impressed all by his saintly demeanor. The young Saint died after a brief illness at the age of seventeen, on the feast of the Assumption, a feast he specially regarded.

Two years after his death, permission was given for the exhumation of the remains in order to give one of the bones to a house of the Order which earnestly pleaded for such a relic.

At the opening of the grave, which had been closed for more than two years, the novices went, vested in surplices, and each bearing a lighted torch, to receive with fitting respect the promised treasure. But no sooner was the coffin uncovered than a fragrance, more delicious than that of the sweetest flower, issued from it. So delicate, so pure, so exquisite was this scent, which, moreover, instead of only delighting the senses, seemed to penetrate to the souls of those present, that one and all felt that it was perfume not of earth but of Paradise. The lid of the coffin was now raised, and everyone pressed devoutly forward to venerate the holy remains which God had honored by this signal grace, when, behold! Stanislaus is again before them, not uncorrupted only, but even as he looked when they had taken their last sorrowful farewell of him before he was committed to the earth: the same smile on his lips, the same unstained fairness on his brow. It is needless to say that no one could think of dismembering the holy body which God had willed that death should not so much as disfigure or discolor; and so, after gazing at him a while, with full hearts and tearful eyes, they were fain to see the coffin reclosed, and to forego the pious hope they had cherished.[1]

On the opening of the tomb a few years later, the mortal remains were found reduced in the normal manner. The bones were then enveloped in silk and placed in a leaden coffin in the novitiate church. They remain today, except for a large part of the cranium which is in the chapel of a Jesuit house in Feldkirch, Germany, enclosed in a beautifully decorated marble urn in the chapel dedicated to the Saint in the Church of S. Andrea al Quirinale in Rome.

St. Stanislaus was canonized in 1726 and is universally regarded as the patron of youth.

---

[1] *The Life of St. Stanislaus Kostka of the Company of Jesus.* Edward Healey Thompson, M.A. Peter F. Cunningham, Catholic Bookseller. Philadelphia. 1876. pp. 280-281.

62

BLESSED MARY BAGNESI

1514—1577

The sickness and death of her mother placed Mary Bartholomew at an early age in charge of the household, which she efficiently and cheerfully managed. By the time she was sixteen, many suitors, attracted by her charm and virtue, requested her hand in marriage. Having made a vow of virginity and desiring at an opportune time to enter the religious life, she turned to Our Lord for guidance when her father one day asked her to choose among the young gentlemen. Her prayers were answered. She became so ill she was put to bed and that bed was transformed into a cross of suffering from which she willingly offered herself as a victim of love. Eight times she was so close to death she was anointed, but upon her recovery, her pains were only intensified by the mysterious illness which affected her eyes, ears, head, stomach, and viscera, causing temporary blindness and deafness and often preventing her from eating or sleeping.

During this trial, she was sustained by the spiritual direction of two holy Dominican priests who led her unfalteringly to the very heights of perfection. At the age of thirty-three, when her father gave up hope for her health and eventual happiness in a married vocation, he suggested that she join the Third Order Secular of St. Dominic, which she did willingly. After spending a year as a novice, she was professed and after this ceremony astonished everyone by rising from her bed and visiting the Basilica of St. Mary Novella, to which she was bound as a Dominican Tertiary. Shortly thereafter, she resumed her sufferings and was never heard to utter a complaint.

Many miracles and extraordinary graces were bestowed on those who requested the prayers of her who was in continual union with God. She was enabled to read the hearts and minds of her visitors, was granted a share in heavenly knowledge, was able to calm troubled souls, and experienced a very high gift of prayer.

She maintained a close friendship with the Carmelite sisters of St. Mary of the Angels, who were to be enormously blessed at a later date by the presence of St. Mary Magdalene de' Pazzi. The Carmelites, unable to accept Mary Bagnesi as a member because of her health, wished at least to have her after her death, and so it happened that after Mary Bagnesi's departure from this world, her body, which was first borne by the Dominican Friars through crowds of people to the Dominican Church of St. Mary Novella, was then obligingly carried, as directed by the codicil attached to the Beata's last testament, to the Carmelite convent, where it was entombed beneath the high altar.

Several years later the coffin was transferred to the cloister and upon its being opened, the body was revealed to be still beautiful and entire, as if it had just been buried.[1] The closed casket was placed in the chapter room of the convent where it served as a constant inspiration to the sisters.

Of the many miracles of healing performed by Mary Bagnesi, the most noteworthy was the one performed in favor of St. Mary Magdalene de' Pazzi who was at the time only eighteen years of age. On June 16, 1584, when St. Mary Magdalene had spent three and a half painful months in the convent infirmary, she asked to be taken to the shrine of the Venerable Mary Bagnesi to pray for a cure. The Saint was immediately cured, and upon visiting the shrine later that day she beheld the Venerable Mary Bagnesi in the glorious company of Our Lord and His Mother.[2]

Mary Bartholomew Bagnesi was solemnly beatified in 1804 by Pope Pius VII.

Her body, which is of a darkened ivory color, is still intact with the features quite distinct. The remains are clothed in the white robes of the Dominican Order, which are made of exquisite brocades, and are enclosed in an urn of silver-plated bronze, which is supported by four small white marble angels. In the chapel of the Carmelo di S. Maria Maddalena de' Pazzi rest the bodies of the Beata and the Saint who await in blessed slumber the glorious day of their promised resurrection.

---

[1]*Seraph among Angels, The Life of St. Mary Magdalene de' Pazzi, Carmelite and Mystic.* Sr. Mary Minima. Translated by the Very Rev. Gabriel N. Pausback, O. Carm. The Carmelite Press. Chicago. 1958. p. 348.

[2]*Ibid.* pp. 53-56.

63

SAINT LOUIS BERTRAND

1526—1581

Believed to be a relative of St. Vincent Ferrer, Louis, on the very day of his birth, January 1, 1526, was baptized at the same font where St. Vincent received the sacrament a century and a half before him. He was exceptionally pious as a child, reciting daily the Office of Our Lady and attending different churches in order to conceal from the knowledge of others his frequent reception of the Holy Eucharist. He was received into Saint Dominic's order when nineteen years old and was ordained before he was twenty-two. He filled many offices in the Order, most notably that of master of novices. By the practice of outstanding virtue, self-denial and penance, he furnished for his novices a perfect model for their imitation.

In the year 1562 he was sent from his native Valencia to South America, where he worked for seven years among the Indians in the northwestern part of the continent, among the tribe of the Caribs in the Caribbean Islands, and among the natives on the Isthmus of Panama. During these missionary years he was favored with the gift of tongues. While speaking to the natives in Castilian, he was understood by all and often spoke in languages with which he was naturally unfamiliar. His preaching was accompanied by many miracles and prophecies. He once raised a girl to life by the application of a Rosary and often attributed to the intercession of Our Lady the miraculous powers he manifested.

After returning to his native land, he again occupied administrative positions in the Order and won the esteem and friendship of St. Teresa of Avila. The Saint died a holy death after suffering a long and painful illness. Many prodigies accompanied his passing. During the process of beatification, witnesses testified that shortly after his death a heavenly perfume arose from his body, that a light which glowed for several minutes proceeded from his mouth and illuminated his whole cell, and that seraphic music was heard in the church before his funeral.[1]

The body of the Saint, which remained incorrupt for over three hundred fifty years, was maliciously destroyed during the Spanish Revolution of 1936.

---

[1] *The Book of Miracles.* Zsolt Aradi. Farrar, Straus & Cudahy Co. New York. 1956. p. 174.

— 64 —

SAINT TERESA OF AVILA

1515—1582

This great reformer of the Carmelite Order was born to a noble family on March 28, 1515, in Avila, Spain. She was very pious as a child, having attempted at the age of seven to journey with her brother to convert the Moors and suffer martyrdom. During her adolescence her fervor languished due to her fascination with the romantic literature of her day, but after a serious illness her devotion was rekindled through the influence of a pious uncle; she became interested in the religious life and joined the Order of Carmel in Avila, where she took her vows in 1534.

At the time of her entrance into this convent, the Order permitted a great deal of socializing and other privileges which were contrary to the original rule. Teresa enjoyed her life there under these relaxed rules until she experienced, during her thirty-eighth year, her "conversion," while reading the *Confessions of St. Augustine*.[1] Finding this atmosphere in opposition to the spirit of prayer for which she felt Our Lord had intended the Order, she began reforming its laxities in 1562 at the cost of countless persecutions and difficulties. Her good friend and advisor, St. John of the Cross, aided her in this endeavor and extended the reformation to the friars of the Order.

Under rigorous interpretation of the rule, she attained the heights of mysticism, enjoyed countless visions, and experienced the phenomenon of levitation. She was also frequently visited by the devil, who appeared in horrible forms, but his taunts and physical abuse were promptly terminated by generous sprinklings with holy water.

There seems to be no phenomenon peculiar to the mystical state which she did not experience, yet she remained a shrewd businesswoman, administrator, writer, spiritual counselor and foundress.

She was a reluctant writer, engaging in this task under obedience, but left three spiritual masterpieces: her *Autobiography, The Way of Perfection*, and, what is considered her greatest work, *The Interior*

---

[1]*Journey to Carith*. Peter-Thomas Rohrbach, O.C.D. Doubleday & Co., Inc. New York. 1966. p. 144.

Castle, the title of which was given her by Christ Himself. Never a healthy woman, the Saint died of her many afflictions on October 4, 1582, while on a visit to her convent at Alba de Tormes. Her constant companion, Mother Anne of St. Bartholomew, who held the dying Saint in her arms, left us this account of her burial.

> The day after her death she was buried with full solemnity. Her body was put into a coffin, but such a heap of stones, bricks, and chalk were put on top of it that the coffin gave way under the weight and all this rubble fell in. It was by the order of the lady who endowed the house, Teresa de Layz, that the rubble was put there. Nobody could prevent her; it seemed to her that by acting thus she was making all the more certain that no one would take Teresa's body away.[2]

The delightful fragrance which frequently enveloped the Saint during her lifetime, and which was so strongly noted at the time of her death that the door and windows of her cell had to be opened, continued to emanate from the grave, and so many wonders were occurring there that the curiosity of the nuns concerning the condition of the body was greatly aroused. Permission to exhume the relic was granted by the provincial of the Order, Fr. Jerome Gracian, during one of his visits to the monastery. Francisco de Ribera, the Saint's confessor and first biographer, described the proceedings in this manner.

> The coffin was opened on July 4, 1583, nine months after the interment; they found the coffin lid smashed, half rotten and full of mildew, the smell of damp was very pungent. . . . The clothes had also fallen to pieces. . . . The holy body was covered with the earth which had penetrated into the coffin and so was all damp too, but as fresh and whole as if it had only been buried the day before. . . . They undressed her almost entirely for she had been buried in her habit— they washed the earth away, and there spread through the whole house a wonderful penetrating fragrance which lasted some days. . . . They put her into a new habit, wrapped her in a sheet and put her back into the same coffin. But before doing this, the Provincial removed her left hand.[3]

[2]*Teresa of Avila.* Marcelle Auclair. Pantheon Books, Inc. New York. 1953. p. 430.
[3]*Ibid.* pp. 430-431.

The provincial, Gracian, gives us an interesting report concerning this relic:

> I took the hand away wrapped in a coif and in an outer wrapping of paper; oil came from it. . . . I left it at Avila in a sealed casket. . . . When I severed the hand, I also severed a little finger which I carry about on my person. When I was captured, the Turks took it from me, but I bought it back for some twenty reales and some gold rings. . . .[4]

A contest soon began between two of her foundations over which one held the greater claim to her body—the convent of San Jose in her native Avila, where she held the position of prioress at the time of her death, and the convent at Alba, where she had requested to be buried. The problem was presented to the chapter of Discalced Friars, who decreed that the body of the Saint should be exhumed and taken to Avila in secret, in order to prevent confrontations with the nuns, the townspeople, and the Duke of Alba. This removal was clandestinely undertaken on November 24 and 25, 1585. As a consolation to the nuns who were being robbed of their treasure, the left arm, from which the hand had already been removed, was amputated and left in their keeping.

The body was entrusted to the sisters at St. Joseph's at Avila, where it was promptly visited by the bishop, Don Pedro Fernández de Temiño, and two doctors, P. Diego de Yepes and Julian de Avila.

> The doctors examined the body and decided that it was impossible that its condition could have a natural explanation, but that it was truly miraculous . . . for after three years, without having been opened or embalmed, it was in such a perfect state of preservation that nothing was wanting to it in any way, and a wonderful odour issued from it.[5]

When the Duke of Alba learned of the secret removal, he immediately petitioned Rome for its return, and the body of the holy mother was eventually brought back to Alba de Tormes on the orders of the Pope.

Of the 1588 exhumation of the body of the Saint, Ribera, who was an eyewitness, left us this interesting description:

---

[4]*Ibid.* p. 431.
[5]*Ibid.* p. 434.

The body is erect, though bent a little forward, as with old people. It can be made to stand upright, if someone props it with a hand between the shoulders, and this is the position in which they hold it when it is to be dressed or undressed, as though it were alive. The colour of the body is of the colour of dates; the face darker, because the veil which was full of dust became stuck to it, and it was mal-treated more than the rest; nevertheless, it is intact, and even the nose is undamaged. The head has retained all its hair, as on the day of her death. The eyes having lost their vital moisture are dried-up, but the eye-lids are perfectly preserved. The moles on her face retain their little hairs. The mouth is tightly shut and cannot be opened. The flesh is that of a corpulent person, especially on the shoulders. . . . The shoulder from which the arm has been detached exudes a moisture which clings to the touch and exhales the same scent as the body.[6]

During later exhumations, parts of the body and bits of flesh were extracted in the name of piety and distributed throughout Europe. One foot is in the Church of Santa Maria della Scala in Rome and a cheek, which was conserved in Madrid, was lost during the Civil War of 1936-39. The left hand, which was kept by the Madres Carmelitas of Ronda, was stolen by the Liberals during the same political upheaval, but during their hurried escape after their defeat, the relic was left abandoned in a valise and eventually found its way into the possession of Generalissimo Franco. At Alba de Tormes, there are exposed for the veneration of the faithful, in their respective silver and crystal reliquaries, the left arm and the heart, which is of partic-ular interest.[7]

The Saint recorded in her *Autobiography* the vision of her trans-verberation, one of her most remarkable experiences:

I saw an angel close by me, on my left side, in bodily form. He was not large, but small of stature and most beautiful—his face burning as if he were one of the highest angels who seem to be all of fire. I saw in his hand a long spear of gold, and at the iron's point there seemed to be a little fire. He appeared to me to be thrusting it at times into my heart and to pierce my very entrails; when he drew it out, he seemed

---

[6] *The Eagle and The Dove.* V. Sackville-West. Doubleday, Doran & Co., Inc. Gar-den City, New York. 1944. p. 90.

[7] The information contained in this paragraph is taken from statements made by the abbess of the Carmelite Monastery at Alba de Tormes.

to draw them out also, and to leave me all on fire with a great love of God. . . .

The wounded heart was meticulously examined in 1872 by three physicians of the University of Salamanca who noted the perforation made by the dart. They unanimously agreed that the preservation of the heart could not be credited to any natural or chemical means.[8]

The last exhumation of the body of the Saint occurred in 1914. The contents of the coffin were found in the same condition as before except that a tube of lead, in which were placed the official documents relating to the Saint, was found reduced to powder, whereas the body of the Saint was in the same condition as in previous exhumations. The sisters at Alba de Tormes were privileged to view the features of their spiritual mother and also perceived the same flowery fragrance which had been noticed so often about her body.

The precious relic is conserved in an urn of silver which is enclosed in a black marble sarcophagus that is delicately embellished with bronze.

St. Teresa of Avila was canonized in 1622 and bore for many centuries the title of Doctor of the Church, an honor conferred on her by public acclamation. On September 27, 1970, Pope Paul VI officially annexed her name to the list of thirty distinguished Doctors; she is the first woman to join such an illustrious group.

---

[8]*Saint Teresa of Avila.* William Thomas Walsh. Bruce Publishing Co. Milwaukee. 1943. p. 136.

SAINT CHARLES BORROMEO

1538—1584

St. Charles, the son of Count Gilbert Borromeo and Margaret de' Medici, was born in the castle of Arona on Lake Maggiore in northern Italy, and was the heir to a large fortune. His uncle Angelo de' Medici became Pope Pius IV on December 26, 1559, and a few days later named his nephew a cardinal, even though the twenty-two-year-old Charles was not a priest. A short time later he was appointed the Archbishop of Milan. He led a virtuous life amid many honors and enjoyed great influence in the affairs of the Church, being credited with the organization and much of the work of the Council of Trent.

A turning point in his life occurred at the time of the sudden death of his elder brother in 1562. Although his life previous to this bereavement was one of great virtue, from that time on he began to live the life of a saint. He resumed his university studies, and after his ordination in 1563, made plans to leave the Roman court, which he did after the death of his uncle. Returning to his archdiocese, which had fallen into a scandalous state, he immediately began the great reform which occupied him until his death. With his inheritance he founded schools, hospitals and seminaries and established many organizations whose functions were the rekindling of devotion and the expansion of the Faith. Because of the reforms, which were not to everyone's liking, he suffered for a time from slander, criticism and even threats of bodily harm. He completely won the faith, devotion, and love of his people, however, during the plague of 1576. While many were fleeing the stricken city, he remained in order to care for the deserted sick, unselfishly giving of his energy and material possessions to relieve their sufferings. Even though he worked closely with the sick, he did not fall victim to the disease and for the next eight years continued to live a holy and austere life.

After his holy death, people from neighboring villages felt obliged to express their love for the Saint by making pilgrimages to his tomb in the Cathedral of Milan.

The crowds became so great that the stone covering the blessed grave had to be surrounded with a railing to protect it from popular pious enthusiasm. Even this did not suffice to restrain the ardor of the multitudes, who kept coming continuously and covered that humble grave with most precious gifts. Rings, necklaces, pearls, diamonds, rubies, massive lamps of gold or silver, were common gifts. In 1610, when the canonization was proclaimed, there were at the tomb of St. Charles, 10,891 silver votive offerings and 9,618 precious gifts.[1]

After his cause for beatification had been well under way, two bishops delegated by Rome were sent to Milan for the identification of the body of the Saint.

For twenty years and four months the body had reposed in that humble tomb under the pavement in the middle of the cathedral, enclosed in a coffin of lead and another of wood. The natural humidity of the place, augmented by certain precautionary measures taken by the canons to prevent the people from kneeling at the slab, had corroded the cover of both coffins in several places and allowed the moisture to penetrate even to the corpse.

On March 6, in the presence of the two bishop delegates, Cardinal Federico, Monsignor Bascape, and notaries for the act of identification, the coffin was opened. These testified that the body was still preserved in spite of the condition to which the coffins had been reduced. It was considered opportune to exhume the body and it was temporarily transported to the south sacristy where it remained, jealously guarded, for an entire year. An iron grill was substituted for the slab which had covered the tomb, and the vault was changed into a little oratory where Mass could be celebrated.

On March 7, 1607, the sacred remains, revested and placed in new coffins of lead and wood, were brought back to their original resting place.[2]

The modest oratory was transformed by Richino in the early seventeenth century into a magnificent octagonal chapel, its ceiling adorned with exquisite handcrafted bas-reliefs, its lower walls and floor covered with beautifully colored marbles set in artistic designs. A silver altar now supports the reliquary, which was presented as a gift by Philip IV of Spain. The jewel-like reliquary is crafted of

---

[1] *Life of St. Charles Borromeo.* Most Rev. Cesare Orsenigo. B. Herder Book Co. St. Louis, Mo. 1943. p. 363.

[2] *Ibid.* p. 364.

geometric pieces of rock crystal set in silver and adorned with numerous miniature angels and religious figures of superior workmanship.

During the examination of the relic in 1880 it was noted, as had been done previously, that the body of the Saint had been embalmed in the usual manner shortly after death, but this was not held directly responsible for the preservation of the body almost three hundred years after the Saint's death.

When John Baptist Cardinal Montini, now Pope Paul VI, was Archbishop of Milan, the face of St. Charles was covered with silver at his request. The body, still incorrupt, is clothed in gem-studded pontifical vestments. Thus does the body of the Saint await in majestic surroundings the day of its glorious resurrection.

VENERABLE CATALINA DE CRISTO

1554—1589

Almost forty years after the birth of the great St. Teresa, there was born in Madrid, in the diocese of Avila, Catalina de Cristo, who was vested in 1572 with the habit of the Discalced Carmelites. Having attained great sanctity, she gained the admiration of the great St. Teresa and served for a time as her companion. The religious reform which Teresa instigated was extended to houses of the Order by Catalina who also established monasteries in Sorio, Pamplona and Barcelona. Having practiced heroic virtues, especially those of obedience, mortification and charity, the Venerable died with a reputation for great sanctity in 1589 at her foundation in Barcelona, where the sweet celestial scent that emanated from the body perfumed the entire monastery. The remains of the Venerable were buried with the customary simplicity in the ground where they were found six months and seven days later, perfectly incorrupt, a condition that has been maintained to modern times. On the instructions of the superior of the Order, the body was placed in an urn that was then kept in the choir for the admiration and inspiration of the sisters. Several years later, in 1604, the body was translated from Barcelona to Pamplona, but before its removal, an arm and hand were detached and left in the keeping of the sisters so they would not be completely deprived of their precious relic. The arm to this day is as perfectly incorrupt as is the body of the Venerable.

Clothed in a Discalced Carmelite habit that is intricately embroidered with brilliant golden threads, the body of Catalina de Christo remains perfectly incorrupt and flexible. Last exhumed in 1961, the precious relic was viewed by throngs of people, who marveled at the excellent condition that has been mysteriously maintained for almost four hundred years.

SAINT BENEDICT THE MOOR

1526—1589

Benedict the Black was the son of Negro slaves who were taken from Africa to San Fratello, Sicily, where they were converted to Christianity. They lived such exemplary lives and fulfilled their duties so thoroughly that their owner, in appreciation, granted freedom to their eighteen-year-old son, Benedict. He continued to work as a day laborer, generously sharing his small wages with the poor and spending his free time in caring for the sick. Because of his lowly origins he was often the object of ridicule, which he bore so patiently and cheerfully that he was called even during his youth, "The Holy Black."

When twenty-one years of age, he became acquainted with Jerome Lanza, a nobleman who had left the world to live under the rule of St. Francis of Assisi. Benedict sold his few possessions, gave the money to the poor and joined the monastic group at San Fratello, later moving with them to Palermo. For many years he was happily employed in the kitchen as a lay brother at the Friary of St. Mary of Jesus, but upon the death of their director, he was chosen the guardian of the friary, even though he could neither read nor write. After serving one term in this office, he was chosen novice master, his counsels being eagerly sought by the novices, professed religious and people of every class. He possessed extraordinary gifts of prayer, was divinely given an infused knowledge of the Scriptures, and had an intuitive grasp of deep theological truths, which astounded learned men and aided him in the direction of souls.

The reports of his sanctity spread throughout Sicily, and the monastery was constantly beset with visitors—the poor requesting alms, the sick in search of a miracle, and people of all ranks seeking advice or prayers. Although he never refused to see anyone, he would have preferred to live a hidden life, unknown to the world. Toward the end of his life he willingly returned to the humble duties of the kitchen when he was relieved of all offices. He died after a short illness at the age of sixty-three, at the very hour he had predicted, and was buried with great solemnity in the common vault behind the sacristy of the church.

Immediately after his death a vigorous cult developed, and his veneration spread throughout Spain, Italy and Latin America. He was beatified by Pope Benedict XIV in 1743 and was canonized by Pope Pius VII in 1807.

The first exhumation of his remains occurred on May 7, 1592, three years after the Saint's death, at which time his body was found perfectly preserved.

In the year 1611, King Philip III of Spain assumed the expense of providing in the same church, a new shrine situated on the left side of the altar of S. Maria di Gesù, to which the Saint's incorrupt remains were transferred with great solemnity.

The sacred relic, still incorrupt but a little dry and hard, is exposed for public veneration. The face of the Saint was covered some time ago with a thin wax mask. Thus has God blessed the virtues of the former slave with the gift of incorruptibility, which blessing has endured for almost four hundred years.

St. Benedict the Black has been proclaimed the "Patron of all Negro Missions in North America."

68

SAINT CATHERINE DEI RICCI

1522—1590

At the age of thirteen, Alexandrina of Ricci, of patrician lineage, willingly left behind a position of honor in the world and entered the Dominican convent of San Vincenzio, at Prato, Italy. She was given the name of Catherine at her profession the following year, and with the assumption of this new name she embraced a life of severe penances, but one distinguished also by unusual mystical experiences. At first she endured many physical afflictions, which seemed to be aggravated by ordinary medical treatment, but her agonies were sanctified by prayer and meditation on the Passion of Our Lord.

During Holy Week of 1542, when Catherine was twenty years old, she experienced the first of her ecstasies, in which she saw enacted, in sequence, the scenes of Our Lord's Passion. The ecstasies, which were repeated every week for twelve years, began at midday every Thursday and ended on Friday at 4:00 p.m. During these raptures her body would move in conformity with the movements of Our Lord, and she would occasionally address exhortations to those witnessing her sufferings.

On Easter Sunday of the same year, Our Lord appeared to her, took a ring from His finger and placed it on the forefinger of Catherine's left hand in commemoration of their mystical espousal. Catherine described the ring as being of gold and set with a large pointed diamond, but others saw it only as a swelling and reddening of the flesh, which various experiments could neither duplicate nor erase.[1]

The wounds of her stigmata, located in her hands, feet, and side and those wounds inflicted by the crown of thorns were variously described by people who viewed them. Some declared that the hands were pierced through and bleeding; others perceived a brilliant light that dazzled their eyes; and still others saw the wounds as being healed but red and swollen.[2]

---

[1] *Lives of the Saints* (Complete Edition). Butler, Thurston, & Attwater. P. J. Kenedy & Sons. New York. 1956. Vol. I, pp. 329-331.

[2] *Ibid.* p. 329.

Another phenomenon recorded of her is that of the conversations which she frequently held with St. Philip Neri while he was in Rome and she in her convent at Prato. While they had exchanged a number of letters, they had never met, except through their mystical visits, which St. Philip Neri readily admitted had occurred and which five reputable people swore they had witnessed.[3]

Even though the life of the Saint seems to have been dominated by her mystical experiences, it might be well to consider the positions of responsibility she assumed in her community. While still very young she was selected as novice mistress and then sub-prioress; later, at the age of thirty-eight, she was appointed prioress in perpetuity. Her reputation for holiness and wisdom brought many laymen and members of the clergy to the convent seeking counsel, including three cardinals, each of whom later became Pope. It is recorded that she energetically fulfilled her responsibilities and was happiest when working among the poor and sick of the city.

After a lengthy illness, the Saint died on the Feast of the Purification of the Blessed Virgin, February 2, 1590, during her sixty-eighth year; she was canonized in 1747.

The Basilica of Prato possesses with pride the incorrupt remains of this saint who has been designated the patroness of the city. The darkened, but still beautiful relic of the Saint lies in an ornate reliquary, which is exposed for public veneration below the major altar of the basilica.

---

[3]*Ibid.* p. 328.

69

SAINT JOHN OF THE CROSS

1542—1591

Known before his religious life as Juan de Yepes, this son of a weaver credited the Blessed Mother with saving his life from drowning on two occasions during his childhood. He received his early education from the Jesuits, but in 1563 he joined the Carmelites at Medina and was ordained five years later after completing an intensive educational program. Feeling himself called to observe a stricter rule, he was considering the Carthusian Order when he met St. Teresa of Avila, who persuaded him to help her in restoring the Carmelites to the strict observance of the original rule of the Order, which included daily and nightly recitation of the Divine Office, perpetual abstinence from meat, and numerous fasts and penances. During the conflicts which ensued among members of the Order, he was kidnapped and imprisoned for a nine-month period and was shamefully persecuted and publicly disgraced. After the separation of the Discalced Carmelites from the Calced Carmelites, which received the approval of the Roman Curia in 1580, he filled a number of important positions in the Order.

For a number of years the Saint served as the confessor of the convent at Avila in which St. Teresa was prioress. In Teresa's estimation, "He was one of the purest souls in the Church of God." It was here at Avila that the sisters witnessed many of his levitations during ecstatic prayer.

His most valuable contributions to the Church are his mystical writings, which include *The Ascent of Mount Carmel, The Dark Night of the Soul,* and *The Spiritual Canticle.* Very appropriately, Bossuet has testified that St. John's works "possess the same authority in mystical theology as the writings of St. Thomas Aquinas possess in dogmatic theology."

At the age of forty-nine the Saint died at Ubeda after a painful illness. His funeral was attended by the faithful, who crowded into the church to touch religious objects to his body. He was buried in a vault beneath the flooring of the church where, on the Monday night following the burial, the friars observed a great light which burned for several minutes.[1]

The relic was found intact when the tomb was first opened nine months after the Saint's death. Doña Ana de Penasola, who wanted the body of the Saint removed to the house she had established for him in Segovia, obtained a legal order for the removal of the bones eighteen months after his death. At that time one of the king's sergeants, Francis de Medina Zavallos, was sent to Ubeda to negotiate the translation. In obedience to the orders, the prior admitted him to the church at night, and upon opening the tomb, they perceived a fragrant perfume and found the body perfectly fresh and supple. The prior refused to have the relic removed, for the official orders called for the removal of the bones. One of the fingers of the Saint was then cut off for Zavallos to present to Doña Ana as proof of the preservation of the body, and when this was amputated, blood flowed profusely, as would be normal in a living person.[2]

After waiting for another nine months, Zavallos was again sent to Ubeda. The grave was opened and the body found still perfectly preserved under a layer of lime, which had been previously applied to it. Zavallos then put the body into a bag and took it away, but the perfume which surrounded the body pervaded the entire area and aroused the curiosity of the people whom he passed along the way, and he was frequently asked about the contents of the bag. At Madrid the Carmelites placed the relic in a coffin so that it could be transported to Segovia in a more fitting manner. Upon its arrival in that city, it was received with all reverence and respect and was exposed for eight days in the chapel, where it was visited by great crowds of people.[3]

The body was exhumed and carefully examined in 1859 and again in 1909. In 1926 an impressive shrine composed of beautifully colored marble and bronze was constructed by national subscription and executed by the best Spanish artists. During the removal of the relic to this magnificent monument, the body was again exposed for the veneration of the faithful.

The last exhumation of the relic occurred in 1955 on the occasion of the visit of the Reverend Provincial General of the Order. The

---

[1]*St. John of the Cross.* Fr. Paschasius Heriz, O.C.D. College of Our Lady of Mount Carmel. Washington, D.C. 1919. pp. 203-204.

[2]*Ibid.* p. 205.

[3]*Ibid.* pp. 205-206.

body at that time was found to be slightly discolored but perfectly moist and flexible.

The Saint was canonized in 1726, and two hundred years later, in 1926, he assumed his rightful position among the Doctors of the Church, being officially designated such by Pope Pius XI.

70

BLESSED ALPHONSUS DE OROZCO

1500—1591

Born in the diocese of Avila fifteen years before the birth of St. Teresa, Alphonsus, the mystic reformer of the Carmelite Order, was attracted to the religious life at an early age, as was that other great saint. He studied at Talavera, Toledo, and Salamanca, where he was further interested in the religious life by the sermons of St. Thomas of Villanova. At twenty-two years of age he joined the Hermits of St. Augustine, and the next thirty years found him engaged in preaching, counseling and teaching—all with great distinction. After serving his order as prior in various monasteries, he was sent to the royal city of Valladolid in 1554 and was appointed court preacher. When Philip II moved his court to Madrid in 1561, Alphonsus remained with it and took up residence in the Friary of San Felipe el Real where he lived an austere and penitential life, which stood in sharp contrast to the splendid functions of the court, which duty dictated he attend.

In response to a vision of the Blessed Mother, he applied his pen with great diligence for the glory of God and produced many classic works of great literary quality and devotional appeal. For thirty-five years he labored in maintaining Christian principles among the nobility and gentry of the court, and upon his holy death at the age of ninety-one, tears of genuine sorrow were shed by many at court over their great loss.

The devotion to his blessed memory remained constant, and at his disinterment twelve years after his death, the discovery of his totally incorrupt body gave even greater impetus to his veneration. At the time of the transfer of his remains, his friends who were witnessing the ceremony were privileged to gaze once more on the features of their dear friend, whose body, though perfectly incorrupt, was found in priestly vestments which had rotted from the effects of the confinement.

The Augustinians of Spain petitioned the ecclesiastical authorities for a judicial inquiry into the sanctity of this humble priest, whom everyone was already proclaiming a saint.

. . . The condition of his body still intact, after lying twelve years in the tomb, invited the closest study, and was pronounced by witnessing physicians as a fact, which was in defiance of the physical laws of nature. The remarkable sight of a flexible body, possessing all the appearances of life, though shrouded in a decayed habit was regarded by all as an evidence of the imperishable happiness the soul possessed in Heaven, and also as a favorable omen of the future laurels, which God would yet bestow upon the memory of His blessed servant on earth.[1]

When Pope Clement VIII was informed of the miraculous preservation by representatives of the Order who petitioned for the inclusion of his name in the ranks of the saints, the Pontiff exclaimed, "I was acquainted with him myself, and regarded him as such; and the intelligence which you now communicate delights me exceedingly."[2]

Alphonsus' sanctity was further affirmed by Pope Urban VIII, who placed his signature on the documents drawn up at the completion of the preliminary investigation by the Papal Nuncio and recommended that the cause of beatification be continued. The heroic virtues of this holy man were officially confirmed in 1882 by Pope Leo XIII during solemn beatification ceremonies in St. Peter's Basilica.

The body of Blessed Alphonsus is no longer conserved, but the precious bones are kept in a silver case and are in the possession of the Augustinian Fathers of Valladolid.

---

[1]*Life of Blessed Alphonsus Orozco, O.S.A.* Rt. Rev. Thomas Camara, O.S.A., D.D. Translated by Rev. W. A. Jones, O.S.A. H. L. Kilner & Co. Philadelphia. 1895. p. 291-292.

[2]*Ibid.* p. 292.

71

SAINT PASCHAL BAYLON

1540—1592

Born at Torre Hermosa in the Kingdom of Aragon to a humble farming family, Paschal tended sheep from the age of seven until his twenty-fourth year. He is alleged to have had a vision of St. Francis and St. Clare, who directed him to join the Franciscan Order, and at a later date he was admitted to the monastery of the Alcantarine Franciscans at Monteforte. As a lay brother he served in various capacities in monasteries of the Order, but his special love was caring for the sick and poor, for whom he often shed tears of compassion and performed miracles of healing.

Devotion to the Holy Eucharist was the dominant theme of his life. His first biographer, Father John Ximenes, who was a personal friend of the Saint, reports that Paschal spent all his free time before the tabernacle, kneeling without support, with his hands clasped and held up above his face. It is also reported that he delighted in serving several Masses in succession and that he often spent the night in prayer before the tabernacle.

While on a journey through France on a mission for his order, he was called upon several times to defend his belief in the Holy Eucharist. For a friar to wear a habit during the time of the religious wars was an invitation to disaster, and he was several times arrested, questioned, and roughly handled by the Huguenots. At one town he was stoned and suffered an injury to his shoulder which afflicted him the rest of his life.

By a coincidence, the very "hour of the holy man's departure from the world exactly coincided with that of his entrance into it. He was fifty-two years old to the day, on Whit Sunday, at dawn," May 15, 1592.[1]

Owing to the great gathering of people who wished to view the remains, the body was carried from the humble cell in which he had died to one of the chapels in the church of Our Lady of the Rosary.

---

[1] *The Saint of the Eucharist.* L. A. de Porrentruy. Translated by O. Staniforth, O.F.M. Cap. Press of Upton Bros. & Delzelle, Inc. San Francisco. 1905. p. 204.

The mourners who filed past the bier were astonished to see the heavenly radiance on his countenance and the perfumed moisture which had collected on his forehead since the time of his death. During the three days of exhibition, the "miraculous sweat which distilled from the members of the Saint flowed copiously and continuously."[2] We are told that armed guards were required to control the people, many of whom were permitted to collect the scented moisture on small cloths, which were later to occasion many cures by their application to previously hopeless maladies.

We are also told that many of the mourners were also permitted to test the flexibility of the body and to draw back the lids to view the unusually bright and unclouded eyes.[3]

Of the prodigies and dramatic miracles of healing which were occurring on all sides, perhaps the most unusual incident which occurred during this solemn period involved the miraculous opening of the eyes of the corpse, a miracle which was viewed by many of the people who filled the church to capacity.

Eleanora Jorda y Miedes, an eyewitness to this event, who had previously been repulsed by dead bodies, related in her deposition:

> . . . I went up to Brother Paschal as though he had been alive, kissed his hands and feet and saw the miraculous dew upon his forehead. In short, I felt so much at my ease, at the side of the holy man, that in order to remain the longer under his blessed influence, I resolved not to quit the chapel before the end of High Mass. I must confess, to my own shame, that I was more attentive in watching what was going on round the holy man, than in following the Holy Sacrifice. When I saw him open his eyes at the Elevation, I was so astounded that I gave a loud scream. "Mamma, Mamma!" I exclaimed to my mother, who had come with me, "Look, Look! Brother Paschal has opened his eyes." She looked and she too saw the eyes of the saint open and then shut at the second Elevation.
>
> All who were witnesses of this miracle, like ourselves, had one and the same idea about it, namely that Our Lord wished in this way to reward Paschal's extraordinary devotion to the Sacrament of the Altar, and that He gave him a new life, so that even on the other side of the tomb, he might still have the consolation of adoring Him in the Holy Eucharist.[4]

---

[2]*Ibid.* p. 212.
[3]*Ibid.* p. 212.
[4]*Ibid.* pp. 216-217.

During the evening hours of the third day following his death, while a receptacle was being prepared under the altar of the Immaculate Conception, the body was reclothed in a new habit, the old one having been torn to shreds by the faithful. Before the burial, the guardian of the house covered the body with a thick layer of quicklime so that the flesh would be quickly consumed, producing glossy white bones, which he felt would look impressive in a shrine. He also acted under the assumption that the lime would quickly destroy the flesh and thus forbid any unpleasant odor from escaping, a fact which would shock the people and detract from the reputation he had acquired by many marvels.[5]

The body rested undisturbed in this caustic agent for eight months when the provincial of the Order, Father John Ximenes, who had been unable to attend the funeral due to illness, visited the shrine for the purpose of secretly exhuming the body. Concerning this incident, Father Ximenes related that in the company of several friars,

> The lid was raised and we all approached the shrine and attested the presence of the crust of lime which concealed the saint from sight. I would not allow anyone else to have the honor of removing this crust; but detached it bit by bit, beginning with the portion which covered the face.
>
> O heavenly joy! In proportion as I lifted the veil, the features of our blessed brother were disclosed, full of life and animation. It was indeed himself, miraculously preserved in the flesh; intact from head to foot, even down to the tip of the nose, ordinarily the first part to show signs of decomposition.
>
> When we raised the eyelids, the eyes seemed to gaze at us and smile. The limbs were so supple and flexible that they lent themselves to every movement we imparted to them. Nothing recalled death, or the presence of a dead body; on the contrary everything breathed life and brought consolation and joy to the soul. Human language is inadequate to portray such a spectacle.
>
> On our knees before the shrine we shed the sweetest tears of our lives. I took the saint's hand in mine, and, drawing it towards me, and raising it to my lips, I kissed it lovingly. A crystalline liquid like balm distilled from the face and hands. When each of the Religious had satisfied his devotion, a fresh layer of quicklime was spread over the body, and then I directly addressed the saint in the following words:
>
> "He Who for eight months hath so miraculously preserved thee beneath the lime, is powerful enough to preserve thee still, for many

[5]*Ibid.* p. 223.

years to come, and thus give greater lustre to the miracle, until the fitting time shall arrive for translating thy glorious remains to a sepulchre less unworthy of thee."

Having replaced the shrine in the niche, and reconstructed the little well of bricks, we retired in silence to prepare a report of this first recognition of the body.[6]

The second exhumation was undertaken on July 22, 1594. The religious of the community found only a few shreds of the religious shroud. The body, except for the extremity of the nostrils and some fragments of skin, continued to contradict corruption, and it was found that a piece of one ear and a finger had been taken previously as relics. It was also discovered that the body remained without support when it was placed in an upright position.[7]

The date of the third private exhumation is not known, but an incident which occurred then is worth noting. One of the religious, in secret and without authorization, amputated both the Saint's feet and carried them off. Upon discovering the sacrilege, the superiors ordered the feet returned under pain of excommunication, and they were forthwith restored to the coffin some hours later. The mutilation proved to be advantageous, however, for it was from the feet that numerous relics were taken.

Nineteen years after the Saint's death an official exhumation was made for the process of beatification. In the presence of the Bishop of Segorbe, the provincial, the postulator of the cause, certain eminent dignitaries of the country, doctors, surgeons and a notary, the three locks on the coffin were opened and the customary formalities observed before the contents were revealed.

As soon as the lid was raised, an agreeable fragrance, resembling the perfume of flowers, or scent, arose from the sepulchre. Armed with a pair of scissors, the Bishop proceeded to cut open the habit of the Saint down to the girdle in order to give the medical faculty every opportunity of making an examination of the body, which had now been nineteen years lying in the tomb. The doctors and surgeons acquitted themselves of the delicate task with the carefulness and reverence to be expected from sincere Christians. The lid was replaced, as soon as they had declared that they had completed their investigations to their own satisfaction. On the following day the Commission

---

[6]*Ibid.* pp. 228-229.
[7]*Ibid.* p. 230.

reassembled to hear the reading of the medical report. The conclusion arrived at, which was based upon the principles of medical science, was in the affirmative as to the miraculous state of the body.

"We, the undersigned doctors and surgeons, affirm on oath before God and according to our conscience, that the body of the said Brother Paschal Baylon is incorrupt, and that the manner of its preservation is supernatural and miraculous."[8]

To the prodigies and miracles previously mentioned must be added another, that of the curious knockings, sometimes called "Golpes," which proceeded from relics or pictures of the Saint during past centuries. The knockings were instinctively interpreted according to their intensity and frequency and were frequently accepted as a friendly warning. Needless to relate, the unusual sounds instilled in the hearts of the beneficiaries an intense religious joy and an overwhelming consciousness of the Saint's presence.[9]

The strange sounds were first heard when a spiritual son of the Saint, Antonio Pascal, began wearing around his neck a reliquary which contained a tiny fragment of bone taken from one of the disjointed feet. The child at first felt light taps on his chest, as though the relic were alive, and its vibrations became almost habitual. To those who discounted the miracle, the child had merely to take off the reliquary, recite devoutly, "Blessed be the most Holy Sacrament of the Altar," and the knockings would immediately resound.[10]

Of the many events involving witnesses of this unique manifestation, we will content ourselves with briefly reporting three of the most unusual.

The first is that concerning Archbishop Don Luis Alphonsus de Cameros, who doubted the prodigy until the child previously mentioned was brought into his presence. After the customary prayer, the knockings were immediately heard proceeding from the reliquary; the archbishop counted fifteen of them. So great was his emotion that he kissed the relic and exclaimed, "Verily, God is wonderful in His saints."[11]

The Venerable Father Diego Danon, who was renowned in the Province of St. John the Baptist for his great holiness, also wore a relic of the Saint about his neck, and the sounds emanating from it

[8]*Ibid.* p. 232.
[9]See the chapter on Bl. Anthony of Stroncone for reports of similar manifestations.
[10]*Ibid.* p. 258.
[11]*Ibid.* pp. 259-260.

were like those of a ticking clock which those about him distinctly heard. The holy priest maintained that the Saint bestowed many favors upon him by means of the relic and that the holy effects produced would be known only on the Day of Judgment.[12]

The celebrated preacher of his day, Father Alphonsus of St. Thomas, a Discalced Trinitarian, testified in his deposition that the relic he had acquired was a source of copious graces and blessings. During one of his meditations, he counted sixty raps, and the sounds were frequently heard during his celebration of the Holy Sacrifice, at which time they filled him with devotion or aided in his recollection.[13]

The devotion to the Blessed Sacrament which Paschal Baylon exhibited so devoutly during his life was reflected in the phenomena and miracles performed by the Saint after his death, all of which contributed in a large measure to the revival of faith or an increase of devotion in the hearts of many. It would then seem more than appropriate that Paschal, having been canonized in 1690, was declared by Leo XIII in 1897 the patron of Eucharistic Congresses and all organizations dedicated to increasing love and devotion to the Holy Eucharist.

---

[12]*Ibid.* pp. 261-262.
[13]*Ibid.* p. 262.

72

SAINT PHILIP NERI

1515—1595

Philip was provided with a happy and comfortable childhood under the direction of an excellent stepmother, his own mother having died during his infancy. At the age of seventeen he was sent to be apprenticed to his uncle, who had a successful business at San Germano, at the foot of Monte Cassino, site of the famous Benedictine monastery. The thought of a prosperous business career repelled Philip, and he placed himself, instead, under the guidance of one of the monks of the monastery. Three years later he was found in Rome studying with the Augustinian Fathers, but instead of being ordained as expected, he abandoned his studies and for the next thirteen years lived a holy life while engaged in the active apostolate. He was eventually ordained on May 23, 1551, and attracted to himself a number of priestly followers, who lived a community life under his direction. This was the beginning of the Congregation of the Oratory, which was approved in 1575 by Pope Gregory XIII. These secular priests who continue to live in community without vows and devote themselves to prayer and preaching, look with a holy pride to Philip as the distinguished founder of their unique organization.

A man of advanced spirituality, Philip numbered among his friends such saints as Ignatius of Loyola, Camillus de Lellis, Charles Borromeo, Catherine dei Ricci, and Francis de Sales, who delighted, as did everyone who knew him, in his congenial and comforting manner. He often employed a gentle jest to veil the miracles which constantly surrounded him until the time of his death in his eightieth year.

The night following his saintly passing, several physicians officiated at the autopsy, during which the viscera were set aside.[1] The doctors opened his chest, which played a prominent part in one of the Saint's most remarkable mystical experiences. The day before Pentecost in the year 1544, while meditating in the catacombs of St. Se-

---

[1] *St. Philip Neri and the Roman Society of His Times.* Louis Ponnelle and Louis Bordet. Sheed and Ward. 1932. p. 556.

bastian, he had felt in an extraordinary way "filled with God." The doctors found that the swelling which had existed since that experience was caused by two broken ribs which were raised to form an arch over his enlarged heart. The pulmonary artery was very large, but the other organs appeared normal. They could not explain how the Saint had lived without experiencing extreme pain, and after a lengthy examination and a detailed consultation, they attested in the form of a written oath that the cause was supernatural and miraculous.[2]

The body was buried after three days, not in the common burial ground, but in a small chapel over the first arch of the nave of the Chiesa Nuovo. Four years later, on March 7, 1599, the coffin was opened. The following quotation is frequently reported in biographies of the Saint:

> They found the body covered with cobwebs and dust, which had got in through a crack in the lid of the coffin, caused by the moisture in the wall which had been built over it; his vestments were like so much dirt; the chasuble had become so rotten that it all fell to pieces, and the plate on which the Saint's name was engraved was covered with verdigris, so that they expected to find his body reduced to dust. On the following evening, however, having removed all the rubbish, they found not only his legs and arms and the whole body entire, but the breast and stomach so fresh and beautiful, and the skin and flesh so natural that everyone was astonished; the breast, moreover, retained its whiteness. The state of the body was considered by Andrea Cesalpino, Antonio Porto, and Ridolfo Silvestri, three of the first medical men of the time, to be undoubtedly miraculous; and they all three wrote upon the subject . . .[3]

The face, which had suffered a little, was covered with a silver mask, thereby fulfilling Philip's prophecy that his head would be placed in silver.[4]

---

[2]*St. Philip Neri, A Tribute.* Doreen Smith. Sands & Co., Ltd. London. 1945. p. 83.

[3]*The Life of Saint Philip Neri.* Father Bacci. Kegan Paul, Trench, Trubner & Co., Ltd. 1902. Vol. II, pp. 125-126. In spite of the opinion of these physicians, the Fathers of the Congregation Oratorii S. Philippi de Urbe do not consider the preservation of the body at this disinterment to be "miraculous" by any means, since the viscera were removed and the body embalmed in a simple fashion after the Saint's autopsy in 1595. The foregoing quotation is given merely to describe the conditions under which the body was found and the state of the relic at that time.

[4]*Ibid.* p. 127.

The body of the Saint, after it was clothed in fresh garments, including the chasuble in which he had said his last Mass, was put into a new coffin of cypress, and in the presence of many distinguished cardinals and bishops, was again consigned to the same tomb in which it had previously been placed.

A wealthy devotee of the Saint, Nero del Nero, who was greatly indebted to Philip for miracles worked in his behalf, having at first resolved to furnish a splendid coffin of silver in token of his appreciation, changed his design and commenced building a magnificent shrine of precious stones and costly materials, which can be seen and admired in the Chiesa Nuovo.

On the completion of the chapel seven years after Philip's death, the body of the Saint was again exposed, and after an impressive ceremony witnessed by the ecclesiastics of Rome and the members of the Saint's community, the relic was borne in solemn procession to this elegant chapel, where it still reposes beneath the altar.

After its solemn exposition during the year of the Saint's canonization, which was solemnized by Gregory XV on March 12, 1622, the body, which had undergone a simple embalmment at the time of the autopsy, was again embalmed in a more extensive manner.[5]

The whole body of the Saint is exposed for veneration under the altar of his chapel; the hands are completely visible but the face is covered by its silver mask. No bones were ever taken from the body. The only first-class relics distributed consist of flakes of skin which were lifted at the time of the last embalmment.

---

[5]This information was taken from the statement prepared by the Congregation Oratorii S. Philippi de Urbe, Rome.

73

SAINT GERMAINE COUSIN

1579—1601

Germaine was born into poor circumstances in Pibrac, near Toulouse, France. Shortly after her birth she unfortunately lost her devoted mother. Her weak constitution, her withered right hand, and her scrofulous neck with its discharging sores made her an object of revulsion to her stepmother, who constantly persecuted her. It is recorded that the father also had little affection for the child, and so it may be rightly assumed, for he permitted her to be ejected from the house when the other children were born. She was forced to sleep in the stable upon a heap of twigs beneath a stair, was begrudgingly fed on scraps, was denied the company of the other children, whom she loved, and was required to shepherd the flocks even at a tender age.

The little shepherdess' virtues and sanctity did not go unnoticed by the villagers, for many of them witnessed unusual occurrences, which they considered miraculous. We are told that it was necessary for her to cross a stream which was often swollen by rain to reach the village church for her daily attendance at Mass. On one occasion, when the current was particularly strong, the villagers were astonished to see the rushing water separate to provide a dry passageway for her. The sheep, which she often took with her to church, never strayed from her staff which she stuck in the ground, and it is known that not once were they threatened by the wolves that inhabited the neighboring forest.

The most celebrated incident involving the little maiden, which is often depicted in her iconography, occurred one winter day when her stepmother was pursuing her with a stick, loudly accusing her of stealing bread to give to the poor. Upon being told to open her folded apron, there fell out only fragrant flowers of a variety unknown to the region. The witnesses of this event, Pierre Pailles and Jeanne Salaires, gave sworn testimony concerning this miracle, which is reminiscent of a similar marvel recorded of St. Elizabeth of Hungary.

One night Germaine died unattended on her pallet of straw, where her father found her sickly body the next morning. We are told that during the night two monks traveling from Toulouse were sleeping in the ruins of a nearby castle when they were awakened by angelic melodies. They saw a great beam of light rising from a distant building and extending into the sky. Heavenly figures were seen descending into the building and later ascending with another figure. Upon reaching Pibrac the next morning, they inquired if anyone had died during the night and were told of the death of the little shepherdess.

In view of her saintly conduct and the many miracles witnessed by the townsfolk, the body of the maiden was buried in the village church of Pibrac. Germaine was almost forgotten until the year 1644 when a distant relative named Edualde died. Two church workers, Gaillard Barous and Nicholas Case, set about preparing a grave for her adjacent to that of Germaine's. Upon lifting the flagstone covering the tomb, the workmen were amazed to find there a beautiful young girl lying in a perfect state of preservation. A tool which one of the men had used to remove the stone had slipped and injured the nose of the corpse, causing it to bleed profusely. The dress and the wreath of flowers upon her head had remained fresh and fragrant. The older villagers identified Germaine (who had died forty-three years before) by the withered arm and the wounds which the scrofulous condition had left on her neck. Her body was kept for many years in the sacristy in a lead casket, which is still preserved in the village church.

The unembalmed body was scrupulously examined sixteen years later and was found not only perfectly conserved but also entirely flexible.

The many miracles ascribed to her encouraged the Church officials to seek a formal authorization of her cultus, which met unfortunate delays, caused by the French Revolution. She was eventually raised to the honors of the altar during her formal canonization in 1867.

The virginal body which remained whole and incorrupt for almost two hundred years was barbarously destroyed in 1795 during the French Revolution. Now only some bones are kept in a figure representing the little Saint, which are clothed in garments of exquisite, lacy fabrics. The figure can be viewed through the Gothic windows of a magnificently crafted golden urn, which resembles a small church. A miniature kneeling figure of the little shepherdess, accompanied by small sheep, adorns the top.

This little Saint, so abused, neglected, and mistreated during her lifetime, has been greatly loved and venerated throughout the world, but especially in Pibrac where, on her feast day, June 15, huge pilgrimages wend their way to the basilica where special ceremonies are observed in her honor.

74

SAINT MARY MAGDALEN DE' PAZZI

1566—1607

St. Mary Magdalen was born to a Florentine family of great wealth and distinction, but from early childhood she shunned the finery and comfort of her station, preferring instead to dress simply and live religiously. The Saint encountered great difficulties in realizing her desire to enter the Carmelite convent, but her dream eventually became a reality during her sixteenth year with her joyful entrance into the Carmelite convent of Santa Maria degli Angeli in Florence.

Always an exemplary religious, the Saint patiently withstood almost unbelievable physical and spiritual distress, which was rewarded by mystical experiences and remarkable visions of Our Lord, the Blessed Virgin, and a number of saints. On many occasions she experienced the phenomenon of levitation, performed many miracles, was granted the privilege of viewing in Purgatory the souls of persons she had known, and was further privileged to view and suffer the Passion of Our Lord.

The holy Carmelite died during her forty-second year after suffering a lengthy and agonizing illness. Her body, clothed in silk, was buried beneath the high altar of the church of the monastery. From the tomb there emanated the sweet odor of sanctity, which has been recognized about the body on numerous occasions even to the present day.

During the year following her death, permission was obtained to move the sacred relic into the cloister and

> . . . when the casket was opened, the corpse was found to be still entire, fresh-looking, and fleshlike in its softness. Blond hairs still adhered to the head; the whole body was flexible. The Saint appeared as one recently deceased. Yet the clothing was wet, for the place of burial was a damp one with running water nearby.[1]

---

[1]*Seraph among Angels, The Life of St. Mary Magdalene de' Pazzi.* Sr. Mary Minima. The Carmelite Press. Chicago. 1958. p. 348.

The body of the Saint soon exhibited the phenomenon of transpiration, the secretion being described as ". . . a liquor as oil, more odiferous [odoriferous] than balm."

> When the nuns took their precious charge back with them into the cloister, they discovered a new circumstance. From the knees of the sacred body trickled a liquid of exquisite scent. It looked like oil, but it was not. It was examined, but its nature could not be ascertained. At any rate, this liquid absorbed into pieces of cloth was distributed to the faithful and carried afar. For twelve years the phenomenon persisted, until the year 1620; then it stopped.[2]

The body of the Saint was carefully examined during the exhumations of 1612 and 1625, and again in 1663 for the trial of canonization. Each time it was testified by all the witnesses that the preservation was of a miraculous nature, ". . . as this body is in no part opened nor embalmed, nor has any artifice been done to it."

The monastery's annals record many visitors and devout persons who are distinguished from an historical point of view. During the last century there were two very noteworthy visitors, one being Pope Pius VII, who visited the shrine twice, the first time while passing through Florence on his way to Paris in 1804, the second time while on a return trip to the Apostolic See in 1815. The other visitor was Thérèse Martin, later to be known throughout the world as St. Therese of the Child Jesus and of the Holy Face. The future saint visited the shrine accompanied by her father, her sister and a group of French pilgrims, all of whom were on the trip home after having visited Pope Leo XIII on the occasion of his sacerdotal golden jubilee. The episode is charmingly related in her autobiography, *The Story of a Soul:*

> In Florence we saw the shrine of St. Mary Magdalen de' Pazzi, in the choir of the Carmelite Church. All the pilgrims wanted to touch the Saint's tomb with their Rosaries, but my hand was the only one small enough to pass through the grating. So I was deputed for this important and lengthy task, and I did it with pride.

At the death of St. Mary Magdalen, her sisters in religion affirmed that the body ". . . did not shed horror as dead bodies do, but on the contrary, at the death of that holy soul, her face remained cheerful

---

[2]*Ibid.* p. 326.

and all her limbs as white as ivory." Today, after three hundred seventy years, the ivory has grown yellow and the face still smiles. A recent description of the relic reads as follows:

> The Saint, delicately laid in the crystal and gilded bronze urn, looks gently asleep awaiting resurrection. Her rather pronounced nose still has fleshy nostrils and the smile of her toothless mouth, (she had lost all her teeth during her life), disappears into a graceful dimple. The hands, slightly large for the person, are still recognized as those that the painter Santi di Tito has left us in the portrait of the Saint at the age of sixteen. The feet, so very intact in flesh and muscles, would seem still able to move nimbly and lightly along the poor rooms of the monastery. Those bare feet that are so in contrast with the rich black and gold brocade of the robe and the white and gold of the mantle, still speak of the exterior and above all the interior poverty that the Saint loved and lived in the bareness of her soul destitute of all except God.[3]

From the day of her death, the Saint's body has been held in great veneration. Even today, after more than three hundred seventy years, principally on occasions of her feasts, whole pilgrimages and individual faithful ascend the hills of Careggi, to the monastery church, to view the perfectly preserved body of this great saint.[4]

---

[3]This description of the Saint was supplied by her convent.

[4]Unless otherwise indicated, all quotations are drawn from the original documents in the archives of the Carmel of Saint Mary Magdalen de' Pazzi, Careggi, Florence. The sisters of this monastery have kindly read and approved the contents of this chapter.

The incorrupt body of St. Mary Magdalen de' Pazzi (d. 1607) in the Carmelite Church of Florence, Italy.

75

SAINT CAMILLUS DE LELLIS

1550—1614

The symbol of the Red Cross, representing mercy and help to persons in need, is thought to have originated in recent times, but it was first used when St. Camillus founded the Order of Ministers of the Sick in 1586. Having received Papal approval for the order, with the added permission of wearing such a symbol on the front of their black habits, the members of the new nursing order, on donning their distinctive robes, fulfilled in a unique fashion the dream of the Saint's mother before his birth, in which she saw a child with a red cross on his breast and a standard in his hand, leading other children who bore the same sign.

In the hope that her babe would draw to himself the blessing of the Child Jesus and the protection of St. Francis of Assisi, Camilla Compellio, wife of John of Lellis, gave birth to the future Saint in a stable. Being sixty years of age at the time, she was henceforth called Lady Elizabeth in honor of the Gospel saint who also gave birth during her advanced years.

The child proved to be of little consolation to the aged mother, being vivacious and troublesome, a participator and instigator of many street brawls, a frequent truant from school, and a compulsive gambler. By the time he was thirteen years of age, he was so tall and robust that only the foolhardy challenged his opinion or tested his physical prowess. It is uncertain exactly how tall the young man grew, but it is known that he towered over his contemporaries and might well have been considered a giant.

Camillus' father had been the captain and commander of the local garrison at the time of Camillus' birth, and his son, at the age of nineteen, joined him in the army to fight against the Turks at Lepanto. The father died soon afterwards, and Camillus found it necessary to seek treatment for an ulcerated leg at the hospital of St. James in Rome. He rejoined the army in 1571 and fought in Dalmatia and Africa. At the time of his discharge in 1574, he had gambled away his inheritance, his military equipment, and his weapons. Feeling little inclination to work, he preferred instead to beg for alms at the Cathedral of Manfredonia, where he was offered the job of a mason's helper by one of the churchgoers. This position brought him into contact with the Capuchin Fathers, whose monastery was under repair. He experienced a complete reform and a rekindling of faith when one of the monks took him aside one day for counseling. He eventually sought admittance into the monastery and proved himself to be an exemplary religious, whose redoubled austerities were intended to atone for a wasted past.

The recurring ulceration of his leg compelled the superiors to dismiss him, but after his cure he was again accepted. Another recurrence of the disease resulted in his final dismissal from the community, to the profound disappointment of Camillus and the superiors. Again he applied for treatment at the hospital of St. James in Rome, where he had been treated twice before. In spite of the affliction, which was to plague him the rest of his life, he diligently saw to the needs of the sick and was eventually appointed procurator, director and master of the house.

Dissatisfied with the servants' lack of cooperation and constant unfaithfulness to duty, he began the establishment of an order whose members were to bind themselves by a fourth vow—to the charitable care of the sick and dying—a vow still made by members of the Order, in addition to those of poverty, chastity and obedience.

With the encouragement of his confessor, St. Philip Neri, he commenced studying for the priesthood and was ordained on June 10, 1584. The Saint was a prodigy of charity, performing the most menial and repugnant tasks and lavishing the most tender care on the most repulsive cases, always seeing hidden beneath the afflictions of the poor, the image of the Creator.

In addition to the diseased leg, the Saint, during his last years, endured also a painful rupture, frequent renal colics, and spasmodic stomach aches.[1] After bidding farewell to the institutions for the sick and dying which he had established throughout Italy, he journeyed to Rome to prepare for his death, which occurred on July 14, 1614. After the usual autopsy and the extraction of the heart, his grieving followers buried the remains in a crypt in the Church of Saint Mary Magdalene, which the Saint had acquired for the motherhouse of the order in Rome. (The old church was completely reconstructed be-

---

[1]*St. Camillus, The Saint of the Red Cross.* P. Mario Vanti, O.S. Cam., Ph.D. Published by the Order of St. Camillus. Rome. 1950. p. 69.

tween 1668 and 1698 and is considered to be one of the most beautiful and artistically endowed of the magnificent churches of Rome.) Eleven years after the death of the Saint, Pope Urban VIII gave permission for the exhumation of the body. Although the outside coffin had rotted in the damp soil, the body was found perfectly conserved, fresh, and flexible in the inner coffin. The vestments had deteriorated and on the face were seen traces of the wax used in making the death mask. The attending doctors were so amazed at the excellent condition of the body that they made an incision to test it and declared that the flesh reacted as though it were alive.[2]

During the nine days that the body was on view, enormous crowds witnessed the flow of a pure, fragrant liquid which proceeded from the incision made by the doctors. The faithful soaked cloths in it, and it affected many cures.

In 1640 the tomb was reopened, and once more the coffin was found in a deplorable condition, which permitted sand and mud to enter the interior. Although the body remained incorrupt, a slight discoloration was noted. After being placed in a new coffin, the relic was interred in what was thought to be a safer tomb, but unfortunately, the flood waters of the Tiber River infiltrated the grave and reduced the relic to a skeleton.

The Order of St. Camillus, or the Camillians, as the order is popularly called, is the custodian of many singular relics and memorabilia of the Saint: in the apartment of Camillus are kept some of his clothes, vestments, autographed writings, and the deathmask. On the altar in the room in which he died are kept, in their separate reliquaries, the incorrupt heart and the right foot of the Saint. The most prized of all the Saint's relics, the bones of his body, are kept in an artistic urn beneath the altar dedicated to him in the Maddalena.

At the time of the holy founder's death his order numbered 330 professed members, who labored in fifteen cities of Italy. Their numbers consistently increased until the suppressions and confiscations of the nineteenth century, when a decrease in the ranks occurred. In 1964 the Camillians were located in eleven countries of Europe, in Canada, the United States, South America, Formosa, and Thailand, its membership numbering almost 1,350 dedicated souls.

Benedict XIV beatified Camillus in 1742 and canonized him four years later. With St. John of God, his Spanish counterpart, St. Camil-

---

[2] *Life of Saint Camillus.* C. C. Martindale, S. J. Sheed & Ward. London. 1946. p. 154.

lus has been given a triple designation by Pope Leo XIII and Pope Pius XI as the patron of the sick, of nurses, and of hospitals.

VENERABLE JOHN OF JESUS MARY

1564—1615

As the son of a renowned physician, Diego de San Pedro, John was provided with an excellent education and came to know the Discalced Carmelites while pursuing his studies in Salamanca. He was professed in that order at Pastrana, was soon thereafter appointed professor at the Colegio Complutense, and was later ordained a priest in 1590.

John extended the reform of the Seraphic Mother, Teresa of Avila, to houses of his order and attended the general chapter that decreed the separation of the Reform from the old Order of Carmel. At the conclusion of the general chapter, he was appointed master of novices at St. Ann's of Genoa and was later transferred to La Scala in Rome, where he again formed and influenced the spiritual growth of many. He was instrumental in founding the Italian Congregation and was elected second definitor and procurator general, finally becoming general in 1611. After completing his term, he retired to the convent of St. Sylvester in Montecompatre, Rome, where he died on Ascension Day after a brief but distinguished life. It is in Montecompatre that his darkened body now reposes in a crystal urn.

The learned writings of this Spanish mystic deal with the proper spiritual formation of both religious superiors and subjects. Although he was a lover of solitude and was retiring by nature, he was nevertheless the counselor of many cardinals, kings and princes and was greatly esteemed by Pope Paul V.

SAINT ROSE OF LIMA

1586—1617

The first canonized saint of the New World was given the name Isabel at her christening, but because of her red cheeks and extraordinary beauty she was affectionately called Rose. At a later time she annexed to this name that of Santa Maria. While still a child she undertook fasts, performed penances and was favored with many visions and mystical experiences. Her parents proved to be obstacles to her embracing the cloistered life, to which she felt attracted, but she found some satisfaction for the solitude she desired by frequently visiting the small hermitage she had built in the garden of her home.

At the age of twenty, Rose joined the Third Order of St. Dominic, took St. Catherine of Siena as her patroness, and increased her already rigorous fasts and severe mortifications. When her Spanish parents were in need of financial assistance, Rose helped them by selling flowers, working in the fields, and taking in needlework. In addition to these labors, she set aside a room in her home in which she somehow found time to help destitute children and the elderly infirm—a social service conducted yet today from part of Rose's old house, which still exists. The Saint was once brought to the attention of the Inquisition. And her prayers are credited with saving Lima from an invasion of pirates.

St. Rose died on the very day she had predicted, but for several days it was impossible to hold her funeral, owing to the crowds of mourners, both rich and poor, who displayed great love and devotion to her. As she had requested, her penitentially scarred and emaciated body was buried in the cloister of St. Dominic's Church, where it was found entire, fresh-colored, and fragrant eighteen months later. In 1630, although still exhaling a delightful perfume, the body was found somewhat wasted and desiccated.[1]

The relics of the Saint are now conserved in two locations. In the Dominican Church of Santo Domingo there is a special altar dedi-

---

[1] *The Physical Phenomena of Mysticism.* Herbert Thurston, S. J. Henry Regnery Co. Chicago. 1952. p. 249.

cated to the Peruvian saints, on which rest three golden chests containing the skulls of St. Rose and St. Martin de Porres and the remains of Bl. John Mathias. Although these cannot usually be seen, they are exposed on special occasions. The rest of her relics are kept a few blocks away in the small church which was built on the very grounds on which Rose lived. This small structure, which was elevated to the dignity of a basilica, also possesses many objects which the Saint wore or used in life, including a cross from which she is reported to have once received the Precious Blood, a ring which was miraculously inscribed to her, and a thorny piece of metal she wore to chastise herself. In the garden can be found the small hermitage and the well into which she threw the key to the lock which bound the chain she had put around her waist as a penance.

Having been canonized by Clement X on April 12, 1671, Rose was promptly proclaimed the patroness of Peru, the Indies, the Philippines and of all America.

78

VENERABLE MARIA VELA

1561—1617

At the age of fifteen, Maria Vela entered the Cistercian Convent of Santa Ana in Avila, where she lived in great sanctity for the rest of her forty-two years on earth. She was an outstanding and useful member of the community, being an accomplished musician and choir director, and skilled with the needle. As sacristan, she performed her tasks with great care and thoroughness, and she exercised tender solicitude and rare tact in dealing with her charges during her tenure as novice mistress.

Maria suffered from both physical and spiritual afflictions, which she endured with heroic patience. At times her jaws became mysteriously locked, preventing her from receiving Holy Communion or from eating, and she experienced frequent fainting spells. She was beneficently supported in her various trials by many visions and was variously encouraged, rebuked, or consoled by locutions, particularly from Our Lord. She was often rapt in ecstasies and levitated frequently during prayer.

Reports of her sanctity spread beyond the walls of her enclosure, and at the time of her death the convent was besieged by crowds seeking relics and requesting to view the remains of the Saint. She was declared a venerable by popular acclamation, which could legally be done in those days with the permission of the Church. The circumstances accompanying her death necessitated a departure from the traditional rules of the convent governing the burial of its members. The bishop, Don Francisco de Gamarra, directed that the body be placed in a coffin and that instead of interment in the cloister, the body should be entombed at the foot of the altar dedicated to Our Lady of the Sun, to whom she had shown particular devotion. The bishop presided at the funeral, which was attended by the canons of the cathedral and the nobles and gentry at Avila.

After the Venerable's death many mysterious occurrences were recorded, and there were instances when her voice was heard speaking to her dear friend and fellow religious, Maria de Avila, during the community recitation of Matins, and her singing voice was recognized accompanying the sisters during Benediction services.[1]

Two years after her death, with the permission of the bishop, the casket was transferred to a new position in the chapel so that it could be seen by both the religious behind the grill and those in the chapel. During this transfer, the body was found in a perfect state of preservation, a condition unaccounted for since the body had not been embalmed.

The coffin has been opened several times since then, in 1664, 1808, 1812, and in 1943.

During the canonical visit made to the convent by the Reverend Bishop Dr. D. Santos Moro Briz on November 6, 1943, the Reverend Abbess Manuel del Pilar Santos asked as a special favor permission to lower the body of Ven. Maria and view it, which the Reverend Bishop graciously granted. The Reverend Abbess described the exhumation and examination of the body in this manner:

> . . . on the fourteenth day of the same month, after previous notice, at four in the afternoon, the afore-mentioned Bishop came in person to the monastery accompanied by his Mayordomo, D. Jesús Jiménez, and the Chaplain of the Community, D. Flavio Aguilera. When they had entered the cloister, the Bishop ordered the nuns to lower the casket, which contains the body, while the afore-mentioned dignitaries went with the Superiors, to the room of Isabella the Catholic there to see and examine the books and The Life of the Venerable, written by this nun herself, which they did with admiration, both for the excellent state of preservation in which they found these documents and for the beautiful handwriting.
>
> With indescribable emotion and enthusiasm, the nuns who remained in the choir proceeded to lower the sarcophagus, which is covered with red damask and curtained with green velvet. Once lowered, it was placed on the table which had been prepared beforehand, and the waiting Bishop, Superiors and other dignitaries were notified. When the community, the Bishop and the Abbess were all together again, they opened the sarcophagus and saw that the body was intact, except for part of the eyes, nose and lips.
>
> By order of the Bishop and Superiors, the body was removed from

---

[1] *The Third Mystic of Avila, The Self Revelation of Maria Vela.* Frances Parkinson Keyes, Translator. Farrar, Straus & Cudahy. New York. 1960. p. 36. See the chapter on Blessed Peter Ghigenzi, whose voice also heard under similar circumstances. Blessed Clelia Barbieri who died in 1870 can still be heard in convents she founded throughout Italy.

the casket with great care and respect and placed on a white cloth. This removal occasioned no disturbance whatsoever in its condition, except for the loss of a tooth which the Abbess offered the Bishop, but which, through delicacy, he did not accept; instead, he insisted upon leaving it with the community as a relic. The Venerable's woolen habit, which had disintegrated, was removed, but her undergarments were like new, fresh, and whole. Another favor, which he granted with his usual graciousness, was then asked of the Bishop: namely, that the body might be left where it was for three days, in order that a new habit might be made for it, like those at present worn by the community; then she was clothed in a cowl, hood and veil, all very clean and well arranged.

On the 17th, at seven in the afternoon, the Bishop, accompanied by his Mayordomo Jesús Jiménez, Flavio Aguilera, Leandro Martin and Venancio Moro, met the community and again viewed the body of the Venerable, now dressed in her new habit. The sarcophagus was closed with two keys, one of which remained in the keeping of the Abbess and the other in the keeping of the Bishop. . . .[2]

The body of the Venerable now rests in a crystal reliquary, which is still situated in its lofty position between the upper and lower choirs and can be viewed by both those in the church and the sisters in the cloistered choir. The rigid but only slightly yellowed body of the Venerable has miraculously contradicted the laws of nature for over three hundred fifty years.

---

[2]*The Land of Stones and Saints.* Frances Parkinson Keyes. Doubleday & Co., Inc. New York. 1957. pp. 330-331.

79

SAINT FRANCIS DE SALES

1567—1622

Born of a distinguished family of Thorens, located twelve miles from Annecy, Francis received an excellent education at Paris and Padua but declined his father's worldly ambitions in favor of a priestly vocation. His brilliant preaching, his artful direction of souls, and his countless conversions brought him to the attention of Church officials, and in 1602 he was appointed Bishop of Geneva. Because of his successes in this post, he was offered the bishopric of Paris but declined the position through humility.

His saintly friends included St. Vincent de Paul and St. Philip Neri. St. John Bosco, the miracle-worker of the nineteenth century, was so attracted to Francis that the religious order he founded, the Salesians, was named for this saintly bishop. Another saint and his good friend, St. Jane Frances de Chantal, assisted him in founding the Order of the Visitation, which now boasts one hundred eighty-five monasteries throughout the world.

St. Francis suffered atrocious pains on his deathbed, which were only intensified by the ignorance of the attending physicians. The day before his death they applied hot irons to his head to revive him from a coma. Although applied with the best of intentions, the irons were nevertheless so ineptly applied as to burn through the flesh to the bone, making marks which are still visible on the skull.[1]

St. Francis died during his fifty-sixth year, and the twentieth of his episcopate. His entrance into Heaven was made known supernaturally to many of his friends and relatives, especially to Madame de Chantal, who was informed of the death by an interior voice.[2]

During his autopsy the body was embalmed[3] and the heart extracted. This was placed in a silver coffer and was given to the

---

[1]The condition of the skull was reported in correspondence with the author by the Sister Archivist of the Visitation Convent of St. Marie, Annecy.

[2]*The Life of St. Francis de Sales.* Robert Ornsby, M.A. D. & J. Sadlier & Co. New York. p. 144.

[3]*Ibid.* p. 145.

Church of the Visitation at Lyons. A clear oil has exuded from this relic at intervals throughout the years.[4]

After much opposition by the local authorities, Louis XIII granted permission for the removal of the body from Lyons (the city in which he had died) to Annecy, where he had requested to be buried. Accompanied on this journey by a great concourse of people and attended by numerous miracles, his body was brought to the first monastery of the Visitation and placed under the altar of the church. The place of entombment was quickly covered with gold and silver ex-votos by his grateful clients.[5]

In compliance with the requirements of the Sacred Congregation of Rites prior to beatification, the body of the holy bishop was exhumed. On August 4, 1632, ten years after his death, it was found perfectly conserved.[6] At a later date, however, only dust and bones were found.

Following a number of translations, one of which was attended by the king and queen, nine bishops, and five hundred thirty-two priests,[7] the remains were placed in the Basilica of the Visitation at Annecy in 1911, where they still repose. The bones of the Saint are connected by silver threads and rest in a composite figure that is clad in exquisitely embroidered episcopal garments. The bronze and crystal urn which contains the relic is situated on one side of the main altar, while the bones of St. Jane de Chantal, which are similarly placed in a religiously vested figure, repose on the opposite side in an almost identical urn.

St. Francis de Sales was beatified in 1661, was canonized in 1665, and was declared a Doctor of the Church in 1877.[8] In view of his excellent writings, of which *Introduction To A Devout Life* and *Treatise On The Love of God* are the most popular, Pope Pius XI, in 1922, designated him the patron of journalists and writers.

---

[4]*The Physical Phenomena of Mysticism.* Thurston. p. 247.

[5]*"Translation des Reliques de Saint François de Sales et de Sainte Jeanne-Françoise de Chantal." Guide-Manuel du Pèlerin à Annecy.* Published by the Visitation Order. Annecy. 1911. p. 45.

[6]*Ibid.* pp. 45-46.

[7]Ornsby. *Op. cit.* p. 146.

[8]Chroniclers frequently disagree on the dates of the occurrences in the life of this saint; however, all the dates mentioned in this entry are taken directly from data supplied to the author by the Visitation Convent of Annecy.

80

SAINT JOSAPHAT

1580—1623

Born at Vladimir, then a part of the Polish Province of Wolyn, John Kuncevyc was baptized in the Ruthenian Orthodox Church, which was officially united to the Roman Church on November 23, 1595, during the Saint's sixteenth year. After some experience as a tradesman, he entered the Monastery of the Trinity at Vilan, which was conducted by the Order of St. Basil the Great, and accepted the name of Josaphat. He was ordained four years later; his quick advancement in the Order culminated in his consecration as the Archbishop of Polotsk in 1617.

Josaphat labored gallantly on behalf of the Roman Primacy, but his efforts to maintain and spread Christian unity were met with acute difficulties from Orthodox factions, who refused allegiance to Peter's successors. Josaphat's courageous sermons, aimed at the dissenters, won for him many enemies, who almost succeeded in murdering him when he refused to accept a usurper's claim to the bishopric. Had it not been for armed guards, the infuriated crowd would have been satisfied with nothing less than his martyrdom.

During one of his sermons, delivered while on a pastoral tour in October, 1623, the holy bishop offered to God the sacrifice of his life for Church unity. "Some of you people in Vitebsk want to kill me. Well, here I am, and I have come here of my own free will. I am your shepherd and I should be happy to give my life for you. If it please God that I should die for unity under the earthly headship of St. Peter's successor, so be it. I am ready to die for truth." Two weeks later, inspired no doubt by these words, a planned confrontation was staged by the followers of the Orthodox priest who antagonized the supporters of the bishop. During the melee that ensued, the dissenters stormed the bishop's residence, hacked and beat the bishop to death, and threw his remains into a nearby river.

The martyrdom having taken place on a Sunday, with the water burial the same day, the body of the Saint remained submerged until the following Friday, when it was retrieved by his followers, who found it beautiful and normal in spite of the ordeal.[1] The mutilated body was then interred at Biala in Podlesie.

Because of the numerous miracles which were occurring through Josaphat's intercession, King Sigmund, with the approval and support of Ukrainian and Polish ecclesiastics and civil authorities, petitioned Pope Urban VIII for Josaphat's canonization. In due time the ecclesiastical process which was initiated required the opening of the sepulcher and the identification of the remains. This was performed by the commission almost five years after the death of the martyred bishop. The body was found perfectly incorrupt and pliable although the vestments and interior clothes had rotted away because of the dampness. In order to satisfy the desires of the thousands of people who had flocked to the church on hearing the news of the miraculous condition of the body, the relic, after being dressed in new garments, was propped upon the episcopal throne for all to see. In an emotional gesture, George Tishkevick, bishop of Milton, raised the right hand of the dead bishop and blessed the throng. The Saint would seem almost to have been touched by the unusual benediction for his face broke out in droplets of sweat which were collected in handkerchiefs.[2]

The Commission again returned to the Church of St. Sophia for another recognition of the body in 1637. Again the vestments were found molded and disintegrated at the slightest touch. The hair and beard also fell away but the body retained its whiteness and suppleness while the skin remained pliant. The great gash over the forehead and the injuries to his face were clearly defined. Other wounds were discovered which were not inflicted during the martyrdom, namely those made by relic seekers who had successfully made off with the little fingers of both hands and one toe of the left foot.[3]

Mention must be made of the costly reliquary donated by Leo Kasimir Sapiha, who had been a friend of the Saint. Crafted of pure silver by skilled goldsmiths, the casket was surmounted by a life-size image of the Saint in a reclining position. Six kneeling silver angels supported the reliquary, whose walls were covered with pictures made of mother-of-pearl, depicting scenes of the martyrdom. It had been five years in the making by the time it was eventually presented

---

[1]*The Physical Phenomena of Mysticism.* Thurston. p. 251.

[2]*Life of St. Josaphat, Martyr of the Union.* Theodosia Boresky. Comet Press Books. New York. 1955. p. 279.

[3]*Ibid.* p. 282.

to the Church of St. Sophia in 1650. When the body of the Saint was being prepared for its occupancy, a new wonder presented itself, for the mortal wound on the forehead of the Saint, then dead twenty-seven years, opened and discharged fresh red blood.[4]

Many translations of the body with its silver reliquary were mandatory to prevent its destruction during periods in Polish history when the country was beset by invasions and wars. During those turbulent times the incorruption of the body was officially verified in 1674, and in 1767 it was again exposed in the monastery's church in Bila.

After a translation to Vienna, where it was taken for safekeeping, it was brought to the Basilica of St. Peter in Rome, where it has been displayed for a number of years. The body is still well preserved. Although the face has predominately skeletal features, it nevertheless remains in an amazing state of preservation, which is remarkable in view of the wounds inflicted during the martyrdom, the hazards it overcame during its initial water burial, the unfavorable conditions it endured in the tombs it occupied, and the frequent translations to which it was subjected.

Josaphat Kuncevyc, "The Apostle of Union," was canonized in 1867 by Pope Leo XIII.

---

[4]*Ibid.* p. 285.

81

VENERABLE MOTHER MARIA OF JESUS

1560—1640

The fragrant odor of jasmines and roses presaged the discovery of the incorrupt body of Venerable Mother Maria of Jesus at the opening of her sepulcher in 1929. To the amazement of witnesses, it was found that the body had exuded an oil which saturated her garments and kept the skin constantly moist. This mysterious oil and other wonders were declared to be unexplainable by the attending physicians and distinguished men of science who were present.

During her lifetime, the sanctity of the Venerable was recognized by none other than St. Teresa of Avila, who intervened when the seventeen-year-old girl's acceptance into the Discalced Carmelite Order was being debated by the sisters of the convent to which she had applied. The other sisters questioned the wisdom of accepting the young girl because of her fragile health, but St. Teresa recommended that she be welcomed "even though it should prove necessary for her to remain in bed all her life."

Mother Maria's religious life was distinguished by her devotion to the Holy Eucharist, and it was observed that she spent entire nights and major parts of the day before the Blessed Sacrament, so rapt in ecstasy that her companions could not detect the least trace of normal breathing motions.

After spending sixty-three years in the religious life, during which she served her order as a novice mistress and prioress, she died in the odor of sanctity at Toledo, where she had spent many fruitful years.

After having been examined several times during the years, the body of the Venerable had been examined carefully in 1915, previous to its last exhumation in 1929. At this time the distinguished personage witnessing the ceremony examined the seals on the sepulcher which had been placed there previously, and after declaring them to be intact, the carpenters proceeded to open the vault. Marveling at the sweet perfume of roses and jasmines, the Cardinal reverently and carefully removed the veil which covered the relic and exposed to view the perfectly preserved body, which was found dressed in the habit of the Order in which it had been placed during the 1915 exhumation. It was carefully removed and placed on a table for a closer examination. It was observed at this time that the body retained its perfect flexibility. The garments were discovered to be saturated with an odoriferous oil, which also coated the flesh of the entire body. A piece of the moistened flesh and a sample of the saturated clothing were taken for laboratory examination, and after being reclothed in fresh garments, the body was returned to the sepulcher.[1]

To the amazement of all, it was observed that everything which the Venerable had used in life retained the flowery fragrance observed about the body. These articles included a torture instrument (consisting of a belt with points), books, manuscripts, and the clothing she had used.[2] This delightful phenomenon was considered particularly mystifying since the Venerable had last touched them two hundred eighty-nine years before.

Her body is now enclosed in a marble sarcophagus at the Carmelite Convent of San Jose in Toledo, Spain, where it is expected to repeat similar manifestations at its next exhumation.

---

[1]*"El Cuerpo Incorrupto de la Venerable Madre Maria de Jesús, Carmelita Descalza.* Fr. Florencio del Niño Jesús, C.D., Provincial de los Carmelitas Descalzos de Castilla. April, 1929.

[2]*Ibid.*

82

SAINT JEANNE DE LESTONNAC

1556—1640

During the time that Calvinism was flourishing in Bordeaux, St. Jeanne's father steadfastly clung to Catholicism while her mother apostatized. Unable to influence a change in her daughter's religion, the mother severely mistreated the child, who only turned more fervently and prayerfully to her faith. When Jeanne was seventeen, she married Gaston de Montferrant, who was related to two royal houses of France. The marriage was a happy one, but her husband died in 1597, leaving her to care for their four small children. When they came of age, she entered the Cistercian monastery of Les Feuillantes at Toulouse, a move her son violently opposed. Two of her daughters later followed her into the religious life, and the youngest daughter married.

After spending six months in the convent, Sister Jeanne suffered a complete breakdown in health and was obliged to leave the Order on the advice of her superiors. She experienced an almost miraculous recovery as soon as she left. Returning to Bordeaux, she attracted many young women, who eventually became the first novices of the order she envisioned, the Institution of Notre Dame,[1] whose rule was approved by Pope Paul V in 1607. Realizing the harmful influence the Calvinistic heresy had on young people, the members of the Order devoted themselves to counteracting the evil by opening schools for girls. Both their institutions and their order met with great success under Jeanne's capable administration and saintly influence.

Mother de Lestonnac was confronted with a great trial, which for two years she bore with heroic patience. One of the sisters invented slanderous stories about her which were believed even by Cardinal de Sourdis. She was deposed as superior and mistreated in every possible way. The patient and humble attitude with which she endured this persecution eventually won the hearts of all, and she was completely vindicated. Because of her advanced age, she refused to be reinstated

---

[1] The order is also referred to as the Company of Mary, and the Religious of Notre Dame of Bordeaux.

as superior; instead, she spent the last years of her life in assisting new foundations and revising the order's rule and constitution.

The Saint died on the Feast of the Purification in 1640. Her body is reported to have remained fresh and supple and exhaling a sweet fragrance for days after her death. Many also noticed a brilliant light surrounding the bier, and numerous miracles occurred. She was buried in the cemetery of the convent on the Rue du Ha, where the body was later found perfectly conserved.

At the time of the French Revolution in 1791, in order to protect the sacred body from defilement, it was taken to the home of friends on the Rue Porte-Dijeaux for concealment, but it was unfortunately found by the revolutionaries, who profaned it and buried it in a hole with the carcass of a horse. In the year 1822, it was found by Mother du Terrail, who transported it to the cathedral. There it was met by a solemn procession which escorted it to the Chapel of the Institution, where it remains to this day.[2]

In 1901 the relic was exhumed for the beatification; the bones were all identified and the body reconstructed. The attending physicians testified that the Saint had been a large and beautiful woman and that she had been left-handed. A few of the bones are conserved in a glass reliquary at the house of the Order in Bordeaux. During the restoration of the chapel in 1956, the greater part of the remains were put into a white marble coffin and placed under the altar where Mass is said each morning.[3]

The former wife, mother, widow, and holy foundress was canonized by Pope Pius XII on May 15, 1949.

---

[2]Information in this paragraph is taken from data supplied by the director of the shrine of the Saint.

[3]*Ibid.*

83

SAINT JANE FRANCES DE CHANTAL

1572—1641

Their eight years of married life were happy ones for the Baron and Baronness de Chantal, the couple being ideally suited to one another. Shortly after the birth of Jane's sixth child, the Baron met his death in a hunting accident and the youthful widow then devoted all her energies to caring for her children and nursing her aged and difficult father-in-law, into whose home she had retired.

Several years later the Saint met St. Francis de Sales, who became her spiritual director, and in 1607 they formulated the plans for the Visitation Order. Three years later, the first house of the Order was established in Annecy, and circumstances permitted the Saint to join it. Two of her children accompanied their mother before completing their education, and her son, who was vehemently opposed to his mother's religious vocation, prostrated himself before the door when it came time to bid farewell, creating the dramatic situation which resulted in the mother stepping over her son's body to answer the divine call. From that date until her death she participated in founding eighty-six monasteries of the Order.

The Saint died at Mouline, December 13, 1641, after outliving her dear friend, St. Francis de Sales, by nineteen years. Her cause for beatification suffered unfortunate delays, but eventually the recognition of her relics was ordered. On December 1, 1722, eighty-one years after the Saint's death, the Bishop of Geneva, the Apostolic Commissioners, Her Most Serene Highness, Princess Éléanor-Philippine, and the sisters of the community of Annecy assembled for the opening of the tomb.

Mother Favre de Charmette, Superior of the Visitation of Annecy, in writing of the event in a circular letter dated January 12, 1729, which was distributed to the houses of the Order, related that when the Bishop of Geneva ordered the leaden case to be opened,

. . . we saw our venerable Foundress clothed in our holy habit, the beads at her side, a crucifix on her breast. Her habit appeared uninjured, save the presence of some white spots caused by the dampness of the vault, which is over one of the canals of the lake. We saw on the head of the venerable servant of God the remains of a crown, which had not lost all its freshness. Nothing was out of order around the person. We recognized her by the original portrait that we have. The air of majesty and holiness that shone upon her face commanded our respect and veneration, and we silently returned thanks to God for making us the custodians of so precious a treasure . . .[1]

Of the numerous translations of the relic, the most unusual occurred in 1793 during the French Revolution when the sisters were ordered to vacate the convent. To protect the relics of St. Jane and those of St. Francis de Sales from defilement, the sisters hurriedly hid the skeletons in a mattress and conveyed them by boat across the lake to the Château de Duingt, which belonged to the family of one of the sisters. The religious authorities were informed that in the urns which formerly contained the relics of the saints, there were placed the bones of other souls. In 1806 when peace was restored, the bones of St. Francis were placed in the cathedral and those of St. Jane were brought to the Church of St. Maurice.[2]

Just as the heart of St. Francis de Sales was attended by a phenomenon, that is, an exudation of oil, so the heart of the foundress displayed an unexplainable prodigy, but one of a different nature. Shortly after its extraction, the heart and eyes of the Saint were placed in the possession of the convent of Nevers. Although the heart remained, for the most part, shrunken in size, it would

. . . swell at times like a heart under the pressure of sorrow. On the eve of great crises that have desolated the Church, it has been seen to expand and swell like a heart about to burst into groans.[3]

This holy wife, mother, widow and foundress was beatified in 1751 and canonized in 1767.

[1]*St. Chantal and the Foundation of the Visitation.* Monseigneur Bougaud, Bishop of Laval. Benziger Bros. New York. 1895. Vol. II, pp. 399-400. The body of the holy foundress is reported by Thurston (*The Physical Phenomena of Mysticism,* p. 240) as having been embalmed, but the excellent condition of the body, though interred in the situation described, can certainly be considered an unusual preservation.

[2]"*Translation des Reliques de Saint François de Sales et de Sainte Jeanne Françoise de Chantal.*" *Guide-Manuel du Pèlerin à Annecy.* Published by the Visitation Order. Annecy. 1911. pp. 48-50.

[3]Monseigneur Bougaud. *Op. cit.* p. 426.

A composite figure of St. Jane, clad in the habit of her order, contains the bones of the Saint which are connected with silver cords. The relic is contained in a bronze and crystal urn that is situated in the sanctuary of the Basilica of the Visitation, which place is doubly sanctified by the presence of the relics of St. Francis de Sales.

84

SAINT JOHN SOUTHWORTH

1592—1654

Of a distinguished Lancashire family who remained staunch in the Faith during the persecutions of penal times, St. John Southworth, after his ordination, heroically ministered to the faithful in Lancaster and London during the same trying period and always under the threat of imprisonment or death. He was apprehended many times for exercising his priestly functions on English soil, but somehow managed to serve only short sentences. During the plague of 1636, assisted by his fellow martyr, St. Henry Morse, he distributed alms to the stricken families in the Westminster district who, known to be Catholic, were deliberately and cruelly denied assistance by the parish officials. After St. Henry Morse fell victim to the disease, St. John continued in his apostolic endeavors, and four hundred families are said to have received material aid and spiritual assistance by his gallant ministrations. His final apprehension occurred in 1654. After refusing to disavow his priesthood, he was sentenced to die and heroically accepted his martyrdom on June 28th, 1654. After being hanged, drawn and quartered, the mangled body was bought by the Spanish Ambassador, Don Flento de Cardenas, who had the remains reconstructed and carefully embalmed by a surgeon, Dr. James Clark. The body was then conveyed to the English College at Douay, France, where the Saint had received his ecclesiastical training and had performed his sacerdotal functions as a newly ordained priest. His grave immediately became a place of pilgrimage and many cures were recorded.

During the time of the French Revolution, in order to save the relic from profanation or destruction, it was secretly hidden on May 4th, 1793, by four students and the prefect general. The place of interment was eventually lost to memory, and the relic remained missing for one hundred thirty-four years, until its accidental discovery on July 15, 1927, by workmen who were digging a new foundation.

The remains were found wrapped in linen bands of a brownish tint.

The trunk had suffered a little from the effects of water, but the flesh of the limbs was mostly unaffected. The sockets of both eyes were empty and the ears and hands had been severed. The head was in a particularly good state of preservation, the skin having assumed a coppery tint; a slight moustache and a beard of a chestnut color were noted.[1]

After definite identification was made, the relic was conveyed back to England and placed in the Douay Room of St. Edmund's College. On Dec. 15, 1929, the holy martyr was beatified, and the following year the body, clad in red vestments, was solemnly translated to Westminster Cathedral and placed in the Chapel of St. George and the English Martyrs, where it still reposes in a crystal reliquary. The face is now covered by a silver mask, and the missing hands were replaced by wooden ones covered with silver leaf. The incorruption of the body is, of course, attributed completely to its having been carefully embalmed.

Pope Paul VI, on October 25, 1970, canonized forty martyrs of England and Wales who were selected from the hundreds of Catholics who died for the Faith during the 16th and 17th centuries. Numbered in this group were John Southworth and his gallant assistant, Henry Morse.

---

[1]*Blessed John Southworth.* Rev. J. L. Whitfield. Catholic Truth Society. London. 1965. pp. 22-23.

85

SAINT ANDREW BOBOLA

1590—1657

A native of Sandomir, Poland, Andrew joined the Society of Jesus at Vilna when he was twenty-one years of age. After his ordination he taught and performed pastoral work in various cities in Poland and achieved marvels by his zeal and preaching, often converting whole villages. In 1624 he won the hearts of the people by his heroic efforts to relieve the sufferings of the plague-stricken. During the social, political, and religious confrontations between Poland and Russia, the Saint was an object of special hatred to recalcitrant schismatics because of his successful religious activities. During the devastation of Eastern Poland in 1657, the Jesuits were forced to flee into the forests and swamps to escape the bloody raids of the Cossacks, who traveled about the countryside beating the Poles into submission. St. Andrew was caught by them, and after they delivered a cruel beating, two Cossacks tied the Saint to their saddles and dragged him to Janow, where he endured other horrendous sufferings.

> No horror in the passions of the early martyrs, nor in the sufferings of the victims of the Indian savages, surpassed what was inflicted on his living body; he was burned, half-strangled, partly flayed alive, and finally dispatched by a saber cut.[1]

Forty years after his death, his inexplicably incorrupt body was discovered in a tomb under the ruins of a Jesuit church in Pinsk, Poland, and devotion to him immediately spread throughout Lithuania and Poland. The cause for his beautification was introduced a short time later, but was delayed because of the suppression of the Jesuits and the death of Pope Pius VIII. He was eventually beatified in 1853 and canonized in 1938.

For over two hundred years the body of the Saint endured many translations. For a while the Dominicans piously guarded the relic,

---

[1] *The Jesuits in History, The Society of Jesus Through Four Centuries.* Martin P. Harney, S.J. The America Press. New York. pp. 272-273.

but later it was given over to the care of the secular clergy. In 1808 it was removed to Polotsk in White Russia and was examined by the Imperial Commission in 1866. The body was again examined, cleaned, and dressed in new garments in 1896, at which time the Bishop of Mohilow took part of the backbone for relics. During the solemn exhibition of the relic on September 17, 1917, the body was found still to be pliable and in a good state of preservation. It was then enclosed in a metal coffin which was sealed and placed under an altar.

A grave sacrilege took place on June 23, 1922, when a cordon of troops of the Red Army surrounded the church and approached the altar to see for themselves if the rumor concerning the incorruptibility of the body were true. After opening the coffin, the soldiers disrobed the body and threw it on the floor. The church officials were put under arrest and the relic was sent by armed band to Moscow, where it was concealed by the Bolshevik government in a museum. Pope Pius XI twice petitioned for the return of the relic, and in 1923 a diplomatic courier of the Vatican Secretariat of State was sent to search through medical museums where the militant atheists had placed the relics of bishops on derisive exhibition. Upon discovery of the body in October, 1923, the Pope successfully persuaded the government to release the relic, and it was quickly taken to Rome. Shortly after the Saint's canonization in 1938, the body was conveyed back to Poland by way of Budapest and Cracow to Warsaw, where it was enshrined in the cathedral. Later the relic was removed to the church bearing his name.

The condition of the body, which has never been embalmed, treated, or conditioned, has many times been declared a miraculous preservation in spite of its mutilated condition, which of course resulted from the Saint's cruel martyrdom. Eighty-eight years after the Saint's death, Doctors Alexander Pascoli and Raymond Tarozzi of the College of Physicians in Rome and professors of medicine in the University of Rome, stated in their medico-physical dissertation that the condition of the body would normally hasten dissolution since it was a corpulent specimen covered with livid wounds. The body was mutilated in many ways during the inhuman attack by the Cossacks. The ears, nose, lips, parts of fingers and one eye had been torn from the body. Large pieces of skin had been ripped away from the legs, arms, chest and sides, leaving gaping wounds in which were found masses of congealed blood. The mutilated body was buried in the summer, in a spot where the ground was moist, and was for sixty years near the contagious elements of decaying bodies, all of which would normally act upon it in a swift and destructive manner. The doctors affirmed that no embalming of the body or other treatment had been administered, yet when they examined it, it had a normal color, was quite flexible, and had soft and lifelike skin. The doctors declared that the survival of the disfigured body, especially under the unfavorable circumstances of its entombment, was beyond their ability to explain; they unanimously declared the preservation to be of a miraculous nature.[2]

For the Acts of Beatification and Canonization, Doctor Marco Cingelo Marcangeli, a physician, professor of theoretical medicine in the University of Rome and Medical Director of the Holy Ghost Apostolic Hospital wrote in his deposition on the medico-physical examination dated 1827:

> . . . having been asked to present my opinion on the question of the preservation of the body of the Servant of God, the Venerable Andrew Bobola, Priest of the Society of Jesus, I do not hesitate to repeat and to confirm the opinion of the many witnesses who have seen and touched the body and who are unanimous in acknowledging its integrity, which experienced persons have described as eyewitnesses and which well known Medical Professors have asserted to be nothing less than miraculous . . .[3]

The doctor elaborated at great length and concluded in favor of a miraculous preservation.

There have been over four hundred ten well authenticated miracles attributed to St. Andrew Bobola, whose feast is observed on May 16.

The body of the holy martyr is at this time rather dark and rigid but still well preserved. The body, dressed in red sacerdotal vestments, lies in a reliquary of silver and crystal and can be viewed below the main altar of the church bearing his name in Warsaw, Poland. The face still bears the disfigurements sustained during the Saint's agonizing martyrdom three hundred twenty years ago.

---

[2] *The Life of Saint Andrew Bobola of the Society of Jesus, Martyr.* Cesare Moreschini. Translated, adapted and augmented by Louis J. Gallagher, S.J. & Paul V. Donovan, LL.D. Bruce Humphries, Inc. Boston. 1939. pp. 203-204.

[3] *Ibid.* p. 205.

The crystal and silver reliquary containing the mutilated but incorrupt body of St. Andrew Bobola (d. 1657) beneath the main altar of the Church of St. Andrew Bobola in Warsaw, Poland.

86

SAINT VINCENT DE PAUL

1580—1660

St. Vincent was born to a peasant family at Poy, France, about the year 1580 and as a child tended sheep until he was sent to the Franciscans at Dax to be educated. He was ordained a priest in the year 1600 at the early age of twenty. On a return trip from Marseilles he was captured by the Moslem corsairs, who took him to Tunis where he was sold as a slave. It is believed that he eventually converted his owner and obtained his release.

It was in Paris that he began his great works of charity and founded the Congregation of Priests of the Mission who are also known as the Lazarists or Vincentians. Later, with the help of St. Louise de Marillac, he founded the Sisters of Charity, who helped him in his work with the poor, the sick, and the aged as well as with orphans and foundlings.

Vincent died in Paris, October 5, 1660, at the house of Saint-Lazare, which belonged to his order of priests, and was buried beneath the choir of the church. In 1712, fifty-two years after his death, the body was exhumed by the Cardinal-Archbishop of Paris, two bishops, two subpromotors of the faith, a medical doctor, a surgeon and a number of priests of his order, including the superior-general, Father Bonnet. An eyewitness gave us this account of the proceedings:

> When they opened the tomb everything was the same as when deposited. The eyes and nose alone showed some decay, I counted eighteen teeth. The body was not moved, but those who approached saw at once that it was entire and that the soutane was not in the least damaged by time. No offensive odour was discernible, and the doctors testified that the body could not be thus preserved for so long a time by any natural means.[1]

---

[1]*History of St. Vincent de Paul, Founder of the Congregation of the Mission (Vincentians) and of the Sisters of Charity.* Monseigneur Bougaud, Bishop of Laval. Translated by Rev. Joseph Brady, C.M. Longmans Green & Co. New York. 1908. p. 364.

During the celebration for the canonization of the Saint, the body was again exhumed, and it was then discovered to be in a state of decomposition due to the effects of an underground flood.

Following many translations, his bones, which are encased in a wax figure, now rest in a magnificent reliquary in the chapel of the headquarters of the Vincentian Fathers, Rue de Sèvres, in Paris. The head of the representation is said to be a true likeness of the Saint.

His still incorrupt heart, however, is enclosed in a golden reliquary which is exposed on the altar of his shrine in the chapel of the motherhouse of the Sisters of Charity, 140 rue du Bac, Paris. A short distance from this relic there is enshrined beneath a side altar the perfectly preserved body of his spiritual daughter, St. Catherine Labouré, the visionary of the Miraculous Medal. Also in this chapel on a side altar can be seen the reliquary which contains the wax figure of St. Louise de Marillac, the co-foundress of the Sisters of Charity. The bones of the Saint are contained in the model.

It was often before the relic of Saint Vincent that Catherine Labouré, as a postulant and young religious, prayed for guidance from the humble priest who had favored her with a number of apparitions.

St. Vincent has been named the Patron of All Charitable Societies, and notably, of course, is patron of the great society which bears his name.

87

SAINT PACIFICO OF SAN SEVERINO

1653—1721

Born of a distinguished Italian family named Divini, in San Severino in the Marches, Pacifico was orphaned at an early age and was left in the care of an uncle who harshly mistreated him. Already advanced in virtue, he accepted the unjust treatment in the spirit of mortification.

When he was seventeen, he entered the Order of the Friars Minor and was ordained a priest at the age of twenty-five. For many years he successfully taught in the villages and hamlets of the Apennine Mountains and, due to his ability to read minds and consciences, he was able to bring many to true contrition and repentence. At the age of thirty-five his active apostolate came to an end when he contracted an illness which left him deaf, blind and crippled. In addition to these infirmities, he added his own mortifications, which he offered for the conversion of sinners. These afflictions did not prevent him from serving as vicar and guardian of the friary at San Severino, to which he was transferred in 1705 and where he spent the rest of his years amid his friends and the scenes of his childhood.

The Saint was endowed with many supernatural gifts. He was often found in ecstasy while celebrating Holy Mass, and his countenance at those times would shine like the sun. He had the gift of prophecy and often healed the sick. The holy friar died on September 24, 1721, and was canonized by Pope Gregory XVI in 1839.

The Saint was buried in the common grave of the religious community, where his body was found incorrupt four years later, although it had been buried without a coffin. After this exhumation the body was placed in a casket and moved to the Altar of the Madonna at the side of the chapel. Between the recognition of 1725 and the second one of 1756, corruption of the body took place due to the excessive humidity of the sepulcher. The year following the Solemn Beatification, which occurred in 1786, the bones were artistically covered with wax in a figure representing the Saint, which has been exposed in an urn ever since. The figure appears in the normal length and is clothed with the Franciscan habit; a stole, the sign of his priestly ministry, is draped around his shoulders.

Behold a great priest, who in his days pleased God, and was found just.

Ecclesiasticus 44:16-17

88

SAINT VERONICA GIULIANI

1660—1727

When Veronica was four years of age, her dying mother entrusted each of her five children to a sacred wound of Christ. Veronica, the youngest, was assigned the wound in the side. This action of the dying mother might well have been of a prophetic nature, for her daughter's interest in the Passion increased. Later she became marked with the stigmata, and on her heart were found the symbols of Our Lord's Passion, as she had indicated before her death.

When Veronica came of age, her father weakened under her insistent pleadings and permitted her to enter the Capuchin Monastery at Città di Castello, where the primitive rule of St. Clare was observed. Her novitiate was very difficult, for she was severely tested by her superiors and endured many interior trials.

She was favored with many visions of the suffering Christ. In one vision she accepted the chalice of Our Lord's sufferings and soon recognized some of the sufferings of Christ in her own body and soul. The following year she was imprinted with the Crown of Thorns, and on Good Friday, 1697, she received the impression of the five sacred wounds.

To guard against fraud, the bishop of the diocese, at the direction of the Holy See, thoroughly tested the phenomenon. She was for a time forbidden to receive Holy Communion, was kept under constant supervision, and was shut off from the rest of the community; her hands were placed in special gloves fastened with the bishop's signet. All medical treatments proved futile. In the sworn testimony submitted for her beatification, her confessor and fellow religious stated that the stigmatic wounds opened and bled at command, and that they closed and healed in a short time while the bishop waited.[1] Her obedience and humble demeanor proved the genuineness of the mystical experiences.

St. Veronica has been likened to St. Teresa of Avila, having been a woman of great common sense and administrative ability, in addition

---

[1]Arradi. *Op. cit.* p. 176.

to having been endowed with many supernatural favors. Her judgments were highly respected, for she served the community as novice mistress for a period of thirty-four years; during the last eleven years of her life she served as abbess. In this position she saw to all the practical aspects of the community, improved the convent's water supply by having pipes installed, and supervised the details of the new additions made to the convent.

In her diary of ten volumes, written at the command of her confessor, she left an invaluable record, which was used during the process of her beatification and which has proved to be of great interest to hagiographers.

Toward the end of her life, she was afflicted with apoplexy and died of the complications of that disease on July 9, 1727. She was canonized in 1839.

Before her death she drew a picture indicating the presence of the symbols of Christ's passion on her heart. A post-mortem examination, performed in the presence of a bishop and many witnesses, revealed on her heart a number of figures corresponding to those she had drawn.

The body of the Saint remained incorrupt for many years, until it was destroyed during an inundation of the Tiber River. Her bones now repose in a composite figure of the Saint, the skull of which is covered with wax. The reliquary is situated beneath the altar of the church. The incorrupt heart, which was extracted after her death, is kept in a reliquary apart and is said by physicians to be well preserved. A museum in the convent contains many of her relics and mementos, and the pilgrims visiting the shrine are permitted access to it when accompanied by the convent's confessor, since the Order is one of very strict enclosure.

89

SAINT LUCY FILIPPINI

1672—1732

St. Lucy was the zealous and holy foundress of the Pontificial Institute Maestre Pie Filippini, which was responsible for improving the social, religious, and intellectual conditions of the women of Italy at a time when compulsory education was unknown. The Saint was born in Tarquinia about sixty miles outside of Rome, on January 13, 1672. While a young girl, she assisted her pastor in teaching catechism, and her zeal and piety came to the attention of Cardinal Marcantonio Barbarigo, Bishop of Montefiascone, who had her join him in Montefiascone to participate in an educational program for the training of teachers which he had established in that city. It was there, in 1692, that she met Bl. Rose Venerini, foundress of the Venerini Sisters, who had founded a similar organization in Viterbo and who gave the new institute the benefit of her vast experience. Under Lucy's direction the work prospered, and educational centers multiplied. On October 15, 1704, the community was formally established, and three years later, after the death of the Cardinal, Pope Clement XI called the Saint to Rome, and she established there a school of the Maestre Pie. The Casa Generalizia of the Order remains in that ancient city.

Her delicate constitution was strained under the burden of numerous and demanding responsibilities, and in spite of the best medical attention, she died a holy death on the day she had predicted, March 25, 1732.

Widely acclaimed for her sanctity and noted for the exercise of great virtue, she was beatified on June 13, 1926, and was canonized June 22, 1930.

On May 20, 1926, one month before her solemn beatification, her body was exhumed and found almost entirely incorrupt. The relic was clothed in fresh robes and was placed in the crystal reliquary in which it is still enshrined. After two centuries, her body is still remarkably preserved. No bones have separated, and these are covered with soft and flexible tissue. Her legs and feet are especially well conserved and "look like a person just after death." The venerable face of the Saint is the only part of the relic which has suffered a little, and this is covered with a silver net, contoured to resemble her features. The teeth are so firmly attached to the jaws that when the late Cardinal Salotti, who prepared the documents necessary for the canonization, tried to extract one tooth to keep as a relic, he could not remove it and lamented: "She does not want to give it to me."[1]

The precious relic of this holy foundress is exposed in her crystal reliquary in the crypt of St. Margaret's Cathedral in Montefiascone.

---

[1] The information contained in this paragraph was taken from statements made in correspondence with the author by the representatives of the Casa Generalizia, Pontificio Istituto Maestre Pie Filippini.

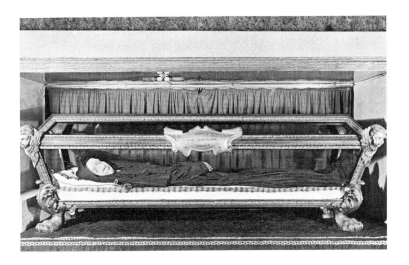

The body of St. Lucy Filippini, foundress of the Pontifical Institute Maestre Pie Filippini (d. 1732), was exhumed in 1926 and found almost entirely intact. It now reposes in the crypt of St. Margaret's Cathedral in Montefiascone, Italy.

90

SAINT TERESA MARGARET OF THE SACRED HEART

(Anna Maria Redi)

1747—1770

Cavalier Ignatius Redi of Arezzo, Italy, and his wife, Camilla Ballati, a native of Siena, were the noble and devout parents of two priests and four nuns. Anna Maria, their second-born, was pious from early childhood and at the age of seventeen entered the Discalced Carmelite convent at Florence. She became an exemplary religious, taking the name of Teresa Margaret of the Sacred Heart, in honor of St. Teresa of Avila, St. Margaret Mary Alacoque, and the devotion to the Sacred Heart, which she dearly loved.

St. Teresa Margaret advanced rapidly in perfection and was always a source of edification to her sisters in religion. During the time she served as infirmarian, many of the sick were miraculously cured when she blessed them with oil from the lamps that burned before the statues of Our Lady and St. Joseph. She experienced a delightful smell and taste when receiving the Sacred Species, was often rapt in prayer, and at times would become so intense in her love for God that the color of her countenance would change from crimson to purple to ash-grey.

Three days before her death, although in seemingly perfect health, she prepared for her last Holy Communion, knowing that she would be too ill to communicate on her death bed. She was suddenly struck down with severe intestinal pains and rapidly developed a gangrenous condition. Although suffering excruciating pain, she was a model of patience and charity, dying fully recollected on March 7, 1770, after an agony lasting eighteen hours.

The circumstances immediately following her death are unique: The gangrenous condition of the body seemed to hasten the process of decomposition, for immediately after the Saint's death, the rigid body became discolored and the abdomen began swelling to such dimensions that by evening the head and shoulders had to be lifted up with pillows in order for the faithful to view the face of the Saint, who lay in state by the grill which opened into the chapel.

After viewing her body, the people who had crowded into the chapel for the funeral rites clamored for relics and information about the young nun who had died in their midst. After the ceremony,

> When her body was being carried below ground to be buried underneath the Monastery, it was discovered that the lividly purplish hue of her face, hands, and feet had changed to a faint rose-like color, which gave her a more angelic beauty than she had when alive. The nuns decided to put off the burial for a while. The ninth of March, that is, two days after her death, the religious went to her uncovered tomb again, and were astonished to see that the lifeless and pallid color of her hands and feet had now changed to the glow of living flesh; her cheeks, now rosy, gave a heavenly look to her face . . . she seemed, truly, to be alive, just quietly sleeping. The Father Provincial and Doctor Antonio Romiti, the Monastery surgeon, marveled at the beauty of her countenance . . . even the eyelids were dewy and in color, even her lips seemed fresh and naturally red. They returned to see the corpse two days later, when their astonishment reached its peak on discovering that the face was even more beautiful and that the body had regained its former size and shape without exuding a drop of moisture. Her limbs had become so pliable and so easily moved as to give the impression of being animated. It was at this time that a new and most delightful odor, not to be compared with any earthy fragrance, clearly revealed what had been brought about in these precious remains . . . God had glorified them by the gift of incorruption.[1]

According to the custom, flowers which had been strewn on the corpse were distributed to the faithful, and these were the cause of many miracles. Parts of the Saint's clothing were cut into small pieces for relics to satisfy the demands of the people who flocked to the church seeking mementos.

On the fifteenth day following her death, the archbishop went to the monastery to view the sacred remains. Accompanying him were Canon Pasquali, the chancellor of the archdiocese, a number of the Florentine clergy, Doctor Romiti, and three surgeons.

---

[1]*St. Teresa Margaret of the Sacred Heart of Jesus (Anna Maria Redi)*. Msgr. James F. Newcomb, P.S., J.C.D. Benziger Bros. New York. 1934. pp. 219-220. Adapted from *Un Angelo del Carmelo* of Friar Stanislaus of St. Teresa, O.C.D.

When they came to the side of the corpse they found it just as it had been described to them, except that the eyes had become a little sunken, and a small amount of moisture had appeared beneath the nostrils. The Archbishop was so deeply touched that he wept. He then ordered one of the nuns to move the Saint's arm; with the greatest ease, the sister lifted the arm outside the coffin and then put it back into its former position. The nuns were now about to close the coffin finally, when the Archbishop suggested that the moisture under the nostrils be removed with a handkerchief . . . another marvel! . . . the cloth and moisture, as if to give further testimony of the innocence of the soul that had once dwelt in that uncontaminated body, sent forth so sweet an odor that the Archbishop could not keep from weeping. Smelling the little piece of cloth, he exclaimed, 'Virgineo fragrat odore . . . fragrance of virginity.' It was a stirring moment. All wept with joy.[2]

The Saint was then buried in a double casket in the wall of the monastery.

After her burial, the sweet odor of sanctity was perceived on all the objects which she had touched in life. Her mother was the first to notice it—on a lock of her hair and on other mementos sent to her by the convent.

Thirteen years after the Saint's death, permission was obtained to move the remains to a drier location in the monastery's wall. On June 16, 1783, in the presence of her father, the Archbishop of Florence, members of the clergy, and distinguished laymen, the body was exhumed and found to be perfectly incorrupt. Doctor Romiti, who had assisted the Saint on her death bed, again inspected the remains and made an official report of his findings. The body was cleaned, dressed in a fresh habit, and placed in a new coffin. Before it was consigned to the tomb, Cavalier Redi placed on a finger of his daughter a valuable ring which had belonged to the Saint's then deceased mother.

The doctors who examined the body on June 21, 1805, declared that it was of a

. . . healthy flesh color, somewhat dry but, nevertheless, surprisingly elastic and pliable, even in the soft parts between the ribs and groin; the color of the hair on the head livid and fresh, that of the eyebrows golden-blond, with the appearance of life in it; the wound made in the right foot by the surgeon that bled her still visible, but healed and of good color . . .[3]

The shrine of the Saint was visited through the years by many members of the royalty and other distinguished persons. Pope Pius VII, whose own mother had entered a Discalced Carmelite convent in her later years, visited the Saint's grave while on a return trip from France, where he had taken part in Napoleon's coronation.

St. Teresa Margaret of the Sacred Heart was canonized on the feast of St. Joseph, March 19, 1934. Her body, now dark and dry but still perfectly incorrupt, lies exposed to public view in the chapel of the Monastery of St. Teresa, Via dei Bruni 12, Florence, Italy.

Everything comes to an end; therefore take heart, for we pass from one thing to another until at last we arrive at eternity. Even seeing how things of this world end so quickly ought to console us, because the nearer and more quickly are we approaching that end towards which all our activities should tend.

—St. Teresa Margaret of the Sacred Heart.

---

[2]*Ibid.* pp. 221-222.
[3]*Ibid.* p. 231.

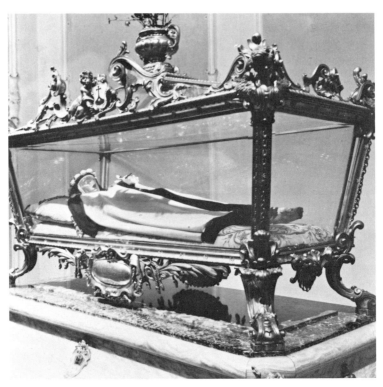

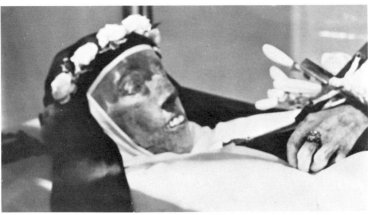

The body of St. Teresa Margaret of the Sacred Heart (d. 1770) was found perfectly preserved in 1783 and now reposes in a glass case at the Monastery of St. Teresa in Florence, Italy.

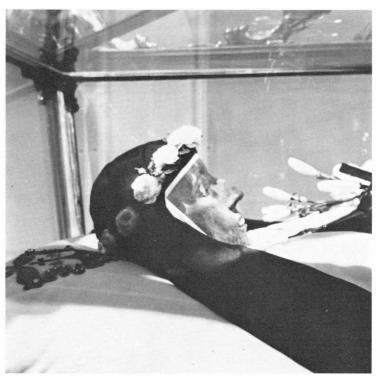

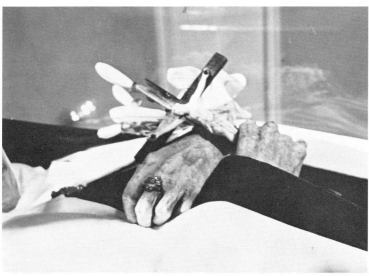

91

SAINT JULIE BILLIART

1751—1816

After witnessing the senseless slaying of her father by an unknown assailant, Julie suffered a nervous disorder which affected her limbs, producing a paralysis which lingered for thirty years. She heroically offered the sufferings she endured to the Sacred Heart in reparation for the sins of the world, especially those committed against the Holy Eucharist. Because of the manner in which she accepted this illness, she became known by the townspeople as the "Saint of Cuvilly."

During the French Revolution and the infamous Reign of Terror, when the churches and convents were destroyed and religious put to death, she managed to escape a mob that rifled her home, only because of the quick thinking of friends who hid her under straw in a cart. During this period she had a vision of the religious order she would found, the Institute of the Sisters of Notre Dame of Namur. In this vision she saw the faces of sisters, whom she recognized years later, gathered around the cross of Calvary.

After she joined in a novena made by Father Engantin, who had been ordained in a barn during the Revolution, she obtained a complete cure in June, 1804. Renewed in health and spirit, she set about the founding of her order, which met with numerous difficulties, but she was supported and encouraged in her work by many visions of its future expansion. During an epidemic of typhoid in 1808, her gift of healing was manifest when twenty-three of her sisters were miraculously cured. There were also instances when the multiplication of food resulted from her prayers. In spite of many difficulties, including many misunderstandings with her bishop, fifteen institutions were in existence before her death in 1816. Having died at the motherhouse of the Order at Namur, Belgium, she was buried two days later, on April 10, 1816, in the city cemetery.

Three months after the interment, in the height of the summer heat, when it was necessary to place a sepulchral slab on the tomb, the coffin was opened for a short time . . .

. . . and there, even as on the day of her death, lay the pure and venerable body of Julie Billiart, incorrupt, sweet, the cheeks still wearing the flush of life, the garments perfectly dry, the limbs quite flexible as they reverently moved them in this direction or that.[1]

The body of the blessed foundress was transferred from the public cemetery to a tomb on the grounds of the mother house at Namur on July 17, 1817. During the translation,

. . . the sisters themselves took off the lid of the coffin, and again their Mother lay before them untouched by the corruption of the tomb, fresh and beautiful as in the previous year, save that the finger-tips were slightly shrivelled. They lifted the body, wrapped it in the linen cloths they had brought with them . . . and, without mishap . . . conveyed it to the Mother House. . . . Nearly sixteen months had elapsed since the death of the Servant of God; the weather was extremely hot, yet the movements necessary to lift the body from the coffin, had absolutely no effect on its integrity. From it exuded a quantity of clear oil which stained the cloths in which it was wrapped, and even the wooden floor of the room whereon it was laid for a moment. It was at once placed in the garden-crypt.[2]

The body was later reduced in the normal manner.

In consequence of the frequent inundations of the Sambre and Meuse, the little vault was often under water, and when in 1842 it was opened to receive the body of Reverend Mother Ignace Goethals, the flesh had crumbled to dust and the bones alone remained; these were now enclosed in a small chest.[3]

St. Julie Billiart was raised to the honors of the altar by Pope Paul VI on June 22, 1969, during impressive services at St. Peter's Basilica in which her venerable name was added to the list of saints.

[1]*Life of Blessed Julie Billiart, Foundress of the Institute of Sisters of Notre Dame.* By a Member of The Same Society. Edited by Father James Clare, S.J. Sands & Co. London. 1909. Second Edition. p. 529.

[2]*Ibid.* pp. 530-532.

[3]*Ibid.* p. 532.

92

BLESSED ANNA MARIA TAIGI

1769—1837

Anna Maria attained her position among the blessed in Heaven by being an exemplary wife and mother amid poor and trying circumstances. As the daughter of an unsuccessful apothecary, she was taken from her native Siena to Rome, where her father sought new employment. At still an early age she worked at various occupations in order to bring financial assistance to her family. In 1790, at the age of twenty-one, she married a butler, Domenico Taigi, a man she dearly loved, but who caused her considerable anguish because of his exacting and temperamental attitudes. She became the mother of seven children, three of whom died in infancy. Those she raised to maturity were provided with the most complete religious and secular education.

Added to the many penances she undertook voluntarily for the conversion of sinners and the welfare of the Church, she patiently endured aridity of spirit, nursed her mother through a lengthy and repulsive illness, faithfully performed her duties as housewife and mother, saw to the needs of her quarrelsome husband, and struggled to maintain peace among members of the family in their overcrowded house. In spite of this seemingly uncongenial atmosphere, she was frequently in ecstasy, worked miracles of healing, foretold deaths, read hearts, and as a tertiary of the Third Order of the Most Holy Trinity, she fulfilled perfectly the obligations of the rule.

Mention must be made here, as it is in all of the Beata's biographies, of the "mysterious sun" which she first saw in 1790 or 1791, shortly after her marriage. The luminous disc, somewhat like a miniature sun, maintained a constant position before her. Above the upper rays was a large crown of interwoven thorns with two rather lengthy thorns on either side, curved downward so that they crossed each other under the solar disc, their points emerging on either side of the rays. In the center of the disc the Beata saw a beautiful woman seated majestically, her face raised toward Heaven in ecstatic contemplation. In this globe Anna Maria saw things of the natural, moral, and divine order and could see present or future events anywhere in the world, as well as the state of grace of living individuals and the fate of those departed. She could also discern the secret thoughts of persons who were present or far off. Anna Maria was granted the privilege of this phenomenon for forty-seven years, a period spanning from the beginning of her marriage to her death.[1]

Because of her holiness and infused knowledge, she was frequently consulted by many distinguished persons, including Pope Leo XII, Pope Gregory XVI, Napoleon's mother, and his uncle, Cardinal Fesh. Among her other friends can be counted St. Vincent Pallotti, St. Gaspar del Bufalo, St. Mary Euphrasia Pelletier, many cardinals, monsignori, and prelates, all of whom gave ample testimony of her outstanding virtues and merits.

Blessed Anna Maria died on June 9, 1837, after suffering many painful afflictions. Her body was left exposed for two days in the Church of Santa Maria in Via Lata and was borne by a devout cortege to the new cemetery in the Campo Verano, where, according to the instructions of Pope Gregory XVI, it was enclosed in a leaden casket, which was sealed and placed near the chapel.

The fame of her sanctity increased, and so many miracles were occurring through her intercession that the people regretted the fact that the body of the Beata rested so far from Rome. Requests were constantly made for the removal of the body to a more convenient location—within the city. Eighteen years after the burial of the Blessed, the Cardinal Vicar gave orders for the removal of the casket to the Church of Our Lady of Peace, where it was opened during the night in complete secrecy. Somehow news of the exhumation spread throughout the district and crowds thronged to the church to view the body of the Blessed, which had been found in a state of perfect preservation, as fresh as if it had been buried the day before.

Pope Pius IX, who held this saintly mother in the highest esteem, on the learning that she had expressed a wish to be buried in the Church of the Trinitarians, had the body removed to the Basilica of San Chrysogono on August 18, 1865.

Three years later the coffin was again opened, and though the clothes of the Beata had decayed, her body was still intact. The sisters

---

[1]*La Beata Anna Maria Taigi, Madre di Famiglia.* Msgr. Carlo Salotti. Libreria Editrice Religiosa, Francesco Ferrari. Rome. 1922. pp. 273-278.

of St. Joseph took off the poor clothing and replaced it by new. For eight days the body was exposed for the veneration of the faithful; the whole neighborhood of Trastevere seemed on the move, and troops were necessary to ensure order. The body, enclosed in a double coffin of lead and of cypress, was near the chapel of the Blessed Sacrament in a memorial tomb, and, later on, in the chapel to the left, under the altar within a large glass shrine which allowed it to be seen in the habit of a Trinitarian Tertiary. The hands were joined in front of the breast. The face, giving an impression of infinte serenity, was covered in a light wax mask beneath the white coif.[2]

The official inquiry for the Process was begun in 1852. Among the thirty sworn witnesses who testified were cardinals, bishops, nobles and servants who had known the Beata. Anna Maria's two daughters also gave evidence of the heroic nature of their mother's virtues, and the Beata's husband, Domenico, then ninety-two years old, gave his wife a glowing tribute.

In 1863, Pius IX introduced the Cause of Beatification; Pope Pius X declared the heroic quality of her virtues on March 4, 1906, and on May 30, 1920, Pope Benedict XV beatified Anna Maria Taigi, mother of a family. He later designated her as special protectress of mothers of families and the Patroness of the Women's Catholic Union.

The body of Anna Maria is unfortunately no longer incorrupt, but her bones are well arranged and enclosed in a figure representing her; the face and hands are composed of plastic. The relic still is enshrined in a glass-sided reliquary beneath the altar of the Basilica of St. Chrysogonus in Rome.

Her children rose up, and called her blessed: her husband, and he praised her. Many daughters have gathered together riches: thou hast surpassed them all.

—Proverbs 31:28-29.

---

[2]*Wife, Mother and Mystic.* Albert Bessières, S.J. Translated by Rev. Stephen Rigby. Edited by Douglas Newton. The Newman Press. Westminster, Maryland. 1952. p. 242.

SAINT VINCENT PALLOTTI

1795—1850

Vincent was born in Rome to a pious couple who were successfully engaged in the selling of foodstuffs. Vincent, who was one of ten children, five of whom died in infancy, was always indebted to his parents for the excellent religious training he received as a child and wrote a touching memoir of his mother, in which he described the virtuous life she lived under trying circumstances and the manner of her saintly death.

Vincent's decision to become a priest was made when he was fifteen years of age and was realized when he was twenty-three. Shortly before his ordination, he began to write a spiritual diary, which he maintained until his death. This work traces clearly the activities, prayer life, resolutions and hopes of this great saint. Two months after his ordination, he took the final examination at the Roman University and received the degree of Doctor of Theology and Philosophy and was awarded the title of Professor of Greek, Philosophy and Arts. He taught theology for ten years before he began to devote himself to spiritual guidance and the active apostolate. He served as spiritual director for several Roman colleges and seminaries and founded three orders: the Pallottines, the Sisters of the Catholic Apostolate, and the Pallottine Missionary Sisters. His charitable activities included spiritual ministrations to soldiers, especially to those who were ill. He assisted condemned prisoners in their last hours, founded several mission colleges and a large orphanage, collected funds for the missions, reorganized guilds for men of various working trades, and founded trade schools for young boys. During the cholera epidemic of 1837, he worked among the sick and organized relief organizations to assist the ill and their dependents. Because of these and other accomplishments, he became known as the second St. Philip Neri among the grateful Roman populace.

In his iconography he is pictured holding in one hand a small boxlike reliquary on which is pictured a likeness of the Blessed Mother and the Child Jesus. It might be explained that during this time in

Italy it was the custom to kiss the hand of a priest when greeting him or bidding farewell. Vincent disliked this custom, but finding it difficult to avoid, he had a special case made in which was enclosed a figure of the Blessed Mother, the outside bearing a likeness of the Mother and Child. It was this small case he offered, instead of his hand, for the customary kiss of respect.

During the course of his work among seminarians, he knew intimately and directed spiritually many men who were later to distinguish themselves throughout the world as dedicated and saintly churchmen. He knew St. Gaspar del Bufalo, Blessed Anna Maria Taigi, Pauline Jaricot of the Society for the Propagation of the Faith, and the Venerable Elizabeth Sanna.

Vincent died on January 22, 1850, the very day he had predicted. For three days, people numbering in the thousands touched medals and rosaries to the body of the humble priest they were convinced would someday be recognized officially as a saint.

Great care and formality were observed at the burial. A leaden tube containing the official documents was placed beside the body, which was clothed in priestly vestments. The body was placed in three coffins, the first of wood, the second zinc, and the third of hardwood, each being carefully sealed. It was lowered into a vault under the floor of the second altar on the left of the Church of St. Salvatore in Onda. A marble stone on which his name was engraved, marked the place of interment.

Many people of unquestionable integrity have stated that for a period of one month following the Saint's death, a sweet fragrance lingered in the room in which he had died, in spite of an open window.[1]

The first official steps toward Vincent's canonization were taken two years after his death. On March 22, 1906, in the presence of the delegates of the Sacred Congregation of Rites, the body was exhumed and found to be intact although a little dry. The body was left exposed until April 10, when it was wrapped in linen cloths and placed in a hardwood casket lined with zinc. Around the body were placed bundles of cotton and wool in an attempt to defend it from humidity. The casket was then placed in another of zinc, which was sealed and interred in a vault in the wall of the church. The tomb was later ornamented with exquisite marble.

---

[1] *The Life of St. Vincent Pallotti.* Rev. John S. Gaynor, Ph.D.,DD. Pallottine Fathers. Clerkenwell, London. 1962. p. 159.

The second exhumation took place on December 2, 1949, a few weeks prior to his beatification. After the monument was dismantled and the casket withdrawn, the body was found to be dry, partially mummified, but in an excellent state of conservation. It was then cleaned with alcohol and formaldehyde and covered with balsam. On January 21, 1950, the day before the beatification, the body was clothed in sacerdotal vestments; on the face of the Saint was placed a silver mask made from the impression of the original death mask, and on his hands were placed similar coverings made from the impression of the hands. The sacred body was placed in a sarcophagus of crystal and bronze and enshrined under the main altar of the Church of St. Salvatore in Onda, where it still reposes.

On the one hundredth anniversary of his death, Pope Pius XII beatified Vincent Pallotti, and Pope John XXIII conducted the solemn canonization ceremonies on January 20, 1963.

The preserved body of St. Vincent Pallotti (d. 1850) with the face covered by a silver mask. Last exhumed in 1950, the body now rests in a silver and bronze shrine beneath the main altar of the Church of St. Salvatore in Onda, Italy.

94

BLESSED ROSE PHILIPPINE DUCHESNE

1769—1852

Born in Grenoble, France, Philippine was the daughter of a man who was active in politics on the local and national level. When eleven years of age she was sent to study at the Convent of the Visitation, Sainte-Marie d'en-Haut, where she became interested in the religious life. Over the protests of her father, she entered the Visitation Order on September 10, 1788, but was forced to leave when her convent was closed as the result of the suppressions of religious houses during the French Revolution. The next ten years were spent in nursing the sick, teaching and caring for the neglected children of Grenoble, and sheltering persecuted priests. When peace was restored, she obtained possession of the convent in which she had studied and entered the religious life, but being unable to assemble the scattered Visitation nuns, she joined the Society of the Sacred Heart, which was founded in 1800 by St. Madeleine Sophie Barat, and the convent she had procured became the second house of this order.

After founding another house of the Order in Paris, she and a few companions were sent by Mother Madeleine to the United States, arriving at New Orleans, Louisiana, in 1818. From that time the Religious of the Sacred Heart played a significant role in the development of the Louisiana territory and in the cultivation of the Church in the United States. Many schools and convents were founded by Philippine in the states of Louisiana and Missouri. Her long-standing desire to work among the Indians was fulfilled during her seventy-second year with the opening of a school for Potawatomi Indian girls at Sugar Creek, Kansas. Being unable to learn the language, she busied herself with the sick and was affectionately named Quah-kah-ka-num-ad, Woman-who-prays-always. For reasons of health she returned to the convent she had established in St. Charles, Missouri, where she spent the last ten years of her life. After her funeral, which was attended by a great number of religious and lay admirers, including many Protestants, the body of the holy mother was deposited in an enclosure arranged in the garden. A few years later, the superior of the house, having built an oratory on the grounds, wished to transfer the remains of Mother Duchesne there and subsequently had the remains exhumed.

> The body having been placed in a coffin made only of wood, and buried in a damp soil, it was fully expected that nothing but bones and ashes would be found. Great therefore was the glad surprise of all the assistants when on opening the tomb Mother Duchesne's form was seen in perfect preservation and emitting no bad smell. The face was so unchanged that it was immediately photographed in order to perpetuate the memory of such a token of Divine protection extended to a frame which penance had, as it were, spiritualized. At the moment when it was removed into a new vault a certain contraction of the limbs took place, and a visible change in the garments. New ones were substituted, and the old ones carefully preserved. The new chapel received the precious remains, before which are often seen in prayer those who, having known this heroic woman, long to glorify, like her, the Sacred Heart of Jesus, and devote themselves to His service.[1]

The holy relic rested in this small building for many years until its transfer into the chapel of the Academy of the Sacred Heart. The body of the Beata has unfortunately been subjected to the normal laws of nature, and only bones and dust remain.

---

[1] *The Life of Mother Duchesne, Religious of the Society of the Sacred Heart of Jesus and Foundress of the First Houses of the Society in America.* Abbe Baunard. Translated by Lady Georgiana Fullerton. Roehampton. 1879. p. 407.

The body of Bl. Rose Philippine Duchesne (d. 1852) as it appeared one year after being disinterred.

95

SAINT JEAN-MARIE-BAPTISTE VIANNEY

(The Curé of Ars)

1786—1859

The humble nineteenth-century French priest, who has endeared himself to Catholics around the world, began life in 1786 as the son of a poor farmer in the small village of Dardilly, France. During his childhood St. Jean Vianney worked as a shepherd and helper in the fields and was unable to begin his education until he was twenty years of age. While an ecclesiastical student he was called for military service and became a delinquent conscript, more or less because of illness, and was obliged for a time to hide in order to escape Napoleon's police.

Knowing nothing of philosophy and finding it difficult to learn Latin, he twice failed the examinations required before ordination. He was eventually ordained a priest at the age of thirty but was thought to be so incompetent he was placed under the direction of Father Balley, a holy priest in the neighboring village of Ecully, for further training. After the death of this good priest he was transferred to the small village of Ars, where he spent the rest of his years on earth.

The Saint lived an austere life, ate the simplest of foods, wore old clothing and slept on a hard bed. It was a known fact that the two hours of sleep he allowed himself each night were frequently interrupted by the devil, who assaulted him with deafening noises, insulting conversation, and physical abuse. These diabolical visitations were occasionally witnessed with alarm by the men of the parish, but the pious Curé accepted the attacks as a matter of course and often joked about them.

This holy priest was the possessor of many heavenly gifts, such as the power of healing and the ability to read the minds and hearts of his penitents. It was this latter gift which caused his fame to spread throughout France, inducing crowds of troubled souls to seek guidance from the humble priest who knew their secret sins and hidden past.

The frail Curé began the hearing of confessions at the unlikely hour of one o'clock in the morning, and it has been reported that he spent from thirteen to seventeen painful hours a day in the cramped, stifling confessional.[1]

Completely exhausted by apostolic labors and by the additional penances he inflicted on his thin, sickly body, the Saint died peacefully on August 4, 1859, after receiving the final consolations of his religion. Forty-five years later, on June 17, 1904, his body was exhumed because of his impending beatification and was found dried and darkened, but perfectly entire. Only his face, which was still perfectly recognizable, suffered a little from the effects of death. After the viscera were removed,

> The precious remains were wrapped in bands of fine linens and clothed in the following vestments: a tunic of white watered silk, a black cassock, a rochet edged with fine lace, and a stole of cloth of gold embroidered with lilies and roses of the same material. A rosary of jasper beads was twined round the darkened fingers, and the face was covered with a wax mask which reproduces the features of the servant of God. When on April 2, 1905, the old men of Ars, who had known M. Vianney well, were shown the relic as it is seen today by pilgrims, they burst into tears and exclaimed with one voice: "Oh, how truly like him!"[2]

During the year of his beatification his perfectly preserved heart was removed and enclosed in a beautiful reliquary, which was placed in a separate building called The Shrine of the Curé's Heart.

The magnificent reliquary which contains the body of the Saint was donated by priests around the world and is situated above an altar of the basilica which was annexed to the old parish church. Before this golden reliquary, which exposes the relic to view, the Holy Sacrifice of the Mass is continually offered during the summer months by pilgrim priests.

Preserved at Ars are the living quarters of the Saint, which have been kept exactly as they were on the day of his death and on whose walls can be seen the pictures which the Curé himself had hung. Also kept there are his personal articles, his breviary, the rosary he fre-

---

[1] *The Curé of Ars, A Pilgrim's Guide.* Editions Xavier Mappus. Lyon.

[2] *The Curé d'Ars, St. Jean-Marie-Baptiste Vianney, According to the Acts of the Process of Canonization and Numerous Hitherto Unpublished Documents.* Abbé Francis Trochu. The Newman Press. Westminster, Maryland. 1950. p. 580.

quently used, a blood stained discipline, and the bed which had been set on fire during one of the devil's frequent visitations.

St. Jean-Marie-Baptiste Vianney, who as a student had such difficulty being accepted for the priesthood, but who exercised his vocation in such an edifying manner, was canonized in 1925 and was named later the Patron of Parish Priests throughout the World.

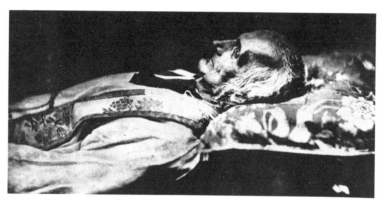

The body of the Curé of Ars, Patron of Parish Priests (d. 1859), situated in a golden reliquary above the main altar in the Basilica at Ars in France. *Opposite page:* The upper picture was taken shortly after the Curé had died. The lower picture shows him as he appears today, his face covered with a wax mask.

SAINT MADELEINE SOPHIE BARAT

1779—1865

Born at Joigny in central France, Madeleine received her early education from her brother Louis, a priest, who took her to Paris to continue her education. While there, she was persuaded by Abbé Joseph Varin d'Ainville to join and reorganize a group of women living under a religious rule. After journeying with them to Amiens, she became at the age of twenty-three, the superior general and principal of their school for girls. Two years later, in 1804, she founded a house of the Society of the Sacred Heart in Grenoble and admitted to the order Blessed Rose Philippine Duchesne, who in 1818 sailed in the company of four religious to found the first schools of the order in America.

The initial success of the order was followed by grave internal dissension, which resulted when various groups attempted to reorganize the rule and constitution. Mother Barat successfully prevented the changes, and this period of conflict was followed by one of great expansion of the order. The Saint was untiring in her efforts to establish houses of the order. At the time of her death almost a hundred institutions were in operation throughout Europe, and several had been already established in America, in the states of Louisiana and Missouri.

Saint Madeleine Sophie Barat died on the day she had foretold, Ascension Thursday, May 25, 1865, at the motherhouse of the order in Paris. The Saint was subsequently beatified in 1908 and canonized on May 24, 1925.

In 1893 the first recognition of her relic took place in the presence of Msgr. Caprara, Promoter of the Faith, Father Muttioll, Procurator General of the Barnabites, Msgr. Baunard, and many other ecclesiastics.

The coffin, which was falling to pieces owing to the damp of the vault, was with great difficulty lifted out, chiefly through the help of a faithful old servant who had seen it placed there twenty-eight years before. It was feared that scarcely anything would be found intact, when Msgr. Caprara cried: 'See, the veil is hanging from her head,' and when the debris of wood and the mildewed garments were removed, the body was found entire, the feaures quite recognizable, the veil well preserved, the slender fingers still clasping a small crucifix. Cardinal Richard, Archbishop of Paris, who was presiding over the ceremony, put the crucifix into the hands of Reverend Mother Lehon. The body was clothed in a new religious habit, the members and even the tongue were found to be quite flexible. Mother de Sartorius placed her own profession ring on Mother Barat's finger, until a new one was provided, then Reverend Mother Lehon, who was quite blind, was led close up to the coffin, and together with Cardinal Richard drew a white silk veil over the holy remains, the body was then laid in a tomb prepared for it in the chapel of Our Lady of Dolours above the crypt where it had previously been buried.[1]

While the cause of Mother Barat was advancing, her religious houses were systematically being confiscated by the Masonic laws of 1901, and within seven years, forty-six convents were closed. During this suppression and expulsion of religious orders from France, the body of the Saint was taken for safekeeping on April 30, 1904, to Jette, Belgium, where it is still enshrined.

During the year of her beatification the remains were again exhumed and found to be perfectly incorrupt and fresh, retaining a certain flexibility.

The body was again found whole and incorrupt and was placed under the predella of the altar of Our Lady of Sorrows in the antechapel of the convent. The Holy Father decided that no relics should be taken from the body which had been so marvelously preserved; a shrine beneath an altar surmounted by graceful Gothic pinnacles was prepared for it. The glass of the shrine is covered by a brass trellis work with moveable panels, through which the reclining figure is seen, clothed in the habit of the Order, the face and hands covered with a silver mask.[2]

In 1934 a special shrine was erected in the Sacred Heart Convent in Jette, and the incorrupt body of the Saint was removed to the reli-

[1]*Life of Saint Madeleine Sophie, Foundress of the Society of the Sacred Heart of Jesus* (1779-1865). Margaret Ward. Convent of the Sacred Heart. Roehampton. 1925. p. 638.

[2]*Ibid.* p. 639.

quary situated beneath its altar. During the celebrations in honor of the canonization, thousands of pilgrims flocked to the reliquary, and local pilgrims still continue to visit the shrine on the first Sunday of each month.

97

SAINT PIERRE JULIEN EYMARD

1811—1868

Parental opposition and delicate health hindered the priestly vocation of Pierre Julien Eymard, and he was forced to leave the novitiate of the Oblates of Mary Immaculate after only three months. After the death of his father in 1831, he entered the major seminary in Grenoble and was ordained in 1834. He performed pastoral duties for five years until he joined the Marist Fathers and served this order in various positions for seventeen years, including provincial superior and rector of the College of La Seine-sur-Mer. He attempted to establish within this order a group especially dedicated to the Blessed Sacrament, but since his superiors felt this was not within the scope of their apostolate, he gained permission to leave the Order and founded in Paris, in 1856, the Blessed Sacrament Fathers, which he served as the superior general until his death twelve years later. In 1858 he founded, together with Marguerite Guillot, a contemplative order of nuns named the Servants of the Blessed Sacrament. The Saint died after a painful illness during which he proved to be a model of patience and resignation. His body, clad in sacerdotal vestments, was buried in the ground a short distance from the church in La Mure d' Isère near Grenoble.

In 1877 permission was obtained by the Blessed Sacrament Fathers to remove the remains of the Saint from La Mure to Paris, and so, nine years after Pierre Julien Eymard's death, his grave was opened. The oak coffin, which contained one of zinc, was falling to pieces, and these fragments were quickly taken by the faithful of La Mure as relics of the Saint whose physical presence they were grieved to lose. The zinc coffin containing the relic was placed inside another of oak, and this was put into a hearse decorated with fresh flowers by his faithful friends. Thus was his body borne to Paris, where it arrived two days later. After being placed in the chapel, the zinc coffin was opened, revealing to his friends the countenance they had all known so well. The event was recorded in *La Revue du Saint Sacrement* in these terms:

. . . The coffin reached Paris on Friday, June 29, 1877. That same day they opened it and found the remains of the Father in such a state of preservation as to greatly astonish the assistants. The flesh, though a little darkened, was intact, and no corpse-like odor was perceived. The features were so natural that not only they who had seen him during life, but they who knew him only by his portrait, exclaimed: 'There he is! It is indeed he!' . . . It was like an apparition, the return, the resurrection of a father whose absence had been wept for nine years.[1]

Many distinguished personages participated in the funeral ceremonies, including the Archdeacon of Notre-Dame and First Vicar General of His Eminence the Cardinal Archbishop of Paris, the Archbishop of Sussex and the Chamberlain of the Pope. After the impressive service the coffin containing its precious contents was sealed and lowered into the tomb prepared for it in the middle of the sanctuary floor at the foot of the Eucharistic throne.

At a later exhumation only his bones were found. Since the year of the beatification, 1925, these have been contained in a waxen image of the Saint which reposes in the chapel of Corpus Christi in a chasse, in which from 1908 to 1925 reclined the incorrupt body of St. John Marie Vianney.

The Congregation of the Fathers of the Blessed Sacrament was privileged to have its founder declared a saint of the Church on December 9, 1962.

---

[1]*La Revue du Saint Sacrement.* II Year, July 15.

98

SAINT CATHERINE LABOURÉ

1806—1876

The visionary of the Blessed Mother to whom the Miraculous Medal owes its existence was born into a large farming family in the peaceful village of Fain-les-Moutiers, France. Her mother died when Catherine was nine years old, and it was then that she chose the Blessed Mother for her mother and protector. She was pious from early childhood, fasting twice a week in spite of the fatiguing chores which she performed on her father's farm, and attending daily Mass in the chapel of the Sisters of Charity a mile from her home. Having decided to enter the religious life, she declined two marriage proposals, and her father, hoping to discourage his daughter, sent her to live with a brother, who conducted a restaurant in Paris, where she obediently waited on tables. Circumstances eventually permitted her to enter the order of the Sisters of Charity on the Rue du Bac in Paris, and it was there that her destiny was fulfilled.

As a young postulant she frequently beheld Our Lord in front of the Blessed Sacrament during Mass, and on three occasions she saw mystical, symbolic visions of St. Vincent de Paul above the reliquary containing his incorrupt heart, which is enshrined in the chapel of the motherhouse where all her visions occurred. Undoubtedly the most extraordinary visions were those which concerned our Blessed Mother.

On July 18, 1830, the eve of the feast of St. Vincent de Paul, the founder of her order, St. Catherine was awakened during the night by her angel, who appeared as a child of about five years, all radiant with light, and conducted her into the chapel. She was met there by the Blessed Virgin, who sat on the chair which was reserved for the director of the sisters. Kneeling before the apparition, Catherine was permitted to rest her folded hands on the knees of the Blessed Mother, who told her, "Come to the foot of this altar. There graces will be showered on you and on all who shall ask for them, rich and poor."

The second apparition occurred on November 27, 1830, while

Catherine was making her afternoon meditation. Hearing the rustle of silk, which she recognized from the first apparition, she looked in the direction of the sound and beheld the Blessed Virgin standing in the sanctuary near a picture of Saint Joseph. The small globe which the apparition held close to her heart slowly disappeared and at once her fingers were covered with rings, from which streamed rays of light, symbolic of the graces which she bestows on all who ask for them. Slowly there appeared around the Virgin an oval frame on which brilliant letters appeared: "O Mary, conceived without sin, pray for us who have recourse to thee." At the same time a voice said, "Have a medal struck from this model. Persons who wear it indulgenced will receive great graces, especially if they wear it around the neck; graces will be bestowed abundantly upon those who have confidence." The vision reversed itself and there appeared the Virgin's monogram, which is found on the back of the Miraculous Medal.

The third vision was almost identical to the second, except that the Virgin moved to a position above and behind the tabernacle, which place is now occupied by a statue made in the likeness of this vision.

The privileged soul reported these visions only to her superior and her spiritual director, and many difficulties had to be overcome before the medals were made and distributed.

After her profession, Catherine was assigned to the hospice on the Rue de Reuilly, where she spent the next forty-six years of her life, performing the most menial and repugnant of tasks for the aged, sick, and infirm. While all the sisters were aware that one in their midst was the celebrated seer of the Miraculous Medal, the identity was not made known until Catherine was on her deathbed. Having often predicted that she would never see the year 1877, she died on December 31, 1876.

In order to comply with the laws of Paris regarding interment in private vaults, the sacred body was placed in a triple coffin and buried in a crypt of the chapel at 77 Rue de Reuilly, where it remained undisturbed for fifty-six years. Following the announcement of her beatification, the customary recognition of the relics took place. On March 21, 1933, the ecclesiastical and medical delegation gathered in the crypt for the exhumation. The outer coffin of wood had fallen to pieces but the second coffin, of lead, was well preserved, and this was lifted out with great difficulty from the place where it fitted exactly and where it had rested for over half a century.

The coffin was then taken to a room which had been especially prepared for the examination of the relic. The undertaker cut the lid of the leaden coffin and lifted it off, disclosing the inner coffin of wood, which was also opened. When the physician lifted the sheet which covered the body, the remains were found to be perfectly intact. One eyewitness wrote:

> The hands had slipped towards the side, but were white and natural looking. The cord of the chaplet had decayed and the beads were loose in the coffin. The skin of the face had the appearance of parchment, but was entire. The eyes and mouth were closed.[1]

Two old ladies who had known Sister Catherine easily recognized the features of their saintly friend.

The community surgeon, Dr. Robert Didier, who witnessed the exhumation recorded:

> . . . On opening this we found a grayish mass of sawdust which had taken the form of the body; on the surface of this were some evidences of mould; but there were no putrefaction, simply a slightly acid odor.
>
> After carefully removing the sawdust by hand the winding sheet could be seen; it was intact, slightly damp and could easily be unfolded.
>
> The body was then cleared of all encumbrance. It seemed to be perfectly preserved in clothing which had kept its color and normal consistency.
>
> The cornette had remained over the face and this with the weight of the winding sheet and sawdust caused the nose to be flattened.
>
> The hands and the face were of a pinkish color slightly tinged with brown, but intact. Two fingers of the left hand were somewhat blackened, but we quickly perceived that this dark color was not due to necrosis of the tissue but to the dye of the habit which had faded on to the hand on the side of the crack in the leaden coffin. These facts being ascertained, we replaced the sheet and sealed the coffin for the transporting of the body.[2]

After this cursory examination, the body was borne in solemn procession to the motherhouse, where the Beata's body was met by the

---

[1]*Blessed Catherine Labouré, Daughter of Charity of St. Vincent de Paul.* Rev. Edmond Crapez, C.M. St. Joseph's Provincial House. Emmitsburg, Maryland. 1933. pp. 235-236.

[2]*Ibid.* pp. 239-240.

sisters, novices, and postulants of her order and the priests and novices from St. Lazare. The leaden casket, covered with a white silk pall on which were embroidered pictures of both sides of the Miraculous Medal, was carried along a path lined by the sons and daughters of St. Vincent de Paul.

At ten o'clock the next day, in the presence of many witnesses including the cardinal and the canon, who was the Promotor of the Faith, the body was again disclosed to view in another especially prepared room. Dr. Didier further recorded:

> The body was carefully taken out of the coffin and placed on a long table.
>
> The face on account of its first contact with the air had slightly darkened since the day before; the clothing perfectly preserved was carefully removed. It is well to note that on the left side of the body, the side in contact with the crack in the leaden coffin, the clothing was a little damp, and some parts of the body (the left arm and shoulder) had undergone a slight attrition.
>
> The skin there was a little swollen, hardened, and showed on its surface some whitish, limelike deposits. In examining the body we noticed the perfect suppleness of the arms and legs. These members have merely undergone a slight mumification. The skin throughout was intact and like parchment. The muscles were preserved; we could easily dissect them in a study of anatomy.
>
> We cut the sternum on the median line. The bone showed a cartilaginous, elastic consistency and was easily cut by the surgeon's knife. The thoracic cavity being opened it was easy for us to remove the heart. It was much shrunken but it had kept its shape. We could easily see within it the little fibrous cords, remains of the valves and muscles. We also took out a number of the ribs and the clavicle. We disjointed the arms—these two will be conserved apart. The two knee caps were taken out. The fingers and toe nails were in perfect condition. The hair remained attached to the scalp.
>
> The eyes were in the orbits; the eyelids half closed; we were able to state that the ball though fallen and shrunken existed in its entirety, and even the color, bluish gray, of the iris still remained. The ears were intact.
>
> To insure the preservation of the body we injected a solution of formaldehyde, glycerine and carbolic acid.[3]

The body of the Saint was later placed in the motherhouse chapel

---

[3]*Ibid.* pp. 240-241.

under the side altar of Our Lady of the Sun, where it still reposes behind a covering of glass. The upturned hands around which a rosary is entwined are made of wax. The incorrupt hands of the Saint, which have been amputated, are kept in a special reliquary, which is now enshrined in the novitiate cloister of the motherhouse. The heart of the Saint was likewise put into a special reliquary made of jeweled crystal and gold, which is reverently kept in the chapel at Reuilly where the Saint had so often prayed between duties at the hospice.

This chapel of the visions is undoubtedly one of the most hallowed in the world, for not only was it visited many times by Our Lord, the Virgin of the Miraculous Medal, and St. Vincent de Paul, but it is also enriched by the presence of many precious relics. Near the incorrupt body of St. Catherine is the altar of St. Vincent de Paul, the founder of the Order, before whose statue there is exposed the reliquary containing his heart. On the opposite side of the chapel, above the side altar is the magnificent reliquary in which can be seen a wax figure containing the bones of St. Louise de Marillac, who, with St. Vincent, founded the Sisters of Charity. On one side of the main altar stands the blue velvet chair on which the Virgin Mary sat during the first apparition. Visitors to the chapel are permitted to touch or kiss the chair and many leave on the seat slips of paper on which are written their petitions.

St. Catherine was canonized on July 27, 1947. The feast of the Saint is observed on November 28, the day after the feast of the Miraculous Medal.

The incorrupt body of St. Catherine Labouré, the visionary of the Miraculous Medal (d. 1876), as it appears today under a side altar in the motherhouse chapel of Our Lady of the Sun on the Rue du Bac in Paris. Her body was disinterred in 1933 following the announcement of her beatification.

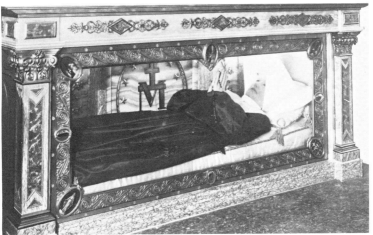

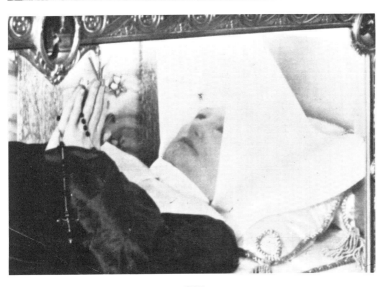

99

SAINT BERNADETTE SOUBIROUS

1844—1879

The celebrated visionary of Lourdes was born to a very poor family on January 7, 1844. As a child she suffered severely from asthma and was such a poor student she was delayed from making her First Holy Communion until the year 1858, when she was fourteen years of age. On February 11 of that year, the first of her visions took place as she was gathering firewood along the river Gave. This drama, known to Catholics around the world, occurred eighteen times in all.

On March 25, 1858, the Blessed Virgin appeared for the last time and identified herself as the "Immaculate Conception." With these words the Mother of God confirmed the pious belief which Pope Pius IX, four years earlier, had raised to the dignity of a dogma of the infallible Church.

The Sisters of Nevers, who operated a school at Lourdes, were later entrusted with Bernadette's care, and at the age of twenty-two, she was admitted to their order. She spent the rest of her days at the motherhouse in Nevers, a short distance from Lourdes.

The Saint was always very sickly but attended patiently to her duties as infirmarian and sacristan. After suffering heroically for years from tuberculosis of the bone in the right knee, and many complications, she died a holy death on April 16, 1879. Burial was in the Chapel of St. Joseph in the convent grounds behind the motherhouse in Nevers.

The body was first exhumed thirty years after her death. On September 22, 1909, in the presence of representatives appointed by the postulators of the cause, two doctors, and the sisters of the community, the coffin was removed by workmen from the place where it had been entombed thirty years before. On opening the lid, they discerned no odor and the virginal body lay exposed, completely victorious over the laws of nature.

Although the clothing was damp, and sawdust and charcoal surrounded the body, the arms and face were completely unaffected and had maintained their natural skin tone. The teeth were barely visible through the slightly parted lips and the eyes appeared somewhat sunken. Her perfect hands held a rosary which had become rusty, and the crucifix which lay upon her breast was coated with verdigris. While the sisters were removing the damp robes, they discovered that while the body was entire and without the least trace of corruption, it was nevertheless emaciated. The left knee was found to be much smaller than the right, which had been affected by tuberculosis.

The sisters, with the best of intentions, thoroughly washed the body and reclothed it in a new religious habit before placing it in a new casket. After the official documents pertaining to the exhumation were placed beside the body, and the double casket officially sealed, the remains were again consigned to the tomb.[1]

The second exhumation took place at the end of the Process on April 3, 1919. The body of the Venerable was found in the same state of preservation as ten years earlier, except that the face was slightly discolored, due to the washing it had undergone during the first exhumation. A worker in wax who had frequently applied such a coating to the faces of the newly dead was entrusted with the task of coating the face of the Saint who had been dead forty years.

The sacred relic was placed in a coffin of gold and glass and can be viewed in the Chapel of Saint Bernadette at the motherhouse in Nevers.

[1] *The Sublime Shepherdess, The Life of Saint Bernadette of Lourdes.* Frances Parkinson Keyes. Julian Messner, Inc. New York. 1947. pp. 162-164.

The incorrupt body of St. Bernadette Soubirous, the visionary of the Lourdes apparitions (d. 1879). First exhumed in 1909 and later in 1919, the body now lies in the Chapel of St. Bernadette in the motherhouse of her order in Nevers, France.

100

BLESSED PAULA FRASSINETTI

1809—1882

Paula's four brothers all became priests, and she was chosen by divine Providence to be the great foundress of the order known throughout the world as the Congregation of the Sisters of St. Dorothy, otherwise known as the Dorotheans.

Born in Genoa, Paula enjoyed the loving presence of her mother for only nine years, and after the death of an aunt who had taken care of the family for three years, she was obliged to assume the full management of the little household. The strain of the responsibilities and the added burden of numerous penances resulted in a decline in her health, which one of her brothers thought would be corrected in the invigorating climate of Quinto, where he was stationed. In this small village near Genoa, Paula's health was completely restored, and she immediately set about assisting her brother in his parish and catechetical work, which labor evolved, with the additional help of devoted friends, into a new religious family. After the transfer of the small group to Genoa and the establishment of a novitiate in that city, the Order increased by great numbers. Before her death, the blessed foundress saw her order established throughout Italy and in Brazil. The Order still continues her missionary labors in several countries of Europe, in several foundations in the United States, as well as in South America and in Africa.

On a number of occasions Paula expressed a wish to retire because of her advanced years, but she was prevented from doing so by her confessor and advisors who saw in her continued direction of the Order the will of God. Paula continued her labors until she began suffering from a number of afflictions, including the effects of three strokes, the third of which left her completely helpless. During her final illness she was visited by St. John Bosco, who told her grieving sisters, "My children, your Mother's crown of merits is completed." Paula entered her eternal reward shortly after this saintly utterance.

At the bier of the foundress in the motherhouse in Rome, the numerous visitors were so convinced of her sanctity that rosaries and medals were continually pressed against her body. On June 13, three days after her death, the remains were laid to rest in the Camp Verano, which is annexed to the Basilica of S. Lorenzo Fuori le Mura. In 1906, after many years of research into the life of this holy mother, Pope Pius X issued a decree permitting the introduction of her cause of beatification. In the same year the remains were exhumed for their translation into a provisional tomb in the chapel of the motherhouse where the Beata had spent so many prayerful hours when her infirmities had prevented her from actively participating in the work of the Order. The body was found perfectly preserved, with the joints as flexible as those of a living person. The clothing was also found undamaged by dampness.[1]

The decree of beatification was read by Pope Pius XI in St. Peter's Basilica on June 8, 1930. After this celebration, the incorrupt remains were removed from the provisional tomb into a silver and crystal casket, a gift of the sisters and pupils of the Brazilian Province.

The body of the blessed foundress has darkened slightly and is somewhat dry, but it remains perfectly preserved. The body is gently turned to the right, the eyes are closed, the lips a little parted, and the legs are slightly bent. The relic lies exposed in its reliquary beneath the tabernacle of the main altar in the motherhouse chapel, in an attitude of peaceful abandon.[2]

---

[1] *Blessed Paula, Paula Angela Maria Frassinetti, Foundress of the Congregation of the Sisters of St. Dorothy.* The Sisters of St. Dorothy. Taunton, Massachusetts. 1958. p. 40.

[2] Taken from a description of the body as supplied by the superior general of the Order in Rome.

The incorrupt body of Bl. Paula Frassinetti, Foundress of the Sisters of St. Dorothy (d. 1882), lies in a silver and glass casket in the chapel of the motherhouse of her order. The body was exhumed in 1906.

101

SAINT CHARBEL MAKHLOUF

1828—1898

Perhaps the most amazing phenomenon in the modern world is the existence of the perfectly incorrupt and life-like body of the holy Maronite monk, St. Charbel Makhlouf, who was born on May 8, 1828, in the village of Biqa-Kafra in the high mountains of Northern Lebanon. Given the name of Joseph at his baptism, he was the last of the five children born to very poor but religious parents. From early childhood he showed a strong attraction to prayer and solitude, and when he attained his twenty-third year, he left home in spite of the displeasure of his family and settled happily in the Monastery of St. Maroun at Annaya. After being received into the novitiate, he was given the name Charbel, the name of an early martyr. Having received a thorough theological education at seminaries conducted by his order, he was ordained a priest on July 23, 1859 and was assigned to the Monastery of St. Maroun, where he spent sixteen years in the practice of monastic virtues. In 1875 he received the permission of his superiors to retire to the Hermitage of Saints Peter and Paul, which was a little distance from the monastery and which was used by the priests during days of quiet retreat. It was in this secluded sanctuary that he spent the remaining twenty-three years of his life in the practice of severe mortification. It is recorded by his companions that he wore a hair shirt, practiced corporal discipline, slept on the hard ground, and ate only one meal a day, that being the remains of the meals of his companions.

Nothing outstanding is recorded of him except his remarkable devotion to the Holy Eucharist and his preference for saying daily Mass at 11:00 a.m., so he could spend almost all the morning in preparation and the rest of the day in thanksgiving.

In 1898 he suffered a seizure while saying Mass, and a priest assisting at the Holy Sacrifice was forced to pry the Holy Eucharist from his grasp. The holy monk died eight days later on Christmas Eve at the age of seventy. Interment was in the monastery cemetery where so many saintly monks before him had been buried. According to monastic custom, the body, which was not embalmed, was dressed in the full habit of the Order and was consigned to the grave without a coffin.[1]

In all probability he would have been forgotten had not a certain phenomenon occurred at his grave in the form of an extraordinary bright light, which surrounded his tomb for forty-five nights following the interment.[2] Because of this and the enthusiasm of the many witnesses of this prodigy, the officials of the monastery requested permission from the ecclesiastical authorities to exhume the body—a ceremony which took place four months after the saint's death.

When the common grave was opened in the presence of the superiors of the Order, the monks of the monastery, and many villagers, the body was found in perfect condition, even though, as the result of frequent rains which had inundated the cemetery several times since the burial, the body was found floating on mud in a flooded grave.[3]

After being cleansed and reclothed in fresh garments, the body was reverently laid in a wooden coffin and placed in a corner of the private chapel of the monastery.

A strange phenomenon accompanied this exhumation, one that has continued to occur to the present day. From the pores of the body there exuded a liquid described as perspiration and blood, which had the distinct odor of blood. As a result of this transpiration, the blood-stained clothing on the relic was changed twice a week. Small pieces of cloth soaked in this mysterious fluid are distributed as relics and these frequently relieve pain and effect cures.[4]

On July 24, 1927, after the body of Father Charbel was minutely examined by two physicians of the French Medical Institute at Beirut, it was clothed in sacerdotal garments and was placed in a new coffin of wood covered with zinc. Various documents drawn up by the physicians, the Judge of the Ecclesiastical Commission, the Defender of the Faith, a notary and superiors of the Order, were placed in a zinc tube, which was firmly closed and placed beside the body. Sealed with the episcopal crest of the Commission, the coffin was

---

[1]*A Miraculous Star in the East, Charbel Makhlouf.* Paul Daher. The Monastery of St. Maron. Annaya-Djebeil, Lebanon 1952. p. 23.

[2]*Blessed Sharbel, The Hermit of Lebanon of the Lebanese Maronite Order.* Monastery of St. Maron. Annaya, Lebanon. p. 15.

[3]Daher. *Op. cit.* p. 25.

[4]*Blessed Sharbel.* p. 15. See entry of Blessed Matthia of Nazzarei. A similar "blood-fluid" still exudes from the body of this Beata, who died in 1300 A.D.

placed in a new tomb especially prepared in the wall of an oratory. The coffin was placed on two stones to prevent contact with the dampness of the soil, and after being carefully sealed with masonry, the tomb was left undisturbed for twenty-three years.[5]

On February 25 of the Holy Year 1950, pilgrims to the shrine noticed a liquid seeping from a corner of the tomb and flowing onto the floor of the oratory. The father superior of the monastery, on examining the liquid and fearing damage to the contents of the tomb, had it opened in the presence of the assembled community. The tomb was found dry and the coffin in the same condition as when it was placed in position, except that a viscous liquid was seen dripping through a crack in the foot of the casket. This liquid flowed in the direction of the west wall, eventually finding its way into the oratory.

Permission to examine the contents of the sealed casket was obtained, and in the presence of many ecclesiastical authorities, officials of the Order and attending physicians, the seal was broken on April 22, 1950. The body was found completely free of any trace of corruption and was perfectly flexible and lifelike. The sweat of liquid and blood continued to exude from the body, and the garments were found stained with blood, the white content of the fluid having collected on the body in an almost solidified condition. Part of the chasuble had rotted and the zinc tube containing the official documents was covered with corrosion.[6]

While the examination of the body was taking place, the monastery and church were thronged with sick and crippled pilgrims who have continued their visits in ever increasing numbers. Estimates have been made of the number of souls visiting the shrine on various days, and these number not less than five thousand each day to approximately ten or fifteen thousand on Sundays and feast days, many people traveling from distant countries in anticipation of a cure or a favor.[7]

Numerous, well-authenticated miracles have been performed at the shrine. After the exhumation of 1950, the monastery began keeping records of the miracles and with in a two-year period had collected over twelve hundred reports.[8]

---

[5]Daher. *Op. cit.* pp. 29-30.

[6]*Ibid.* pp. 32-36.

[7]*Ibid.* p. 43.

[8]*Ibid.* p. 79.

Two of the cures acknowledged as being miraculous and accepted by Pope Paul VI as the required miracles for the beatification occurred during 1950. The first involved Sr. Maria Abel Kawary, S.S.C.C., who suffered for fourteen years from a gastric ulcer which neither surgery nor medication could cure or relieve. Unable to eat and compelled to stay in bed, she was in such grave condition that she was anointed three times. After fervent prayers at the tomb of St. Charbel, she was completely and spontaneously cured. The doctor who examined the nun after the miraculous cure recorded it as "a supernatural happening which is beyond man's power to explain."[9]

The second miracle accepted by the Sacred Congregation occurred to Mr. Alessandro Obeid, who was blinded when the retina of his eye was torn when it was struck by the branch of a tree. His sight was miraculously restored at the tomb, and he was privileged to see his heavenly benefactor in a vision. The physician who had treated Mr. Obeid during his blindness and who examined the effects of the miracle attributed the cure to an "Almighty Will which operated only by divine grace. There is no other explanation and it is certain that we have seriously sought an explanation without finding one."[10]

Probably the most startling and frequently mentioned miracle involved a fifty-year-old seamstress, Miss Mountaha Daher of Bekassin, Lebanon. Since childhood she had been the object of ridicule because of a disfiguring hunchback, which several doctors could not reduce. Her cure was obtained after a visit to the tomb, during which she prayed not for herself, but for certain needy relatives. Her physician testified that he had examined her many times before the cure and declared that besides the deformity of the huge hump she had other deformities, including a "chicken-breast" and misshapen shoulders. The figure of the woman after the cure was of normal proportions.[11]

For 67 years the body of the saint remained perfectly preserved and exuded a blood fluid described by all accounts as being supernaturally sustained. However, at the time of the beatification in 1965, the body was found to have complied with the laws of nature. Only bones remained, and these were of a curious red-

---

[9]*Ibid.* pp. 90-96.

[10]*Blessed Sharbel.* p. 17.

[11]Daher. Op. cit. pp. 104-107.

dish color.[12] The fluid, of course, had ceased, but enough had been gathered before the beatification to furnish a supply from which small quantities are still distributed. Small pieces of cloth from St. Charbel's garments and those that were saturated in the fluid are likewise distributed. After more than 20 years the bones still maintain their reddish tint.

---

[12]Taken from information contained in a letter to the author from Francis M. Zayek, Bishop of St. Maron diocese.

Christ gives us the relics of saints as health-giving springs through which flow blessings and healing. This should not be doubted. For if at God's word water gushed from hard rock in the wilderness—yes, and from an ass's jawbone when Samson was thirsty—why should it seem incredible that healing medicine should distill from the relics of saints? —St. John Damascene

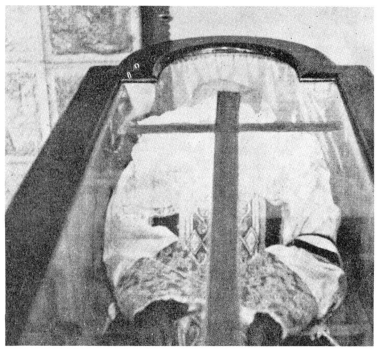

The incorrupt body of St. Charbel Makhlouf (d. 1898) as it appeared prior to his beatification in 1965. For 67 years the body remained incorrupt and exuded a liquid reported to have been accompanied by many miracles. St. Charbel was canonized in 1977.

St. Charbel Makhlouf as he appeared toward the end of his life.

102

BLESSED MARIA ASSUNTA PALLOTTA

1878—1905

Born in Piceno, Italy, Maria was obliged as a youth to work in many lowly positions in order financially to assist her poor parents. She acquired only a minimum of formal education, but attracted everyone by her modest and edifying demeanor. After her investiture with the holy habit of the Franciscan Missionaries of Mary, she was sent to the Congregation's convents in Rome, in Grottaferrata, and in Florence, where she was occupied variously as a housekeeper, gardener, infirmarian, and catechist.

In 1904 she knelt before St. Pius X to ask his blessings before setting out on her journey to the Chinese mission of Tong-Eul-Kiou. She was assigned to duties in the orphanage, but within one year after her arrival she contracted typhus from the plague-stricken people she was assisting, and died a holy death at the early age of twenty-seven. Pagans as well as Christians prayed at her grave, and when her remains were transferred to Tai-Yuan-Fou in April, 1913, eight years after her death, her body was found perfectly preserved.

In 1949 the Communists took over the Mission and it is impossible to obtain any information concerning the present condition of the relic. It is also not known if the grave of the Beata has been respected.

Maria Assunta Pallotta was beatified by Pope Pius XII on November 7, 1954, and April 7 has been designated as her feast day.

AFTERWORD

It would seem appropriate to quote here the opinion of some distinguished physician who has devoted time to a comparative study of preservations such as those recorded in this book. It is regrettable, however, that, with the exception of the physicians and men of science who examined individual remains of saints, the writer could find no one who, to any depth or degree, had made a study of any sort concerning this subject. We must rely, then, on the opinions of those physicians who, after careful examination of the saints' bodies in question, variously declared them to be unaccountably, mysteriously, or miraculously preserved.

How else can the existence of these relics be explained when it is considered that many of these saints died of diseases and infirmities that so vigorously assaulted their bodies as to extinguish life? How else can we explain their existence when they were not embalmed and when their internal parts contained all manner of corruptible materials? How could some have resisted extreme dampness, which encourages dissolution, or burial without benefit of a coffin? How could they resist the countless bacteria which are attracted not only to living bodies, but, especially, to those that are devoid of living forces to challenge them? If living flesh is so delicate and prone to infirmities, how can these bodies, which are unable to heal or restore themselves, endure throughout the centuries exposure to various climates, fluctuating levels of humidity and temperature, frequent reclothings, the taking of relics, and countless probings during periodic examinations? That some bodies which are now somewhat discolored exist at all, in spite of these factors, is no less a marvel. But what of those that are *perfectly* preserved?

While we can conjecture about their existence, who can explain why this favor was denied to some saints and awarded to others, many of whom are less known and who would seem, "less worthy?" Some of our most illustrious saints—Saints Francis and Clare of Assisi, St. Anthony of Padua and St. Frances Cabrini, to name but a few—did not escape the ravages of the tomb. When a novice suggested to the dying St. Thérèse of Lisieux, the Little Flower, whom the Popes have consistently lauded, that God would surely work a miracle to preserve her body incorrupt, the dying Saint humbly replied, "Oh, no.

Not that miracle . . ."[1] and indeed the miracle was not vouchsafed her.

It would be folly to weigh the holiness and merits of one saint against the good works and accomplishments of another, and it would further prove an impossibility to understand the reason of the Power who ordained this privilege to some and not to others.

Nonetheless, considering the unusual circumstances of these saintly preservations, as well as the phenomena and miracles which have surrounded many of them, we must concur with the opinion of St. Cyril of Jerusalem, who declared, "Even when the soul is gone, power and virtue remain in the bodies of the saints because of the righteous souls which have dwelt in them."

---

[1]*Soeur Thérèse of Lisieux, The Little Flower of Jesus.* T. N. Taylor, Priest of the Archdiocese of Glasgow, Editor. P.J. Kenedy & Sons. New York. 1912. p. 414.

SELECTED BIBLIOGRAPHY

Abtei St. Walburgh. *St. Walburg Eichstätt Kloster-und-Pfarrkirche.* Druck: Funk-Druck. Eichstätt. 1967.

Albertson, Clinton, S.J. *Anglo-Saxon Saints and Heroes.* Fordham University Press. New York. 1967.

Alfonsi, Fr. Tommaso M., de' Predicatori. *La B. Maria Bartolomea Bagnesi, Vergine Fiorentina del Terz' Ordine de S. Domenico.* Firenze. 1904.

Angelini, Father Atanasio, O.S.A. *The Life of St. Rita of Cascia.* Poligrafico Alterocca. Terni, Italy.

Annales de Sainte-Germaine de Pibrac. Redaction et Administration: M. le Curé. Pibrac. June 1968 and October 1968.

Aradi, Zsolt. *The Book of Miracles.* Farrar, Straus & Cudahy Co. New York. 1956.

Arigo, Iris. *The World of San Bernardino.* (A Helen & Kurt Wolff Book). Harcourt, Brace & World, Inc. New York.

Attwater, Donald. *A Catholic Dictionary.* The Macmillan Co. New York. 1956.

A Dictionary of Saints. (Based on *Butler's Lives of the Saints,* Complete Edition). P. J. Kenedy & Sons. New York. 1958.

Auclair, Marcelle. *Teresa of Avila.* Pantheon Books, Inc. New York. 1953.

Bacci, Father. *The Life of Saint Philip Neri.* Kegan Paul, Trench, Trubner & Co., Ltd. London. 1902. Vol. II.

Barlow, Frank. *The Life of King Edward.* (Attributed to a monk of St. Bertin). Thomas Nelson & Sons, Ltd. London. 1962.

Basilica of St. Nicholas. *The Shrine of St. Nicholas of Tolentino.* Tolentino.

Baunard, Abbé. *The Life of Mother Duchesne, Religious of the Society of the Sacred Heart of Jesus and Foundress of the First Houses of the Society in America.* Translated by Lady Georgiana Fullerton. Roehampton. 1879.

Bede the Venerable, Saint. *Ecclesiastical History of the English Nation.* J. M. Dent & Sons, Ltd. London. 1910 & 1958.

Benedictine Monks of the St. Augustine's Abbey, Ramsgate. *The Book of Saints.* The Macmillan Co. New York. 1947.

Bessieres, Albert, S.J. *Wife, Mother and Mystic.* The Newman Press. Westminster, Maryland. 1952.

Blessed Eustochia Calafato. V Centenary of the Foundation of the Convent of Montevergine, 1464-1964. (A paper).

Blessed Sharbel, The Hermit of Lebanon of the Lebanese Maronite Order. Monastery of St. Maron. Annaya, Lebanon.

Bonniwell, William, O.P. *The Story of Margaret of Metola.* P. J. Kenedy & Sons. New York. 1952.

Boresky, Theodosia. *Life of St. Josaphat, Martyr of the Union.* Comet Press Books. New York. 1955.

Bougaud, Monseigneur, Bishop of Laval. *History of St. Vincent de Paul, Founder of the Mission (Vincentians) and of the Sisters of Charity.* Translated by Rev. Joseph Brady, C. M. Longmans, Green & Co. New York. 1908.

St. Chantal and the Foundation of the Visitation. Benziger Bros. New York. 1895.

Bowden, Henry Sebastian. *The Following of the Saints.* Edited and revised by Donald Attwater. P. J. Kenedy & Sons. New York. 1959.

Brevisimo Compendio de la Vida del Insigne Lego Franciscano San Diego de Alcala. Alcala de Henares. 1955.

Brodrick, James, S.J. *The Life and Work of Blessed Robert Francis Cardinal Bellarmine, S.J.* Burns, Oates & Washbourne, Ltd. London. *1928. Vol. II.*

St. Francis Xavier. The Wicklow Press. New York. 1952.

Brusher, Joseph S., S.J. *The Popes through the Ages.* D. Van Nostrand Co., Inc. New York. 1959.

Butler, Thurston, & Attwater. *Lives of the Saints.* (Complete Edition in 4 Volumes). P. J. Kenedy & Sons. New York. 1956.

Butler, Rev. Alban. *Lives of the Saints with Reflections for Every Day in the Year.* Benziger Bros. New York.

Butler, N. V. Pierce. *A Book of British Saints.* The Faith Press, Ltd. Westminster. 1957.

Callen, Louise, R.S.C.J. *Philippine Duchesne, Frontier Missionary of the Sacred Heart.* The Newman Press. Westminster, Maryland. 1957.

Calvet, J. *Louise de Marillac.* P. J. Kenedy & Sons. New York.

Camara, Rt. Rev. Thomas, O.S.A., Bishop of Salamanca. *Life of Blessed Alphonsus Orozco, O.S.A.* Translated by Rev. W. A. Jones, O.S.A. H. L. Kilner & Co. Philadelphia. 1895.

Camillus de Lellis, The Hospital Saint. Benziger Bros. New York. 1917.

Canonici, Luciano, O.F.M. *Antonio Vici, Principe Conteso.* Edizioni Porziuncola. Assisi. 1961.

Capecelatro, Alfonso Cardinal. *The Life of St. Philip Neri, Apostle of Rome.* Benziger Bros. New York.

Cenni, Ellero. *Vita della Beata Eustochia.* Monastero di Montevergine. Messina. 1966.

Centi, P. Timoteo M. *Sant'Agnese Segni Domenicana, Patrona di Chianciano Terme.* Santuario S. Agnese. Montepulciano. 1966.

Charboneau, Rev. Damian Mary, O.S.M. *Saint Peregrine Laziosi, O.S.M. The Cancer Saint.* Servite Fathers, St. Joseph Province. Chicago. 1954.

Charles, Archbishop of Glasgow. *The History of St. Cuthbert*. Burnes & Oates, Ltd. London. Catholic Publications Society Co. New York. 1887.

Cioni, Raffaello. *S. Veronica Giulani*. Libreria Editrice Fiorentina. Citta di Castello. 1951.

Collet, M. *Life of St. Vincent of Paul, Founder of the Congregation of The Mission and of The Sisters of Charity*. John Murphy & Co. Baltimore.

Cook, G. H. *The English Cathedral Through the Centuries*. Phoenix House Ltd. London. 1957.

Cooledge, Eric. *The Mediaeval Mystics of England*. Charles Scribner's Sons. New York.

Corcoran, Rev. M. J., O.S.A. *Our Own St. Rita, A Life of the Saint of the Impossible*. Benziger Bros. New York. 1919.

Cordara, Dal P. Giulio. *Vita, Virtu e Miracoli della Beata Eustochia*. Goi Tipi della Minerva. Padova. 1836.

Crapez, Rev. Edmond, C. M. *Blessed Catherine Labouré, Daughter of Charity of St. Vincent de Paul*. St. Joseph's Provincial House. Emmitsburg, Maryland. 1933.

Curé of Ars, A Pilgrim's Guide. Éditions Xavier Mappus. Lyon.

Curley, Edmund F. *St. Camillus*. The Bruce Publishing Co. Milwaukee. 1962.

Daher, Paul. *A Miraculous Star in the East, Charbel Makhlouf*. Monastery of St. Maron. Annaya-Djebeil, Lebanon. 1952.

Charbel Un Homme Ivre de Dieu. Monastère S. Maron d'Annaya. Jbail, Lebanon. 1965.

Daniel-Rops, Henri. *Monsieur Vincent, The Story of St. Vincent De Paul*. Translated by Julie Kernan. Hawthorn Books, Inc. New York. 1961.

Daughter of Charity of St. Vincent de Paul. *Little Catherine of the Miraculous Medal*. Benziger Brothers. New York. 1937.

De Grunwald, Constantin. *Saints of Russia*. The Macmillian Co. New York. 1960.

De la Bedoyers, Michael. *François de Sales*. Harper & Bros. New York. 1960.

De Robeck, Nesta. *St. Clare of Assisi*. The Bruce Publishing Co. Milwaukee. 1951.

De Spens, Willy. *Saint Rita*. Translated by Julie Kernan. Hanover House. Garden City, New York. 1960.

Di Donato, Pietro. *Immigrant Saint, The Life of Mother Cabrini*. McGraw Hill Book Co., Inc. New York. 1960.

Diotallevi, P. Ferdinando, O.F.M. *Breve Vita della B. Mattia Nazzarei*. Arti Grafiche-Gentile. Fabriano. 1962.

Drane, Augusta Theodosia. *The History of St. Catherine of Siena and Her Companions*. Longmans, Green & Company. London. 1899. Vol. II.

Englebert, Omer. *The Lives of the Saints.* Translated by Christopher and Anne Fremantle. Collier Books. New York. 1951.

Farges, Mgr. Albert. *Mystical Phenomena.* Burnes, Oates & Washbourne, Ltd. London. 1926.

Ferrers, A. G. S. *Bernardino of Siena.* Howell, Methuen & Co., Ltd. London.

Florencio del Ninò Jesús, C.D., Rev., Provincial de los Carmelitas Descalzos de Castilla. *El Cuerpo Incorrupto de la Venerable Madre Maria de Jesús, Carmelita Descalza.* 1929.

Fullerton, Lady Georgiana. *The Life of St. Frances of Rome, of Blessed Lucy of Narni, of Dominica of Paradiso, And of Anne de Montmorency.* D. & J. Sadlier & Co. New York. 1855.

Gaustad, Edwin Scott. *Religious History of America.* Harper & Row Publishers. New York. 1966.

Gaynor, John S., S.C.A. *The Life of St. Vincent Pallotti.* Pallottine Fathers. Clerkenwell, London. 1962.

Gentili, P. Domenico, Agostiniano. *Un Asceta e un Apostolo, S. Nicola da Tolentino.* Editrice Ancora. Milano. 1966.

Gherardi, Luciano. *La Beata Clelia Barbieri.* Utoa. Bologna. 1969.

Gueranger, Rev. Prosper, Abbé de Solesmes. *Life of Saint Cecilia, Virgin and Martyr.* P. J. Kenedy & Sons. New York.

Guglielmo, D., Can. Co. Malazampa. *Un Fiore de Santita Benedettina S. Sperandia, Vergine.* Cingoli. 1952.

Gusmini, Giorgio Cardinal. *Beata Clelia Barbieri, Fondatrice delle Minime dell'Addolorata.* Casa Generalizia, Suore Minime dell'Addolorata. Bologna. 1968.

Haffert, John M. *The World's Greatest Secret.* Ave Maria Institute. Washington, N.J. 1967.

Harney, Martin P., S.J. *The Jesuits in History, The Society of Jesus through Four Centuries.* The America Press. New York. 1941.

Heriz, Fr. Paschasius, O.C.D. *St. John of the Cross.* College of Our Lady of Mount Carmel. Washington, D.C. 1919.

Hodges, George. *Saints and Heroes to the End of the Middle Ages.* Books for Libraries Press. Freeport, New York.

Hofer, Rev. John. *St. John Capistran, Reformer.* B. Herder Book Co. St. Louis, Missouri. 1943.

Jones, Charles W. *Saints' Lives and Chronicles in Early England.* Cornell University Press. Ithaca, New York. 1947.

Jörgensen, Johannes. *Saint Catherine of Siena.* Longmans, Green & Co. New York. 1939.

Journal of the British Archeological Association. 3rd Series. Vol. XVII.

Keyes, Frances Parkinson, Translator. *The Third Mystic of Avila, The Self-Revelation of Maria Vela.* Farrar, Straus & Cudahy. New York. 1960.

Keyes, Frances Parkinson. *The Land of Stones and Saints.* Doubleday & Co., Inc. New York. 1957.

The Sublime Shepherdess, The Life of Saint Bernadette of Lourdes. Julian Messner, Inc. New York. 1947.

Tongues of Fire. Coward-McCann. New York.

Three Ways of Love. Hawthorn Books. New York. 1963.

Lavedan, Henri. *The Heroic Life of St. Vincent de Paul, A Biography.* Longmans, Green & Co. New York. 1929.

Life of Blessed Julie Billiart, Foundress of the Institute of Sisters of Notre Dame. By a Member of the Same Society. Fr. James Clare, S.J., Editor. Sands & Co. London. 1909.

Life of St. John of God, Founder of the Order of Hospitallers. R. Washbourne. London. 1875.

Lovasik, Rev. Lawrence G., S.V.D. *Saint Cecilia, Model of Purity.* Divine Word Publications. Techny, Illinois.

Martindale, C. C., S.J. *Life of Saint Camillus.* Sheed & Ward. London. 1946.

Maynard, Theodore. *The Odyssey of Francis Xavier.* The Newman Press. Westminster, Maryland. 1950.

Great Catholics in American History. Hanover House. Garden City, New York.

Minima, Sister Mary. *Seraph among Angels, The Life of St. Mary Magdalene de'Pazzi.* Translated by the Very Rev. Gabriel N. Pausback, O. Carm. The Carmelite Press. Chicago. 1958.

Monica, Sister M. *Angela Merici and Her Teaching Idea.* Longmans, Green & Co. New York. 1927.

Moreschini, Cesare. *The Life of Saint Andrew Bobola of the Society of Jesus, Martyr.* Translated by Louis J. Gallagher, S.J. and Paul V. Donovan, LL.D. Bruce Humphries, Inc. Boston. 1939.

Newcomb, Msgr. James F., P.A., J.C.D. *St. Teresa Margaret of the Sacred Heart of Jesus (Anna Maria Redi).* Benziger Brothers. New York. 1934.

Nigg, Walter. *Warriors of God, The Great Religious Orders and Their Founders.* Edited and translated by Mary Ilford. Alfred A. Knopf. New York. 1959.

Ornsby, Robert, M.A. *The Life of St. Francis de Sales.* D & J. Sadlier & Co. New York.

Orsenigo, Most Rev. Cesare. *Life of St. Charles Borromeo.* B. Herder Book Co. St. Louis, Missouri. 1943.

Pellegrinaggio Spirituale Ossia Guida del Monastero di S. Veronica Giuliani. Tipografia Orfanelli S. Cuore. Citta di Castello. 1927.

Polson, C. J.; Brittain, R. P.; and Marshal, T. K. *The Disposal of the Dead.* Charles C. Thomas, Publisher. Springfield, Illinois. 1962.

Ponnelle, Louis & Bordet, Louis. *St. Philip Neri and the Roman Society of His Times.* Sheed & Ward. New York. 1932.

Porrentruy, L. A. *The Saint of the Eucharist.* Translated by O. Staniforth, O.F.M.Cap. Press of Upton Bros. & Delzelle, Inc. San Francisco. 1905.

Rampa, T. Lobsang. *The Third Eye, The Autobiography of a Tibetan Lama.* Doubleday & Co., Inc. Garden City, New York. 1957.

Raymond of Capua, Blessed. *Life of Saint Catherine of Siena.* P. J. Kenedy & Sons. New York.

Repplier, Agnes. *Mère Marie of the Ursulines, A Study in Adventure.* Doubleday, Doran & Co., Inc. Garden City, New York. 1931.

Revue du Saint Sacrement. II Year. July 15.

Ricognizione Canonica delle Venerate Spoglie di S. Bernardino da Siena. L'Aquila. 20-22 Agosto 1968. Estratto da: Acta Provinciae Apurtinae, Sancti Bernardini Senensis, Ordinis Fratrum Minorum. Tipografia Labor. Sulmona. 1968. XXII. fascicola 1.

Rohrbach, Peter-Thomas, O.C.D. *Journey to Carith.* Doubleday & Co., Inc. New York. 1966.

Sackville-West, V. *The Eagle and the Dove.* Doubleday, Doran, & Co., Inc. Garden City, New York. 1944.

Saint Catherine Labouré. The Association of the Miraculous Medal. Perryville, Missouri. 1948.

Saint Julie Billiart, Foundress of the Institute of the Sisters of Notre-Dame of Namur. Editrice Ancora. 1969.

Salotti, Msgr. Carlo. *La Beata Anna Maria Taigi, Madre di Famiglia.* Libreria Editrice Religiosa, Franceso Ferrari. Rome. 1922.

Schwertner, Thomas M., O.P. *St. Albert the Great.* The Bruce Publishing Co. New York. 1932.

Short Lives of the Dominican Saints. By a Sister of the Congregation of St. Catherine of Siena. Kegan Paul, Trench, Trubner & Co., Ltd. London. 1901.

Shirley, Canon John, D.D. *Canterbury Cathedral.* Pitkin Pictorials, Ltd. London. 1969.

Sighart, Doctor Joachim. *Albert the Great of the Order of Friar Preachers, His Life and Scholastic Labours from Original Documents.* R. Washbourne. London. 1876. Wm. C. Brown Reprint Library. Dubuque, Iowa.

Simon, Edith and the Editors of Time-Life Books. *The Reformation.* Time, Inc. New York. 1966.

Sisters of Notre Dame of Namur. *St. Wilfrid.* B. Herder Book Co. St. Louis, Missouri.

Sisters of St. Dorothy. *Blessed Paula, Paula Angela Maria Frassinetti, Foundress of the Congregation of the Sisters of St. Dorothy.* Published by the

Sisters of St. Dorothy. Taunton, Massachusetts. 1958.

Sitwell, Sacheverell. *Monks, Nuns and Monasteries.* Holt, Rinehart and Winston. New York. 1965.

Smith, Doreen. *St. Philip Neri, A Tribute.* Sands & Co., Ltd. London. 1945.

Stern, Karl. *The Third Revolution, A Study of Psychiatry and Religion.* Harcourt, Brace and Co. New York. 1954.

Tenaillon, Rev. Edmond, S.S.S. *Venerable Pierre Julien Eymard, The Priest of the Eucharist.* The Sentinel Press. New York. 1914.

Tesniere, Rev. Albert, S.S.S. *Blessed Peter Julian Eymard, The Priest of the Eucharist.* Fathers of the Blessed Sacrament. New York. 1936.

Thompson, Edward Healy. *The Life of St. Charles Borromeo.* Benziger Bros. New York.

The Life of St. Stanislas Kostka of the Company of Jesus. Peter F. Cunningham, Catholic Bookseller. Philadelphia. 1876.

Thurston, Herbert, S.J. *The Life of St. Hugh of Lincoln.* Benziger Bros. New York. 1898.

The Physical Phenomena of Mysticism. Henry Regnery Co. Chicago. 1952.

Tomatis, Benedetta Maria & Lynk, Rev. F. M., S.V.D. *The Housewife Saint, Anna Maria Gianetti.* Divine Word Publications. Techny, Illinois. 1959.

Translation des Reliques de Saint François de Sales et de Sainte Jeanne-Françoise de Chantal. Guide-Manuel du Pèlerin à Annecy. Published by the Visitation Order. Annecy. 1911.

Trochu, Abbé Francis. *The Curé d'Ars, St. Jean-Marie-Baptiste Vianney, According to the Acts of the Process of Canonization and Numerous hitherto Unpublished Documents.* The Newman Press. Westminster, Maryland. 1950.

Undset, Sigrid. *Stages on the Road.* Translated by Arthur G. Chater. Alfred A. Knopf. New York. 1934.

Saga of Saints. Translated by E. C. Ramsden. Longmans, Green & Co. New York. 1934.

Van Rensselaer, Mrs. Schuyler. *English Cathedrals.* The Century Co. New York. 1892.

Vanti, P. Mario, Ph.D., O.S. Cam. *St. Camillus, The Saint of the Red Cross.* Published by the Order of St. Camillus. Rome. 1950.

Vita e Miracoli della Beata Arcangela Girlani. Trino. 1960.

von Gorrës, Johann Joseph. *Christliche Mystik.* (In *Collected Works of Gorrës*). Bachem Verlag. Cologne. 1936.

von Hügel, Baron Friedrich. *The Mystical Element of Religion as Studied in Saint Catherine of Genoa and Her Friends.* E. P. Dutton & Co. New York. 123. Vol. I.

von Pastor, Baron Ludwig. *The History of the Popes.* Kegan Paul, Trench,

Trubner & Co. London. 1933. Vol. XXIV.

Walsh, William Thomas. *Saint Teresa of Avila.* Bruce Publishing Co. Milwaukee. 1943.

Walsh, Rev. James G., C.S.P. *Saint Catherine of Genoa, Patroness of Purgatory.* The Paulist Press. New York.

Ward, Margaret. *Life of Saint Madeleine Sophie, Foundress of the Society of the Sacred Heart of Jesus (1779-1865).* Convent of the Sacred Heart. Roehampton. 1925.

Watkins, E. I. *Neglected Saints.* Sheed & Ward. New York. 1955.

Whitfield, Rev. J. L. *Blessed John Southworth.* Catholic Truth Society. London. 1965.

Wiener, Claude. *Pontigny.* Zodiaque. 1964.

Wilcocks, Elisabeth. *Saint Etheldreda.* Catholic Truth Society. London. 1961.

Williams, Margaret, R.S.C.J. *St. Madeleine Sophie, Her Life and Letters.* Herder & Herder. New York. 1965.

Williamson, Claude, O.S.C. *Great Catholics.* The Macmillan Co. New York. 1946

Woodgate, M. V. *Saint Francis de Sales.* The Newman Press. Westminster, Maryland. 1961.

Xavier, Mother Mary, O.S.U. *St. Angela Merici.* Divine Word Publications. Techny, Illinois.

Yeo, Margaret. *St. Francis Xavier, Apostle of the East.* The Macmillan Co. New York. 1932.

If you have enjoyed this book, consider making your next selection from among the following . . .

Prices subject to change.

Prices subject to change.

St. Vincent Ferrer. *Fr. Pradel, O.P.* 9.00
The Life of Father De Smet. *Fr. Laveille, S.J.* 18.00
Glories of Divine Grace. *Fr. Matthias Scheeben* 18.00
Holy Eucharist—Our All. *Fr. Lukas Etlin* 3.00
Hail Holy Queen (from *Glories of Mary*). *St. Alphonsus* 9.00
Novena of Holy Communions. *Lovasik* 2.50
Brief Catechism for Adults. *Cogan.* 12.50
The Cath. Religion—Illus./Expl. for Child, Adult, Convert. *Burbach* 12.50
Eucharistic Miracles. *Joan Carroll Cruz.* 16.50
The Incorruptibles. *Joan Carroll Cruz* 16.50
Secular Saints: 250 Lay Men, Women & Children. PB. *Cruz.* 35.00
Pope St. Pius X. *F. A. Forbes* 11.00
St. Alphonsus Liguori. *Frs. Miller and Aubin* 18.00
Self-Abandonment to Divine Providence. *Fr. de Caussade, S.J.* 22.50
The Song of Songs—A Mystical Exposition. *Fr. Arintero, O.P.* 21.50
Prophecy for Today. *Edward Connor* 7.50
Saint Michael and the Angels. *Approved Sources* 9.00
Dolorous Passion of Our Lord. *Anne C. Emmerich.* 18.00
Modern Saints—Their Lives & Faces, Book I. *Ann Ball.* 21.00
Modern Saints—Their Lives & Faces, Book II. *Ann Ball* 23.00
Our Lady of Fatima's Peace Plan from Heaven. *Booklet.* 1.00
Divine Favors Granted to St. Joseph. *Père Binet.* 7.50
St. Joseph Cafasso—Priest of the Gallows. *St. John Bosco.* 6.00
Catechism of the Council of Trent. *McHugh/Callan* 27.50
The Foot of the Cross. *Fr. Faber.* 18.00
The Rosary in Action. *John Johnson* 12.00
Padre Pio—The Stigmatist. *Fr. Charles Carty* 16.50
Why Squander Illness? *Frs. Rumble & Carty* 4.00
The Sacred Heart and the Priesthood. *de la Touche* 10.00
Fatima—The Great Sign. *Francis Johnston* 12.00
Heliotropium—Conformity of Human Will to Divine. *Drexelius* 15.00
Charity for the Suffering Souls. *Fr. John Nageleisen* 18.00
Devotion to the Sacred Heart of Jesus. *Verheylezoon* 16.50
Who Is Padre Pio? *Radio Replies Press* 3.00
The Stigmata and Modern Science. *Fr. Charles Carty* 2.50
St. Anthony—The Wonder Worker of Padua. *Stoddard.* 7.00
The Precious Blood. *Fr. Faber* 16.50
The Holy Shroud & Four Visions. *Fr. O'Connell* 3.50
Clean Love in Courtship. *Fr. Lawrence Lovasik* 4.50
The Secret of the Rosary. *St. Louis De Montfort.* 5.00
The History of Antichrist. *Rev. P. Huchede.* 4.00
St. Catherine of Siena. *Alice Curtayne* 16.50
Where We Got the Bible. *Fr. Henry Graham* 8.00
Hidden Treasure—Holy Mass. *St. Leonard.* 7.50
Imitation of the Sacred Heart of Jesus. *Fr. Arnoudt* 18.50
The Life & Glories of St. Joseph. *Edward Thompson* 16.50
Père Lamy. *Biver.* 15.00
Humility of Heart. *Fr. Cajetan da Bergamo* 9.00
The Curé D'Ars. *Abbé Francis Trochu* 24.00
Love, Peace and Joy. (St. Gertrude). *Prévot* 8.00

At your Bookdealer or direct from the Publisher.
Toll-Free 1-800-437-5876   *Fax 815-226-7770*

Prices subject to change.

NOTES

NOTES

NOTES

NOTES